Protecting Individuals Against the Negative Impact of Big Data

Information Law Series (INFO)

VOLUME 42

Editor

Prof. P. Bernt Hugenholtz, Institute for Information Law, University of Amsterdam.

Objective & Readership

Publications in the Information Law Series focus on current legal issues of information law and are aimed at scholars, practitioners, and policy makers who are active in the rapidly expanding area of information law and policy.

Introduction & Contents

The advent of the information society has put the field of information law squarely on the map. Information law is the law relating to the production, marketing, distribution, and use of information goods and services. The field of information law therefore cuts across traditional legal boundaries, and encompasses a wide set of legal issues at the crossroads of intellectual property, media law, telecommunications law, freedom of expression, and right to privacy. Recent volumes in the Information Law Series deal with copyright enforcement on the Internet, interoperability among computer programs, harmonization of copyright at the European level, intellectual property and human rights, public broadcasting in Europe, the future of the public domain, conditional access in digital broadcasting, and the 'three-step test' in copyright.

The titles published in this series are listed at the end of this volume.

Protecting Individuals Against the Negative Impact of Big Data

Potential and Limitations of the Privacy and Data Protection Law Approach

Manon Oostveen

Wolters Kluwer

Published by:
Kluwer Law International B.V.
PO Box 316
2400 AH Alphen aan den Rijn
The Netherlands
E-mail: international-sales@wolterskluwer.com
Website: lrus.wolterskluwer.com

Sold and distributed in North, Central and South America by:
Wolters Kluwer Legal & Regulatory U.S.
7201 McKinney Circle
Frederick, MD 21704
United States of America
Email: customer.service@wolterskluwer.com

Sold and distributed in all other countries by:
Air Business Subscriptions
Rockwood House
Haywards Heath
West Sussex
RH16 3DH
United Kingdom
Email: international-customerservice@wolterskluwer.com

Printed on acid-free paper.

ISBN 978-94-035-0131-4

e-book: ISBN 978-94-035-0141-3
web-PDF: ISBN 978-94-035-0150-5

Printed in the United Kingdom.

Table of Contents

Acknowledgements

This book would not exist without the support that I received from many different people and organisations while conducting my PhD research. I am particularly grateful for my years in the Institute for Information Law at the University of Amsterdam, where I had the privilege of spending my time with great people, which made work a pleasure. I thank my supervisors Kristina Irion and Mireille van Eechoud for their guidance and patience and for pushing me to make the most of myself. Bernt Hugenholtz, Frederik Zuiderveen Borgesius, Joris van Hoboken, Lucie Guibault, Nico van Eijk, and Tarlach McGonagle also deserve special mention, for creating opportunities, sparking my curiosity, and boosting my motivation at decisive moments during the past few years. Many thanks to professors Corien Prins, Egbert Dommering, Mireille Hildebrandt, Natali Helberger, and Nico van Eijk for being part of the reading committee of my PhD thesis.

I am indebted to my family and friends for their continuous support while writing this work and for lifting my spirits whenever I was struggling in the process. I cannot mention you all, but know that I am very happy having you around. Special thanks to Yedan, who has not only been an awesome friend but also mentored me on my academic journey. I consider myself to be extremely lucky with my parents Jan and Adrienne and my sister Babette. You always provided me with help, encouragement, and loving support, and I am grateful for your efforts that aided me in bringing this project to a successful end. And finally, my love, gratitude, and deep appreciation for Remmelt. Thank you for sharing both my happiness and troubles and for always being there for me.

The research for this book was completed in July 2017. Subsequent developments are not reflected in this research.

Manon Oostveen
Amsterdam, 20 March 2018

Chapter 1
Introduction

1.1 BACKGROUND

At this very moment, massive amounts of data are being processed. The processing is aimed at deriving knowledge from the data, which is then used as a basis for decisions, to improve products and services or to target individuals: big data. Because of big data, data have become the main ingredient for digital knowledge creation and decision-making.

In many ways, big data is a positive and promising development. It holds the potential to enable corporations to generate large revenues, to let scientists solve vital issues and to help governments make informed policy decisions. Yet the massive collection and use of data also raises a host of issues, particularly for individuals' privacy and data protection rights. It is not surprising that privacy and data protection are focal points in ethical and legal discussions on big data, because often personal data are processed, or big data is used to profile individual users.[1] As a result, the attention of researchers and policy-makers is directed at privacy and data protection, both in terms of defining the issue and pinpointing the appropriate laws and legal

1. Big data projects do not necessarily process the personal data of individuals, although much personal data are processed in big data projects. *See* for example on how big data not involving personal data could aid in the prevention of world hunger: Paul Rubens, 'Can Big Data Crunching Help Feed the World?' (*BBC News*) <www.bbc.com/news/business-26424338> accessed 24 April 2015, or on the potential of big data in the oil and gas industry: Robert K. Perrons and Jesse W. Jensen, 'Data as an Asset: What the Oil and Gas Sector Can Learn from Other Industries about "Big Data"' (2015) 81 Energy Policy 117.

solutions. However, the effects of big data on the life of individuals transcend privacy and data protection. Big data applications and algorithmic decision-making produce a cascade of effects on the lives of individuals, going beyond privacy and data protection. Big data affects, for example, the personal autonomy of individuals and the rights to non-discrimination and freedom of expression.

However, the focus on privacy and data protection law in ethical and legal discussions on big data may not be inappropriate. In addition to their value as stand-alone fundamental rights that merit protection as such, the rights to privacy and data protection can function as instruments that protect other fundamental rights and freedoms. For example, data protection regulation facilitates the right of non-discrimination, through creating opportunities to close off from the general public personal information on the basis of which people can be discriminated against. Likewise, the rights to privacy and data protection potentially create a personal zone of protection that shields people from surveillance. This fosters freedom of expression, as it promotes the gathering of information and conception of ideas free from chilling effects that can occur when these processes are visible to others. This facilitative role of the rights to privacy and data protection for the protection of other rights and freedoms is recognised by both the European Court of Human Rights (ECtHR) and the Court of Justice of the European Union (CJEU), as well as in academic literature.[2]

From the perspective of the protection of individual rights and freedoms in the context of big data, this brings up the question of the potential and limitations of the privacy and data protection law framework for protecting people against the negative impact that big data has or may have on their lives. To what extent does the existing legal framework on privacy and data protection protect individual rights and freedoms affected by big data? Is the focus on privacy and data protection in the discussions on big data justified? Or should we focus on the possibilities of tackling issues through other areas of law, or maybe even find new solutions to cope with the dark side of big data?

1.2 RESEARCH DESIGN

1.2.1 Research Question

This research answers the following question:

> What are the potential and limitations of the European Union legal framework on privacy and data protection with respect to protecting individuals' rights and freedoms against the negative impact of big data?

2. Subsection 1.2.4 of this chapter details these concepts.

To answer this question, it is necessary to first understand what is meant by big data, and the potential negative impact it can have on individual rights and freedoms. Second, we need to understand what the European Union (EU) legal framework on privacy and data protection consists of and how it functions in the light of big data, to be able to carry out a legal analysis of the potential and limitations of this framework with respect to protecting these individual rights and freedoms against the negative impact. The methods used to answer these questions are set out in subsection 1.2.5 below.

The starting point of the research is an explanation of what happens in, and because of, big data and how this affects the rights and freedoms of individuals. Big data starts with the collection of data, which often triggers privacy and data protection interests. But throughout the big data process, and in society in general due to the increasing use of big data, the exercise of other rights and freedoms may be impeded as well. Big data's effect on the lives of individuals should be seen as a cascade: it often starts with an effect on the rights to data protection and privacy, but later in the process the consequences become more far-reaching and also affect other individuals' rights and freedoms. The EU framework on privacy and data protection has the potential to protect these individual rights and freedoms. Because of this, and because privacy and data protection are widely regarded as the regulatory framework *par excellence* for big data, the potential and limitations of the EU privacy and data protection framework for countering the negative effects of big data on individual rights and freedoms are researched in this work. The analysis of the EU legal framework on privacy and data protection focuses on fundamental rights and the General Data Protection Regulation (GDPR) to evaluate whether the EU legal framework on privacy and data protection comprehensively addresses the detrimental effects of big data on these individual rights and freedoms. The answers to these questions lead to a conclusion on the potential and limitations of the EU legal framework on privacy and data protection with regard to the protection of individual rights and freedoms. The final chapter supplements this conclusion by exploring how data protection law could be amended and possible alternative solutions to the gaps identified in the protection of individual rights and freedoms.

1.2.2 Academic and Social Relevance

This subsection explains this book's contribution to the literature and the social relevance of the research. Essentially, this research fills two gaps in the legal literature: the lack of analysis of big data as a process, including the diverse array of its consequences, and the lack of careful analysis of the potential and limitations of the EU legal privacy and data protection framework to mitigate these negative consequences. From these analyses, the question arises whether the current informational privacy paradigm indeed provides a sound and comprehensive solution for the negative consequences of big data for individuals. This question and its answer expose the social relevance of this research: the protective potential of the EU legal privacy and data protection framework is limited, and this needs to be addressed and solved if individual rights and freedoms are to be protected in the age of big data.

The contribution to the literature starts with the careful investigation of the concept of big data, perceiving it as a process that consists of many different actions and effects. The term 'big data' is complicated because its definition is dependent on the context in which it is used. Its meaning varies, even within the ever-growing body of academic literature. Occasionally the term is used to attract the attention of a large audience. It is, after all, a very popular term that seems to promise attention and money to those who claim it as their expertise. The actual analysis of the term, what happens in big data, and the changes it causes that influence the lives of individuals, is not usually thoroughly explored in the legal literature. Research from the humanities does focus on big data's impact, and recent years have seen an increase in legal literature combining a single negative effect with legal analysis, such as big data and discrimination.[3] The contribution of this research in this domain is its combination of a thorough analysis of the different actions big data comprises, with a comprehensive analysis of its effects on individual rights and freedoms. All too often big data is equated with personal data processing in legal literature, and the applicability of the EU legal privacy and data protection law framework is not questioned. From this analysis flows a more refined image of big data as a process. This process view shows that big data consists of many different actions and effects, leading to two conclusions on how big data issues should be approached. First, how the law pertains to these actions differs; they cannot be lumped together under the denominator 'big data' and declared subject to privacy and data protection law. Second, not all effects of these actions can be described in terms of privacy and data protection. Big data affects other individual rights and freedoms as well, and there may be a cascade of effects of particular aspects of big data for individuals' future lives.

The social relevance of this research project lies mainly in exploring how the negative effects that big data has and can have on the lives of individuals can be mitigated. In the contemporary information society, public and private organisations increasingly rely on large-scale data collection and analysis as a basis for their decisions. The collection and analysis of data, as well as the application of the knowledge derived therefrom, can have substantial consequences for the individual, but these processes take place largely beyond the individual's knowledge. The opacity of the big data process, the fundamental values that are at stake, and the speed of

3. For example Solon Barocas and Andrew Selbst, 'Big Data's Disparate Impact' (2016) 104 California Law Review 671.

technological developments compared to the pace of legal reform call for an in-depth analysis of what happens in big data, what problems it causes, and how to solve them.

In conclusion, for a long time the discussion of big data in the legal literature has taken place almost exclusively within the boundaries of privacy and data protection, although the number of exceptions to this rule has risen since the start of this research. Since personal data are often collected and processed in big data, big data is perceived as a problem to be solved by data protection law. The European legal debate focuses primarily on the strain that big data puts on current data protection principles and legislation. Through being more comprehensive in its discussion of big data's potential negative effects, and more nuanced in its analysis of what happens in and because of big data, this research reveals that a fixation on privacy and data protection law for regulating big data could actually be detrimental to the protection of individual rights and freedoms in the context of big data. Herein lies both its academic and its social relevance.

1.2.3 Scope of the Research

This research is about individuals, about human beings, and about protecting them against harm they may experience from big data. Its starting point is the idea expressed in Recital 2 of the Data Protection Directive:[4]

> Whereas data-processing systems are designed to serve man; whereas they must, whatever the nationality or residence of natural persons, respect their fundamental rights and freedoms, notably the right to privacy, and contribute to economic and social progress, trade expansion and the well-being of individuals.

Extrapolating this idea to the research question and the chosen perspective of the protection of individuals in a big data context, the first part of the quotation could be replaced by big data: big data should be designed and employed with respect for fundamental rights and freedoms, with the well-being of individuals in mind. The use of big data in ways that do not ultimately serve mankind is perceived as detrimental, which is a justification for curbing the freedom to engage in such uses.

The big data phenomenon and current legal framework are thus reviewed from the perspective of individual human beings and their rights and freedoms. This deliberate focus on individuals and their (fundamental) rights is neither a rejection of the legitimate interests of companies, governments, or other organisations in big data nor a disregard for the

4. Directive 95/46/EC of the European Parliament and of the Council of 24 October 1995 on the protection of individuals with regard to the processing of personal data and on the free movement of such data 1995 (OJ L281/31).

positive impact that big data can have. It does, however, influence the position taken with respect to big data: because of the exclusive focus on the rights and freedoms of individuals, the chapters critically scrutinise big data, those who employ it, and its negative impact. This is a choice for a perspective that is coherent from an academic point of view and of added value to the general discourse on big data. What companies, governments, and other organisations are permitted to do with big data under the current regulatory framework is an important question, particularly due to the links between big data, innovation, and economic growth, but many academics and practitioners are already looking into this topic. It is not the intention of this research to give a conclusive overview of where the boundaries of what is allowed with big data lie, from the point of view of those desiring to engage in big data. Because of the focus on *individuals* and *individual rights and freedoms*, there is also less focus on possible detrimental consequences of big data for society at large, or on aspects of rights that are particularly valuable for society at large instead of being aimed at individual human beings, like big data's possible impact on democracy through, *inter alia*, potentially limiting freedom of expression.

This research is territorially limited to the EU. It therefore focuses on the law that applies in the EU, although the discussion of the effects of big data does not maintain a similarly sharp division between EU and non-EU literature and examples, as both can be relevant in the EU territory now or in the future. At the fundamental rights level, the jurisdiction of the Council of Europe (CoE) and the EU are included, as they are the most important in the EU.[5] They contain fundamental rights instruments, the European Convention on Human Rights (ECHR or Convention) and the Charter of Fundamental Rights of the European Union (CFREU or Charter), that can amongst others be invoked in supranational courts.[6] The CJEU, based in Luxembourg, decides cases regarding the CFREU. Complaints on the basis of the ECHR can be lodged with ECtHR based in Strasbourg.[7] European notions of privacy and data protection and the secondary legal framework on data protection developed largely under the influence of these courts.[8]

Throughout this book, the focus will be first and foremost on commercial uses of big data, because of, amongst others, the scale of commercial data processing, the limited capacity for independent oversight, and the

5. *See* further the methodology section below, particularly subsection 1.2.5.2.
6. Convention for the Protection of Human Rights and Fundamental Freedoms 1950 (2007/C 303/02); Charter of Fundamental Rights of the European Union 2009 (OJ C83/02).
7. Both the ECtHR and the CJEU are occasionally referred to as 'Court' under their respective jurisdictions in the next paragraphs. The Court of Justice of the European Union has been renamed over the course of the years; throughout this work the Court will be referred to by its current name and abbreviation (CJEU), which it acquired with the entry into force of the Lisbon Treaty in 2009.
8. The choice of jurisdictions is elucidated and justified in the methods section of this introduction, *see* 1.2.5 below.

expected prevalence of interferences with individuals' rights. Big data for criminal investigations and surveillance by governments or intelligence agencies are distinct in terms of laws and issues that apply in these contexts. The principal difference is that in these situations there is a vertical relationship whereby fundamental rights have direct effect, whereas for companies the protection is vested in the government or EU. Criminal investigations and surveillance are excluded from the scope of this research.

1.2.4 Terminology[9]

The research question contains concepts that merit further explanation because they are multi-interpretable and their conceptualisation influences the scope of the research. These concepts are 'big data' and 'individual rights and freedoms', the latter consisting of a selection of rights originating from the CoE and EU jurisdictions. Chapter 2 maps out the concept of big data in detail, explaining the origin of the term, what happens in practice and the positive and negative consequences for individuals. Here, the concept of big data is only succinctly explained, as a background against which to read the ensuing subsections on the individual rights and freedoms affected by it. 'Individual rights and freedoms' is explained in more detail, as it is the normative framework against which to test the current EU legal framework and possible alternative solutions. The explanation is divided into two parts: first the rationale and delineation of the notion 'individual rights and freedoms' is discussed, after which a specification of the selected rights and freedoms follows. Subsection 1.2.5 below discusses the selection and methodological choices behind the conceptualisations of this subsection.

1.2.4.1 Big Data

Big data is a multi-interpretable term, whose meaning differs according to who is using it and in what context it is used. However, most definitions have a few characteristics in common, which makes it possible to give the following general description. In big data, data are collected and analysed. The data that are used as input often constitute personal data, i.e., data that relate to identifiable natural persons (*see* Chapter 4), but this need not be the case. In many big data projects, no personal data are processed at all, such as when meteorological data are used to make predictions about weather and climate. On the basis of the acquisition and analysis of the data, information is extracted from it leading to general knowledge or models and predictions on the basis of which individuals can be categorised or clustered. Specific characteristics place them in a group, which results in them being included

9 Parts of this section, particularly subsection 1.2.4.2.2, have been previously published.

or excluded from certain decisions, based on one or (usually) more variables. As such these models or predictions target people individually or as groups. Alternatively, general decisions can be made based on the knowledge derived from big data. Even though these decisions do not target individuals, they have the potential to affect the individual rights and freedoms discussed below. In this work, big data is thus seen as a process, not as the mere collection of large amounts of data.[10] At the same time, with this perception of big data, it can also be regarded as a socio-technological phenomenon with distinct legal implications (or, occasionally, a lack thereof).

1.2.4.2 Individual Rights and Freedoms

This research builds on the premise that big data potentially negatively affects the protection of multiple rights and freedoms of the individual. Whereas big data discussions often focus on privacy and data protection, here it is explained that even though these rights are of intrinsic value and great importance for individuals, there is more at stake.

The content of 'individual rights and freedoms' is derived from the content of fundamental rights, disregarding their procedural context. The selection is made on the basis of the expected detrimental effects of big data on these rights which is explained in detail in section 2.5.2 of Chapter 2. Together, these individual rights and freedoms are the normative framework, the benchmarks of what constitutes desirable protection with a basis in the fundamental rights, against which to test future conclusions on the scope of the EU legislative privacy and data protection framework and possible alternative ways to protect individuals against the negative impact of big data. The liberty that is taken in the approach of the concept of individual rights and freedoms also partially holds for the content of some of the rights and freedoms, such as personal autonomy. In the subsections below, specific attention is paid to these aspects where relevant. Most of the rights and freedoms are discussed succinctly, as their relevance in the big data context is discussed in section 2.5.2 of Chapter 2. Where their content is ambiguous, more attention is paid to their conceptualisation in the subsections below.

1.2.4.2.1 Personal Autonomy

Personal autonomy can be referred to as 'the capacity to be one's own person, to live one's life according to reasons and motives that are taken as one's own and not the product of manipulative or distorting external forces',[11] or summarised as individuals' capability to choose how to live their

10. *See* subsection 2.4 of Chapter 2 on the three-phase model of big data.
11. John Christman, 'Autonomy in Moral and Political Philosophy' in Edward N. Zalta (ed), *The Stanford Encyclopedia of Philosophy* (Spring 2015, Metaphysics Research Lab,

own lives.[12] It is a value underlying many (if not all) fundamental rights and freedoms, but it receives particular attention in relation to the ECHR's right to privacy.[13] It is argued to be a core rationale for protecting privacy in general.[14] Personal autonomy is often put on a par with (individual) self-determination. But personal autonomy is not only linked to privacy or the fundamental rights of the ECHR. It is also a key rationale for data protection, evidenced by, for example, the principles of consent and access to information which aim to give the individual control over her personal data and the consequences of processing. In Germany, this link is particularly visible through the constitutional right to informational self-determination that, although derived from the right to human dignity,[15] gives the individual the right to control personal data relating to herself. Moreover, personal autonomy is a precondition for living a life in freedom and constructing personal identity. Personal autonomy is of key importance in this work because of this close connection to individual freedom, its significance as an aspect underlying other fundamental rights, and the severe impact that big data can have on it.

1.2.4.2.2 Privacy and Data Protection

'Privacy', and to a lesser extent 'data protection', can mean different things. Data protection is not the same as privacy, although they are strongly related, and conceptually data protection is often considered a subspecies of privacy called informational privacy or data privacy.[16] Yet their exact definition is, amongst others, dependent on the subject area in which the terms are used; privacy can mean something different when it is used in law, computer science, or sociology. And even within these areas different interpretations

---

Stanford University 2015) <plato.stanford.edu/archives/spr2015/entries/autonomy-moral> accessed 8 December 2016.

12. Nelleke Koffeman, '(The Right to) Personal Autonomy in the Case Law of the European Court of Human Rights' (Leiden University 2010) 55–56. (Personal) Autonomy can be defined in many ways, *see* for example; Gerald Dworkin, *The Theory and Practice of Autonomy* (Cambridge University Press 1988) 3–6, 20, but in this work the concept is linked to the ECtHR's case law, *see*, *Pretty v UK* [2002] ECtHR 2346/02 [61–62].
13. Koffeman (n 12) 6–7, 62–64; Bernadette Rainey, Elizabeth Wicks and Clare Ovey, *Jacobs, White and Ovey: The European Convention on Human Rights* (Oxford University Press 2014) 383. *See also* subsection 3.5 of Chapter 3.
14. *See* amongst others Beate Rössler, *The Value of Privacy* (Polity Press 2005), Paul Bernal, *Internet Privacy Rights: Rights to Protect Autonomy* (Cambridge University Press 2014).
15. *Volkszählungsurteil* [1983] Bundesverfassungsgericht Az. 1 BvR 209/83, 1 BvR 484/83, 1 BvR 440/83, 1 BvR 420/83, 1 BvR 362/83, 1 BvR 269/83.
16. Gloria González Fuster, *The Emergence of Personal Data Protection as a Fundamental Right of the EU* (Springer International Publishing 2014) 75–94; Bert-Jaap Koops, 'The Evolution of Privacy Law and Policy in the Netherlands' (2011) 13 Journal of Comparative Policy Analysis: Research and Practice; Lee Bygrave, *Data Privacy Law: An International Perspective* (Oxford University Press 2014).

exist, for example because of national differences, e.g., the European versus the United States (US) perception of privacy, or because it is used with regard to specific subject matter, such as locational privacy or informational privacy.[17]

For this work, it is not necessary to fully map out the different theoretical conceptualisations of privacy, because the scope of the research is the law that applies in the EU.[18] Here, the normative concepts of privacy and data protection are derived from how the fundamental rights to privacy and to data protection of Article 8 of the ECHR and Articles 7 and 8 of the CFREU as interpreted by the ECtHR and the CJEU apply to big data. Below, some extra attention is spent on mapping the two concepts as interpreted by the two courts, because their scope is often conflated, which is inaccurate, particularly in the context of big data. Chapter 3 contains a detailed analysis of the fundamental rights to privacy and data protection, mapping out the scope of normative concepts of privacy and data protection in the EU as benchmarks for protection through secondary legislation and assessing its effects in vertical relationships.

Privacy protects the right to respect for private life and it covers a broad range of interferences.[19] Private life refers to a personal sphere (that can also exist in public spaces) over which an individual should have a high level of control.[20] Data protection refers to control over, or protection of, *personal data,* which are data related to identifiable individuals.[21] Data protection applies when personal data are processed and does not necessarily coincide with privacy: a private life element is not necessary for data protection.[22]

The concepts of privacy and data protection become clearer by comparing their history and scope. Privacy is a fundamental right with a long history, whereas data protection first appeared in national legislation of the Member States, international principles, and secondary EU legislation, and

---

17. *See* for example James Whitman, 'The Two Western Cultures of Privacy: Dignity Versus Liberty' (2004) 113 Yale Law Journal 1151. Locational privacy concerns privacy in certain places or spaces. Informational privacy refers to privacy with respect to information, which can also encompass confidentiality of communications.
18. *See* for such conceptualisations amongst others Ferdinand David Schoeman (ed), *Philosophical Dimensions of Privacy: An Anthology* (Cambridge University Press 1984); Daniel J. Solove, *Understanding Privacy* (Harvard University Press 2008); Adam D. Moore, *Privacy Rights: Moral and Legal Foundations* (Pennsylvania State University Press 2010).
19. Private life and privacy can be and are used interchangeably. *See* for more details on the usage and interchangeability of the term González Fuster (n 16), particularly pp. 81–84 regarding the Convention.
20. Christopher Kuner, 'An International Legal Framework for Data Protection: Issues and Prospects' (2009) 25 Computer Law & Security Review 307, 309.
21. *Ibid* 308.
22. *The Bavarian Lager v European Data Protection Supervisor* [2007] CJEU T-194/04 [118–119]; Maria Tzanou, 'Data Protection as a Fundamental Right Next to Privacy? "Reconstructing" a Not so New Right' (2013) International Data Privacy Law 88, 90; González Fuster (n 16) 205.

has only recently acquired fundamental rights status in the EU.[23] The historical relationship between privacy and data protection has been portrayed as the relationship between Zeus and Athena, Athena appearing from Zeus' head and thereafter regarded as his daughter.[24] But the prime difference between privacy and data protection lies in its subject matter. Privacy is broader than data protection because it not only concerns information; it can also be about for example physical spaces or certain choices people make.[25] But at the same time privacy is narrower, because data protection applies irrespective of whether there is an interference with the personal sphere.[26] For example, unwanted physical contact falls under privacy but not under data protection. Alternatively, when someone gives her address to a hotel and the hotel uses it solely for sending her a bill, data protection rules apply, but it will generally not be a privacy issue. In sum, privacy functions, amongst others, as a shield against interferences with the personal sphere, while data protection's nature is more enabling; it is more centred on channelling others' behaviour and controlling the flow of personal information.[27] Detailed rules and principles on data protection can be found in secondary EU legislation (e.g., the Data Protection Directive and the upcoming GDPR) and national laws.

Privacy and data protection can apply individually, but they are not mutually exclusive.[28] Personal data can be, and are often, covered by the right to privacy, but privacy does not encompass data protection per se.[29] To determine whether privacy is at stake, it is not solely the identifying character of the data that is decisive: the context in which the data are collected or processed also matters. It is difficult to determine exactly where the boundary

---

23. Cf. Gesetz zum Schutz vor Missbrauch personenbezogener Daten bei der Datenverarbeitung 1977; Loi n° 78-17 du 6 janvier 1978 relative à l'informatique, aux fichiers et aux libertés 1978; OECD Guidelines on the Protection of Privacy and Transborder Flows of Personal Data 1980; Directive 95/46/EC (n 4); Convention for the Protection of Individuals with regard to Automatic Processing of Personal Data 1981; Paul De Hert and Serge Gutwirth, 'Data Protection in the Case Law of Strasbourg and Luxemburg: Constitutionalisation in Action', *Reinventing Data Protection?* (Springer 2009) 5–8.
24. Tzanou (n 22) 88.
25. Raphaël Gellert and Serge Gutwirth, 'The Legal Construction of Privacy and Data Protection' (2013) 29 Computer Law & Security Review 522, 526.
26. Gloria González Fuster and Raphaël Gellert, 'The Fundamental Right of Data Protection in the European Union: In Search of an Uncharted Right' (2012) 26 International Review of Law, Computers & Technology 73, 526.
27. Paul De Hert and Serge Gutwirth, 'Privacy, Data Protection and Law Enforcement. Opacity of the Individual and Transparency of Power', *Privacy and the Criminal Law* (Insertia 2006) 67–80.
28. Gellert and Gutwirth (n 25) 524–526.
29. Cases in which only the right to data protection has been deemed to apply are for example *SABAM/Netlog* [2012] CJEU C-360/10 [48]; *Commission v Hungary* [2014] CJEU C-288/12 [47] *See also* Juliane Kokott and Christoph Sobotta, 'The Distinction Between Privacy and Data Protection in the Jurisprudence of the CJEU and the ECtHR' (2013) 3 International Data Privacy Law 222, 223–224.

lies between instances in which personal data are within, and those where they are beyond the scope of privacy. However, based on the case law of the ECtHR, circumstances that influence whether or not the right to privacy is triggered include the amount of data processed, whether the data are systematically collected and stored, whether the individual has a reasonable expectation of privacy, how sensitive the data are, and/or what impact the data can have on the private life of the individual.[30] It is, however, a fallacy that public data can never fall under the right to privacy.[31] Moreover, often privacy and data protection apply at the same time: a situation can give rise to both privacy and data protection issues. Part of the explanation for why this is so often the case is that one of the purposes of data protection is the protection of privacy. When this function is interfered with, privacy also applies. In addition, the amount of digital data keeps growing, and the private life of individuals is increasingly taking place online. Consequently, situations that trigger privacy will more and more involve a data protection component. This is very visible in the case law of the CJEU, where the two concepts keep coming closer together in the form of references to the 'right to privacy with respect to personal data'.[32]

Privacy and data protection are stand-alone fundamental rights that have intrinsic value, ends in themselves, which require protection as such. But through their protection of private life and personal data, they also support the protection of other individual rights and freedoms and are as such of instrumental value for these rights and freedoms. This latter value of the rights to privacy and data protection is referred to as the 'enabling function' (of privacy and data protection) in this work. Both aspects of privacy and data protection are discussed in greater detail in Chapters 3 and 4.

1.2.4.2.3 Freedom of Expression

Freedom of expression is guaranteed by Article 10 of the Convention and Article 11 of the Charter. It consists of three parts: (1) the right to hold opinions, (2) the right to *receive* information and ideas, and (3) the right to *impart* information and ideas. As such, it does not only encompass a right to disseminate information or express oneself. Freely holding opinions and receiving information and ideas are also protected by freedom of expression, and an interference with one of these elements constitutes an interference

30. *S and Marper v UK* [2008] ECtHR 30562/04 and 30566/04 [76]; *Rotaru v Romania* [2000] ECtHR 28341/95 [43–44]; *P.G. and J.H. v UK* [2001] ECtHR 44787/98 [57].
31. Cf. *Rotaru v Romania* (n 30) [43].
32. *Volker und Markus Schecke and Eifert* [2010] CJEU C-92/09 and C-93/09 [52]; *Digital Rights Ireland* [2014] CJEU C-293/12 and C-594/12 [62]; *Schrems* [2015] CJEU C-362/14 39.

with freedom of expression. Additionally, under freedom of expression one also has the right *not* to express oneself.[33]

Freedom of expression is of primary importance in the context of big data when there are actual or potential chilling effects, which means that people are reluctant to exert their right to freedom of expression, because they fear negative consequences for their person. These negative consequences range from criminal liability to social stigma, identity theft, increased government surveillance, or simply feelings of embarrassment, which may all result in self-censorship.[34] The doctrine of chilling effects has primarily developed in relation to the right to impart information and ideas in the context of state measures curbing people's liberties and the resulting social stigma, e.g., journalists facing far-reaching defamation legislation.[35] Over the years, however, attention for chilling effects on the right to receive information and ideas and hold opinions and its influence on eventual expression has developed, generally in the context of extensive (knowledge about covert) government surveillance.[36] This is based on the idea that governmental or corporate surveillance chills the receiver's gathering of information and ideas, i.e., that individuals may be reluctant to search for particular information or to express themselves because they feel watched by others.[37] Chilling this receiver aspect of freedom of speech may also chill subsequent free expression of information and ideas of this person.

Additionally, freedom of expression may be at stake in the case of selective offering of choices or information, or manipulation of people's ideas. In both cases, depending on the severity of the external influence on the individual, the gathering of information and ideas can be argued to be unfree.

1.2.4.2.4 Non-discrimination

The last individual right under discussion is the right not to be discriminated against. Discrimination means making a difference between similar people in similar cases. The non-discrimination right concerns making a difference in a negative way, i.e., when people receive disadvantageous treatment in comparison to others. Discrimination on grounds such as race, religion, ethnic origin, or gender is prohibited by Article 14 of the ECHR and Article

33. Rainey, Wicks and Ovey (n 13) 161.
34. Daniel J. Solove, 'A Taxonomy of Privacy' (2006) 154 University of Pennsylvania Law Review 447, 487–488, 495–496.
35. Cf. Frederick Schauer, 'Fear, Risk and the First Amendment: Unraveling the "Chilling Effect"' (1978) 58 Boston University Law Review 685; Rónán Ó Fathaigh, 'Article 10 and the Chilling Effect Principle' (2013) 3 European Human Rights Law Review 304.
36. Jonathon W. Penney, 'Chilling Effects: Online Surveillance and Wikipedia Use' (2016) 31 Berkeley Technology Law Journal 117, 129–134.
37. Neil Richards, 'Intellectual Privacy' (2008) 87 Texas Law Review 387, 403–404.

21 of the Charter.[38] The language of the Articles show that this list of grounds is non-exhaustive.[39] Secondary EU law has many instruments that combat discrimination in specific sectors, such as employment, welfare and social security, and access to justice, as do national laws.[40]

The scope of discrimination can be interpreted in many different ways, and in this work a broad concept is maintained. This allows for the discussion of borderline cases where distinctions between (groups of) people are made that are deemed unfair but not necessarily unjustified, and measures that reinforce existing inequalities in society, without having to focus solely on clearly demarcated discrimination towards targeted individuals in the legal sense. The exact scope of discrimination and how discrimination occurs in big data are discussed in section 2.5.2 of Chapter 2.

1.2.5 Methodology

This section explains how the enquiry into the EU legal framework on privacy and data protection and the negative impact of big data is conducted; what the approach is; what choices have been made; and what methods are used to answer the questions that lie at its foundation.

Two key assumptions underlie this research into the EU legal framework on privacy and data protection and the negative impact of big data. The first is that big data has (potential) negative effects on individual rights and freedoms; the second is that data protection law has a role to play in the protection of these individual rights and freedoms. The first assumption rests on a review of popular and scientific publications on the effects of big data.[41] This review has led to a diversified image of the impact that big data can have, including many consequences that can be perceived as detrimental to individuals that go beyond their privacy and data protection rights.[42] The

38. Article 14 ECHR is a 'parasitic' right, in the sense that it only applies when people are discriminated against in the enjoyment of their fundamental rights under the ECHR. However, the ECtHR's case law as well as Article 1 of Protocol 12 extend the scope of the right not to be discriminated against on the previously mentioned grounds in general. *See* David Harris and others, *Harris, O'Boyle & Warbrick: Law of the European Convention on Human Rights* (Oxford University Press 2014) 784, 819–821.

39. Rainey, Wicks and Ovey (n 13) 577.

40. European Union Agency for Fundamental Rights, *Handbook on European Non-Discrimination Law* (Publications Office of the European Union 2011) 64–78.

41. All literature reviews conducted in this work broadly follow the structure described by Hutchinson and Duncan, *see* Terry Hutchinson and Nigel Duncan, 'Defining and Describing What We Do: Doctrinal Legal Research' (2012) 17 Deakin Law Review 83, 112.

42. Part of this review, geared towards the conceptualisation of individual rights and freedoms, is summarised in the literature review in subsection 2.1.1 of Chapter 2.

second assumption is based on a review of the legal literature on big data.[43] Conducted at the start of this research in 2013, this review led to the observation that there was a widespread consensus that data protection law was the starting point of the discussion of how to deal with big data, undoubtedly under the assumption that personal data are processed in big data. Data protection was (and is) often regarded as the sole or main legal instrument to solve big data issues in the EU.

Resting on these assumptions, this research enquires into the potential and limitations of the EU legal framework on privacy and data protection with respect to protecting individuals' rights and freedoms against the negative impact of big data. Essentially, the research question can be split into three parts. First, it is necessary to ascertain what big data and its negative effects on individual rights and freedoms are (Chapter 2). Individual rights and freedoms as conceptualised above and justified below, serve as benchmarks for adequate (and necessary) protection of individuals. Second, the research must analyse what the scope of the rights to privacy and to data protection should be with respect to the protection of private life and personal data in the context of big data, and with respect to the other selected individual rights and freedoms, in order to assess what protection is required from the implementation of these norms into secondary EU legislation (Chapter 3). Third, it has to evaluate what secondary EU legislation achieves in terms of protection, i.e., to what extent the protection on the secondary EU level meets the normative concept of the fundamental rights to privacy and to data protection conceptualised in the second step of the research, and what its protective potential is with respect to big data's negative impact on all individual rights and freedoms (Chapter 4).

On the basis of the answers to these questions, a conclusion can be drawn that answers the main question. This conclusion shows what protection contemporary EU data protection law offers, and what gaps in protection it leaves against big data's negative consequences. On the basis of the normative concepts of the fundamental rights to privacy and to data protection, the conclusion then evaluates the scope of data protection law with respect to individual rights and freedoms, i.e., the task of data protection law with respect to reducing these negative effects of big data, based on the normative concepts of the rights to privacy and data protection. After this conclusion (also Chapter 4), possible legal alternatives to mitigate the negative impact of big data on individual rights and freedoms are reviewed, based on what the scope of data protection law ought to be, how it can be complemented by alternatives from other areas of law, and how these alternatives address the negative impact on individual rights and freedoms (Chapter 5).

43. The part of this review that considers data protection law is summarised under subsection 4.1.1 of Chapter 4.

In principle the research question is a normative question that takes an internal legal perspective.[44] It evaluates the capacity of the EU legal framework on privacy and data protection to mitigate the negative impact that big data has on individual rights and freedoms, and the extent to which it is the task of the framework to do so under the normative concepts of the fundamental rights to privacy and to data protection, from *within* the current EU law system.[45] But the research question contains many descriptive elements and consists of a mix of questions that require different methods to answer them. As the methodological approach differs for each subquestion, the following subsections discuss the methodological considerations for each part of the main research question separately.

1.2.5.1 Part I: Conceptualisation of Big Data and Individual Rights and Freedoms

Part I answers the questions what big data is and what its (potential) negative consequences on individual rights and freedoms are. It corresponds to Chapter 2 on big data and therefore also relates to the conceptualisation of the term 'individual rights and freedoms' in subsection 1.2.4.2 above.

The crux of the legal analysis of big data and the problems that it can cause for individuals lies in finding the balance between complexity and simplification. The subject is complex, and to a certain extent elusive because of the many meanings assigned to big data in practice. Yet simplification is necessary for the legal analysis, as the application and design of rules require specific events; no definite statements can be made about abstract concepts whose content is not described, nor can such abstract concepts be regulated. At the same time a (too far-reaching) simplification can lack nuance and consideration for the issues at stake. It can, amongst others, lead to the unjustifiable reduction of the negative effects of big data to privacy and data protection problems, and to proclaiming the EU legal privacy and data protection framework applicable to big data as a whole, without any reservations. This work opposes both assumptions.

To operationalise big data for normative and legal analysis while maintaining a nuanced view on the phenomenon, big data is conceptualised as a process that is divisible into three phases, being acquisition, analysis, and application. This division is compatible with commonly accepted definitions of big data. Moreover, it is general enough to accommodate the diversity of big data projects. At the same time, it is sufficiently specific to allow for the analysis of the different actions that occur throughout the

---

44. Richard L. Schwartz, 'Internal and External Method in the Study of Law' (1992) 11 Law and Philosophy 179, 180, 187–190.
45. Christina Eckes, 'European Union Legal Methods – Moving Away From Integration' in Ulla Neergaard and Ruth Nielsen (eds), *European Legal Method – Towards a New European Legal Realism?* (Djøf Publishing 2013) 166–168.

process, the risks that exist with respect to individual rights and freedoms, and how the legal framework applies to the different phases.

In the literature review, many possible negative effects of big data for individuals have been found. The review has not been limited to legal literature; negative effects of big data are often described in other social sciences.[46] The concept of 'individual rights and freedoms' serves as a framework in which to fit the negative effects, so that they can be adopted as benchmarks against which to test the current legal privacy and data protection framework. A selection of five rights and freedoms form the scope of the concept of 'individual rights and freedoms' as employed in this book (personal autonomy, privacy, data protection, freedom of expression, and non-discrimination). This selection is based on the detrimental effects identified in the literature on big data and the EU fundamental rights framework.

In the EU, there is multilevel protection of individuals: protection on the fundamental rights or constitutional level, on a secondary EU legislation level, and in the Member States on a national constitutional level and at the level of national legislation. The fundamental rights are enshrined in the ECHR and the CFREU which are addressed to states.[47] Notwithstanding the origin of fundamental rights and their moral justification, the selection of individual rights and freedoms that are researched in this work are enshrined in, or can be derived from, European fundamental rights treaties. Beneath this approach to the law lies the personal assumption that the fundamental rights and freedoms, including respect for privacy and the protection of personal data, are valuable and that their protection is a precondition for individual liberty.[48]

Most of these individual rights and freedoms correspond to a fundamental right as protected in the ECHR and the CFREU, and all of them have a basis in the case law of the ECtHR and CJEU. Because these fundamental rights instruments are in principle addressed to states, they are generally not applicable to relations between private parties, including individuals, such as social networking sites and individual users.[49] This means that when governments engage in big data which affects these individuals, these individuals are within its protective scope, but not necessarily so when it is private entities that they are faced with. Nevertheless, states have the obligation to protect individuals' fundamental rights and freedoms, and in spite of doctrinal or procedural aspects, individuals have fundamental rights that are to be protected. Moreover, the ECHR and CFREU may have an

46. Cf. Chapter 2, particularly (sub)sections 2.1.1 and 2.5.
47. The choice of the ECHR and the CFREU as the sources of fundamental rights is deliberate; *see* the next subsection for an explanation of the EU fundamental rights landscape and the choice of the Convention and the Charter.
48. Mark van Hoecke, *Methodologies of Legal Research Which Kind of Method for What Kind of Discipline?* (Mark van Hoecke ed, Hart Publishing 2011) vi.
49. *See* in detail Chapter 3.

effect on disputes between private parties. An example is the doctrine of positive obligations, with such positive obligations having been accepted under most of the rights referred to below. Also, in spite of no full horizontal effect of the CFREU being formally accepted, the CFREU influences relationships between private parties, amongst others because the CJEU takes fundamental rights into account in its interpretation of and decisions on secondary EU law.[50] These instances of pseudo-horizontal effects serve as an indication that these rights of individuals should be protected, whether it be against states or private entities. It is important to protect individuals' rights and freedoms irrespective of the nature of the party instigating the big data project, because making the necessity of protection dependent on whether a public or private entity is the actor does not match with contemporary digital reality. Public bodies invest in big data, but in terms of data accumulation, investment and market power, and processing capabilities, the commercial sector trumps many governments.[51] Individuals are faced with sometimes omnipresent private sector entities that are in some respects just as powerful as states, this power of states being the original concern behind fundamental rights. Individuals need similar protection of their rights and freedoms in commercial settings, for example, by effective and sufficiently protective legislation, otherwise notions such as a right to privacy or a right not to be discriminated against become hollow. 'Individual rights and freedoms' is thus interpreted broadly here. One should not think of them as positive rights that are necessarily enforceable between individuals and private parties in EU courts, but as normative concepts that are inextricably linked to the freedom of the individual.

1.2.5.2 Part II: Normative Scope of Privacy and Data Protection

Chapter 3, Part II of this book answers the question of what the scope of the right to privacy and data protection are. The eventual aim of this analysis is to show what the rights to privacy and data protection can and should protect in terms of negative consequences of big data for individual rights and freedoms.

The scope of the right to privacy and data protection is elaborated on the basis of the fundamental rights to privacy and data protection in the EU. Although there are many constitutional instruments that protect the right to

50. Jean-Paul Jacqué, 'The Charter of Fundamental Rights and the Court of Justice of the European Union: A First Assessment of the Interpretation of the Charter's Horizontal Provisions' in Frederico Casolari and Lucia Serena Rossi (eds), *The EU after Lisbon* (Springer 2014). *See* for an example in the area of data protection law *Google Spain* [2014] CJEU C-131/12.

51. Except for arguably the surveillance capacities of some states, such as the USA. Government surveillance is explicitly excluded from the scope of this work, *see* subsection 1.2.3.

privacy or similar rights, this research is limited to privacy in the EU, and this chapter therefore analyses these rights in the jurisdiction of the CoE and the EU. The ECHR and CFREU are arguably the most important fundamental rights instruments for individuals in the EU, principally because they encompass rights that can be invoked by individuals against states, amongst others, in the supranational ECtHR and CJEU.[52]

The CFREU is the fundamental rights treaty of the EU and it protects the right to privacy in Article 7 CFREU and the (separate) right to the protection of personal data in Article 8 CFREU. Yet an analysis of solely the CFREU for the normative concept of the rights to privacy and data protection in the EU is not sufficient for two reasons. First of all, all EU Member States are party to the ECHR.[53] Individuals can be plaintiffs before the ECtHR and states defendants, and the ECHR has a long history of case law that has been of supreme importance for the protection of fundamental rights and freedoms in the EU.[54] The second reason why an analysis of the ECHR cannot be omitted is of great dogmatic significance and concerns the relationship between the ECHR and the Charter, as established by Article 52 (3) CFREU read in conjunction with Article 53 CFREU. According to Article 52 (3) CFREU the meaning and scope of Charter rights that correspond to ECHR rights are identical to that of the ECHR rights. An exception is made when Charter rights provide more extensive protection, in which case the scope and meaning of the Charter prevail. Article 53 CFREU continues the explanation by stating the Charter shall not be interpreted in a way that restricts or adversely affects fundamental rights and freedoms as protected by, amongst others, the ECHR. The ECHR thus functions as a floor for the protection of fundamental rights in the EU (instead of as a ceiling). As such, the CFREU cannot be considered in isolation, as it strongly depends on the right to privacy as enshrined in Article 8 ECHR and interpreted by the ECtHR.

The research question enquiring into the normative conceptual scope of the fundamental rights to privacy and data protection essentially consists of four parts: history and interpretation of the ECHR and CFREU, the substantive scope of Article 8 ECHR and Articles 7 and 8 CFREU, respectively, a comparison of the scope of these rights in order to derive a general concept of the fundamental rights to privacy and to data protection with respect to big data, and an explanation of procedural aspects that influence the extrapolation of the normative concepts to the sub-constitutional level. As there are two jurisdictions, the comparative legal method is used to answer the question on the normative scope of privacy and

52. *See* Articles 1 and 32–34 ECHR and Article 51 CFREU and sections 3.2.1 and 3.3.1 of Chapter 3 on the history and interpretation of both instruments.
53. *See* <https://www.coe.int/en/web/conventions/full-list/-/conventions/treaty/005/signatures> accessed 26 May 2017.
54. Harris and others (n 38) 6, 34–37.

data protection.[55] A functionalist approach is taken to this micro-comparison of the right to privacy (CoE) with the rights to privacy and to data protection (EU), respectively.[56] This means that the comparison focuses on the function of the rights and not solely on the rule or provision as such. An absolute comparison of rights would exclude Article 8 CFREU on the right to data protection, whereas at least certain parts of personal data protection are deemed to be covered by privacy and Article 8 ECHR.[57] When comparing the case law of the CJEU with the ECHR and the ECtHR's case law there is a significant risk of mixing the two jurisdictions due to frequent references by the CJEU to the ECHR and the case law of the ECtHR, particularly prior to the drafting of the CFREU. To avoid accidentally mixing the two jurisdictions at the descriptive phase, successive analysis is chosen as a method of comparison, discussing both jurisdictions completely and separately, only comparing them at the end of this successive analysis.[58]

To gain an understanding of the main developments and landmark cases and to write the general descriptive parts, general commentaries are the sources that are used and referred the most. For the description of the scope of the rights and the analysis of the scope with respect to big data, the case law databases of both Courts were consulted.[59] The search encompassed cases decided on the basis of the right to privacy and/or the right to data protection, with a focus on cases that concern personal data. This selection of cases was determined by their possible relevance for the big data process, mainly where personal data are concerned, the scope of interferences is set, or the relevance of privacy or data protection for other fundamental rights and freedoms is discussed. The selection encompasses both cases in which a violation was found, and cases in which no violation was found because the case was, for example, deemed to be beyond the scope of application or the interference was justified.

The analysis of the rights to privacy and data protection in each section uses the doctrinal method of legal research.[60] The analysis first maps out the origin, interpretation, and applicability of the two fundamental rights treaties, because a number of particularities in these areas have a strong influence on the conceptualisation of the fundamental rights in the context of big data.

---

55. Konrad Zweigert and Hein Kötz, *Introduction to Comparative Law* (Tony Weir tr, Clarendon Press 1998) 1–47.
56. Esin Örücü, 'Methodology of Comparative Law' in Jan Martien Smits (ed), *Elgar Encyclopedia of Comparative Law* (Elgar 2006) 442–454.
57. Lee Bygrave, 'Data Protection Pursuant to the Right to Privacy in Human Rights Treaties' (1998) 6 International Journal of Law and Information Technology 247, 283–284.
58. As opposed to simultaneous analysis, in which for example comparable subparts of the jurisdictions or rights are discussed together or after each other, before continuing with the other parts of the analysis.
59. These databases are Hudoc (ECtHR) and Curia (CJEU), *see* <hudoc.echr.coe.int> and <curia.europa.eu> accessed 10 July 2015.
60. Terry Hutchinson, 'Doctrinal Research: Researching the Jury' in Dawn Watkins and Mandy Burton (eds), *Research Methods in Law* (Routledge 2013) 9–15.

Notably, how the instruments developed over time and the interpretative doctrine of both Courts determines how the rights are able to accommodate technological developments and changes in society. The second part, on the substantive scope of the fundamental rights, is divided according to jurisdiction. These sections essentially consist of two parts: descriptive analyses of the fundamental rights and evaluative parts where the scope with respect to big data is examined. The next parts analyse the rights, maintaining the tripartite structure of the provisions of the rights and their interpretation by the courts. The interests that are protected by the respective rights are discussed first, limited to aspects that are relevant in the context of big data. What follows is a discussion of the scope of interferences and the possible justifications for these interferences, insofar as they are relevant. The conclusions on the scope distinguish between the different phases as set out in the three-phase model of big data. Both the section on the ECHR and the section on the CFREU follow this structure, but as the CFREU section contains two rights (Articles 7 and Article 8 CFREU), the analysis is done twice. Overlap between the two sections will be kept to a minimum; where relevant the section on the CFREU refers back to subsections in the ECHR section. In the penultimate part of the chapter, the outcomes of both jurisdictions are compared, after which procedural aspects regarding the effects on the sub-constitutional level are mapped out. Taking into account the differences between the ECHR and CFREU, the chapter concludes with a general concept of privacy and data protection on a European fundamental rights level in the context of big data.

For the analysis both primary sources, i.e., legal instruments and case law, and secondary sources, i.e., (academic) literature, are used. In the analysis, the legal hierarchy of sources is maintained. This method of interpretation corresponds to the traditional (civil law) hierarchy of legal sources adhered to in this book, which makes a hierarchical distinction between the law itself, case law, and secondary interpretative sources like academic literature.[61] This means that the law itself is the starting point, i.e., Article 8 ECHR and Articles 7 and 8 CFREU, respectively. The method on treaty interpretation of the Vienna Convention on the Law of Treaties is used for the interpretation of the law.[62] This means that the provisions need to be interpreted in accordance with their ordinary meaning in context and in accordance with the object and purpose of the Convention and the Charter and the application of their provisions by the two Courts in practice.[63] Context refers to, amongst others, the preamble and annexes of the treaty, and other agreements or instruments relating to the treaty.[64] In the context of

61. Hutchinson and Duncan (n 41) 13, 22–23.
62. Vienna Convention on the Law of Treaties 1969; *Golder v UK* [1975] ECtHR 4451/70 [29].
63. Articles 31–33 Vienna Convention on the Law of Treaties.
64. Article 31 Vienna Convention on the Law of Treaties.

the right to privacy, the CoE's Convention 108 on Data Protection (Convention 108)[65] is an 'instrument relating to the treaty' and must therefore be taken into account when interpreting Article 8 ECHR. Additional interpretative principles flow from the judgments of the ECtHR itself, which has established its own doctrines of interpretation.[66] For the interpretation of the Charter this means, amongst others, the Explanations to the Charter and secondary legislation like the GDPR are part of the interpretative context.[67] Where the case law is ambiguous or leaves gaps in the interpretation of the law, use is made of the secondary sources such as academic literature.

1.2.5.3 Part III: Evaluation of Secondary EU Data Protection Law

Part III evaluates the protection offered by secondary EU data protection law. It evaluates its potential and limitations with respect to mitigating big data's potential negative impact on individual rights and freedoms as mapped out by Part I, to answer the question of what the potential and limitations of data protection law are with respect to protecting individuals in the context of big data. Second, it compares the protection offered to the normative concept of the rights to privacy and to data protection established by Part II, to assess whether and to what extent EU data protection law is lacking with respect to its tasks under the fundamental rights. Together, these analyses provide the answer to the question of to what extent secondary EU data protection law protects and should protect individual rights and freedoms against big data's negative impact.

Part III largely follows the doctrinal methodology and approach as described above, including the hierarchy of sources. As the future *lex generalis* of EU data protection law, the text of the GDPR is the point of departure for this chapter. Although the GDPR will only enter into force in May 2018, the analysis is not based on the current rules of Directive 95/46/EC, since existing problems may dissolve under the GDPR and the Directive's rules will be replaced soon.[68] The focus is solely on EU law and principles; national implementation is not taken into account in the analysis. The doctrinal method of legal research is used for the legal analysis and evaluation, as elucidated above.[69]

For the answer to the question to what extent EU data protection can mitigate big data's negative impact on individual rights and freedoms, the

65. Convention 108 (n 23).
66. *See* subsection 3.2.1 of Chapter 3.
67. Jean-Marc Sorel and Valérie Boré Eveno, 'Article 31', *The Vienna Conventions on the Law of Treaties: A Commentary* (Oxford University Press 2011) 825; Article 52 (7) Charter; Explanations Relating to the Charter of Fundamental Rights 2007.
68. Directive 95/46/EC (n 4).
69. Mark van Hoecke, 'Legal Doctrine: Which Method(s) for What Kind of Discipline?' in Mark van Hoecke (ed), *Methodologies of Legal Research – Which Kind of Method for What Kind of Discipline?* (Hart Publishing 2011) 11–17.

chapter will first and foremost focus on the scope of application and the substantive norms of EU data protection law, first analysing how data protection law applies to big data, after which the protective potential of the substantive norms is evaluated. The scope of data protection raises many questions in the context of big data. For example, is data protection applicable to all phases of the big data process? Or are some parts of big data beyond the scope of data protection per se, because of the legal criteria that determine applicability? A positive answer to this last question would mean that data protection is insufficient to protect individuals against the negative consequences of big data. Therefore this enquiry into the scope of application of data protection is cardinal: if it turns out that the big data process is not fully covered by data protection law, there is an immediate need to explore other (legal) solutions to big data issues that its rules do not address. When data protection law applies to big data, the question arises to what extent its substantive norms protect the individual. For the clarity of the argument, it is necessary to focus on aspects of the GDPR that have the most protective potential for the protection of individual rights and freedoms of big data in this discussion. Automated individual decision-making regulation, consent, and limitations on processing receive the most attention due to their potential vis-à-vis big data issues. There is also special attention for specific innovations of the GDPR, to see to what extent the new regulations add to the protective potential of EU data protection law. Given the fact that the enforcement of the law is inextricably linked with its protective potential in practice, this topic forms the final part of the discussion of EU data protection law.

The assessment of the EU data protection law framework culminates in an analysis of the lacunae in the protection offered. On the basis of this analysis, conclusions are drawn about the potential and limitations of EU data protection law to protect individuals against the negative (potential) impact of big data on individual rights and freedoms in general, showing where additional protection is necessary. These conclusions are first matched with the normative concepts of the rights to privacy and data protection as derived from Chapter 3, to see whether the fundamental rights to privacy and data protection would require a different implementation on the sub-constitutional EU level. On the basis of this assessment it is shown that there is a need for additional protection through other legal alternatives, which is the subject matter of Chapter 5.

1.2.5.4 Part IV: Recommendations

Part IV brings the phases, lacunae, and legal alternatives together. It gives an overview of the possibilities for changing the EU data protection law framework and discusses possible legal alternatives that address the negative effects on individual rights and freedoms. It is the goal of this overview to present the range of options and eliminate those that do not merit much further research, to show which ones seem promising and where the attention of further discussion and research should best be directed. Whereas the aim is to be comprehensive in showing the range of possibilities, the goal is not to be comprehensive in the exploration of each option; the overview serves as a well-founded inspiration for further research and not as policy advice.

Each subsection first provides contextual information on the suggested solution and the gaps and phases it addresses. Then the solution is appraised on the basis of its benefits, drawbacks, and feasibility. Feasibility primarily looks at doctrinal aspects and legal coherence for the targeted solutions of subsection 5.3.2, whether they can be enacted and could count on support in practice,[70] and whether new laws are necessary and proportionate given how much promise the less drastic solutions are deemed to show for the innovations of subsection 5.3.3. Here it must be borne in mind that that this book is written from the perspective of the protection of the individual and her rights and freedoms, but that a solution to advance the protection of individuals should by no means be judged in isolation. In particular, the rights and interests of others should be respected, including those of big data entities and society at large, that benefit from both personal data processing and the yields of big data. Lesser feasibility does not rule out a specific solution per se, but caution is required and it needs to be balanced with the benefits. If less invasive measures can tackle the same issues, this influences the conclusion on the suggested approach.

1.3 READING GUIDE

The question of the protective potential of the EU legal privacy and data protection framework against the negative effects of big data on individual rights and freedoms and how protection could be improved is answered in four chapters, followed by a conclusion. Chapter 2 explains big data and its (positive and negative) effects. The third and fourth chapters analyse the EU legal privacy and data protection framework, divided between the fundamental rights level and the secondary EU legislation level. Chapter 5 discusses alternative regulatory measures to solve the gaps in protection identified in the previous chapters.

Chapter 2 is about big data as a process of iterative processing activities. It gives an overview of the development of the term 'big data' and the many definitions it has, followed by three practical examples. The chapter continues with a conceptualisation of big data as a process divisible into

70. *See* for this argument emphasised in the context of data protection law and big data Lokke Moerel and Corien Prins, 'Privacy voor de homo digitalis: proeve van een nieuwww toetsingskader voor gegevensbescherming in het licht van big data en internet of things', *Homo Digitalis* (Wolters Kluwer 2016) 55–61.

three phases: acquisition of data, analysis of data, and application of the outcomes of the analysis. This process view helps to illuminate what is new about big data and underpins big data's normative and legal analysis. The second part of the chapter explains big data's effects on individual rights and freedoms. This part commences with a short overview of the positive potential of big data, followed by a more detailed description of big data's negative influence on personal autonomy, privacy and data protection, freedom of speech, and non-discrimination. These individual rights and freedoms provide the framework against which to test the current EU legal framework and possible alternative solutions.

Chapter 3 contains an analysis of the fundamental rights to privacy and data protection in the Council of Europe jurisdiction (ECHR) and the EU jurisdiction (Charter). After an analysis of each jurisdiction, geared towards the big data process and the possible negative impact on individual rights and freedoms, i.e., the different processing actions in big data and the enabling function of the rights to privacy and data protection, the content of the rights is compared. This comparison results in a normative concept of the rights to privacy and to data protection with respect to big data in the EU.

Chapter 4 concerns the ability of the EU data protection regulation, i.e., the legislative, sub-constitutional law, to protect individuals in the context of big data. The focus is on core aspects of data protection that directly influence EU data protection law's ability to protect individual rights and freedoms. EU data protection law's material scope of application is the first topic of discussion, as it determines the applicability of the regulation, while also revealing some gaps in protection offered when it comes to big data. Second are the substantive data protection norms, which are selected on the basis of their relevance and potential with respect to the negative effects as discussed in Chapter 2 on big data. This section is divided into the topics of transparency, control, and risk mitigation. The penultimate section briefly discusses remedies, liability, penalties, and enforcement of data protection law in the context of big data. At the end of the chapter the potential and limitations of data protection are evaluated, gaps in the protective framework are analysed, and a conclusion on the role of data protection in the context of big data is drawn.

Chapter 5 looks ahead by exploring possible solutions to fill the gaps in protection, thereby also evaluating the need for new legislative measures. The chapter gives an overview of the current discourse and a brief analysis of whether competition law, consumer law, non discrimination legislation, and sector or issue specific regulatory interventions can be(come) additional means to protect individuals against the negative impact of big data, featuring recommendations and areas for further research.

In the conclusion in Chapter 6, the findings of all the chapters are summarised and predictions regarding the findings are made. The chapter and book end with a discussion of the implications of this conclusion.

Chapter 2
Big Data

2.1 INTRODUCTION

To clarify the subject matter of this research and describe how big data affects individuals in society, this chapter describes big data and the consequences it has for individual rights and freedoms. This research is about big data, but the term *big data* is problematic. It is a popular and non-self-explanatory expression, a 'catch-all term for data that doesn't fit the usual containers'.[71] Its exact meaning varies depending on the context in which it is used, and the concepts and techniques that are employed in big data projects predate the definition itself.[72] In sum, big data is difficult to delineate and there is no consensus on its definition. But at the very least it signifies a shift in the thinking about and handling of data. As such it represents socio-technical development that merits close scrutiny, because of the consequences it has and might have for individuals and society.

This chapter starts with a literature review that gives an overview of the various descriptions of big data and its effects. The ensuing subsection elaborates what big data is in general terms, and explains the definition of big data as employed in this research. Subsection 2.3 follows with three examples of big data in three different sectors. These examples serve as a practical complement to the theoretical discussion of big data and function as

---

71. Thomas H. Davenport, *Big Data at Work: Dispelling the Myths, Uncovering the Opportunities* (Harvard Business Review Press 2014) 1.
72. Gregory Piatetsky-Shapiro, 'From Data Mining to Big Data and Beyond' (*Inside Analysis*) <insideanalysis.com/2012/04/data-mining-and-beyond> accessed 23 March 2015.

illustrations for big data use cases throughout the book, notably in the explanation of big data's consequences. In subsection 2.4 the definition of big data is worked out in greater detail through explaining the process view of big data. This three-phase model of the big data process enables the analysis of different aspects of big data from a legal angle in the subsequent chapters. Subsection 2.5 explains the effects of big data, commencing with positive developments, after which the focus shifts towards the negative impact of big data on individual rights and freedoms.

2.1.1 Literature Review

Information technology research company Gartner is often credited with introducing the general ingredients for big data in 2001, and consultancy firm McKinsey with introducing the term in 2011.[73] However, neither the expression nor what it is often said to represent are new.[74] Most importantly, the concept of extracting knowledge from (large) databases has been researched for years, under the terms data science, data mining, knowledge discovery from databases, and many more.[75] What marked the shift between 2001 and 2011 is that the datasets that companies sought to process were too big for the then-conventional data processing systems. New technological solutions such as Hadoop[76] were needed to work with these quantities of data.[77] Much was expected from these technological developments and big data became a popular term, particularly in business. Consequently, a wealth of technical literature on big data was published.[78] This type of literature is largely not used in this research, as it does not aid the understanding of big data from a legal perspective.

---

73. Doug Laney, '3D Data Management: Controlling Data Volume, Velocity, and Variety' (2001) Meta Group; James Manyika and others, 'Big Data: The Next Frontier for Innovation, Competition, and Productivity' (June 2011) McKinsey Global Institute Report.
74. 'A Very Short History of Big Data' (*Forbes*) <http://www.forbes.com/sites/gilpress/2013/05/09/a-very-short-history-of-big-data> accessed 22 April 2015.
75. *See* for example Usama Fayyad, Gregory Piatetsky-Shapiro and Padhraic Smyth, 'From Data Mining to Knowledge Discovery in Databases' (1996) 17 AI Magazine 37; Piatetsky-Shapiro (n 72). Although these terms often overlap with parts of big data, they cannot be equated with big data. For example big data is different from data science, as data science is a general term for the extraction of knowledge from data. Big data is also different from data mining, which refers to the computational process in which patterns are sought in large databases. The definition of big data as employed in this work is explained in detail in section 2.2.
76. Hadoop is an open source software platform that enables the distributed storage and processing of large quantities of data across multiple networks of connected computers.
77. Foster Provost and Tom Fawcett, *Data Science for Business* (O'Reilly Media 2013) 8.
78. Technical literature here primarily refers to books, journal articles, and reports from areas like statistics and computer science, including contributions from the academic and commercial research communities.

As big data became a more popular and common concept and its practical applications increased, the content of the term broadened, because it was used in an increasingly diverse array of contexts. The Internet saw a surge in popular 'sales-literature' on big data: writings that are presented as adding to existing knowledge and debate, but in fact only use the term 'big data' to attract a large audience for marketing-related purposes or to challenge having to abide by existing data protection principles.[79] Big data also became increasingly covered in academic and popular science literature.[80] These publications often focus on the effect, be it positive or negative, of big data on society. Big data has received particular attention from renowned scholars from the humanities field that researches the impact of digitisation on society and individuals.[81] Discussions of big data in *legal* literature increased as well.[82] Crossovers between the social sciences and law also exist, particularly in more popular scientific literature.[83] In the legal literature most articles focus on informational privacy, usually discussing the extent to which (parts of) current data protection paradigms are or will be shattered as a result of big data, or are in need of reconceptualisation.[84] Topics such as ownership and access to the data are covered as well, and

---

79. This material holds no relevance for an academic enquiry into big data. On the contrary: this kind of material dilutes the meaning of the term 'big data' and complicates informed discussion on its merits and risks. Obviously, this type of work is excluded from this work.
80. Tal Zarsky, '"Mine Your Own Business!": Making the Case for the Implications of the Data Mining of Personal Information in the Forum of Public Opinion' (2003) 5 Yale Journal of Law and Technology; Omer Tene and Jules Polonetsky, 'Judged by the Tin Man: Individual Rights in the Age of Big Data' (2013) 11 Journal of Telecommunications and High Technology Law 351; Kate Crawford, 'Big Data: Why the Rise of Machines Isn't All It's Cracked Up to Be' (2013) *Foreign Policy*; Jonas Lerman, 'Big Data and Its Exclusions' (2013) 66 Stanford Law Review; Cathy O'Neil, *Weapons of Math Destruction: How Big Data Increases Inequality and Threatens Democracy* (Crown 2016).
81. *See* for example danah boyd and Kate Crawford, 'Critical Questions for Big Data: Provocations for a Cultural, Technological, and Scholarly Phenomenon' (2012) 15 Information, Communication & Society. In the humanities, notably sociology, there is also much research in which big data is employed. These publications are outside the scope of this research, as big data is a method instead of the object of study.
82. *See* for example Christopher Kuner and others, 'The Challenge of "Big Data" for Data Protection' (2012) 2 International Data Privacy Law 47; Chris Jay Hoofnagle, 'How the Fair Credit Reporting Act Regulates Big Data' <papers.ssrn.com/abstract=2432955> accessed 28 May 2014; Fred H. Cate and Viktor Mayer-Schönberger, 'Notice and Consent in a World of Big Data' (2013) 3 International Data Privacy Law 67; Julia Lane and others (eds), *Privacy, Big Data, and the Public Good: Frameworks for Engagement* (1 edition, Cambridge University Press 2014).
83. *See* for example Viktor Mayer-Schönberger and Kenneth Cukier, *Big Data: A Revolution That Will Transform How We Live, Work, and Think* (Houghton Mifflin Hartcourt 2013).
84. Omer Tene and Jules Polonetsky, 'Big Data for All: Privacy and User Control in the Age of Analytics' (2013) 11 Northwestern Journal of Technology and Intellectual Property 239; Ira Rubinstein, 'Big Data: The End of Privacy or a New Beginning?' (2013) 3 International Data Privacy Law 74.

other articles focus on broader topics related to big data, such as ethics.[85] Frequently articles refer to big data but do not define it, and seem to equate big data with personal data processing in general.[86] There are also a growing number of policy documents that discuss the potential and risks associated with big data.[87] Much of the literature referred to in this chapter does not mention big data specifically, but deals with (parts of) big data as defined in this chapter in explaining how it works or what the effects of particular features of the big data process are.[88]

2.2 THE SUBSTANCE OF BIG DATA

As mentioned in the introduction to this chapter, the meaning ascribed to big data is dependent on the context in which it is used; there is no consensus on its definition. Nevertheless, it is possible to find general characteristics that receive much support in literature and policy documents, which is the approach adopted in this subsection on what big data entails. The conceptual analysis starts with a descriptive summary of the developments that have paved the way for the introduction of the term, followed by an analysis of descriptions that have received much support from academics, policy-makers, and industry experts. The common aspects of these views are analysed to come to a general understanding of big data, which is the concept that will be used in this work.

The most important development for big data is of course the creation of the digital computer. Digital computers and advances in their storage and processing capabilities have steadily increased data processing possibilities

85. Neil Richards and Jonathan King, 'Big Data Ethics' (2014) Wake Forest Law Review 393.
86. In some of these cases big data seems to be used to attract reader's attention, with the core of the article being largely a reiteration of issues in data protection that predate big data.
87. *See* amongst others European Data Protection Supervisor, 'Privacy and Competitiveness in the Age of Big Data: The Interplay between Data Protection, Competition Law and Consumer Protection in the Digital Economy' (2014) Preliminary Opinion; John Podesta and others, 'Big Data: Seizing Opportunities, Preserving Values' (2014) White House Report; John P. Holdren and Eric S. Lander, 'Big Data and Privacy: A Technological Perspective' (2014) White House Report; Council of Economic Advisers, 'Big Data and Differential Pricing' (2015) White House Report.
88. Mireille Hildebrandt, 'Profiling and the Rule of Law' (2008) 1 Identity in Information Society 55; Bart Schermer, 'The Limits of Privacy in Automated Profiling and Data Mining' (2011) 27 Computer Law & Security Review 45; Michal Kosinski, David Stillwell and Thore Graepel, 'Private Traits and Attributes Are Predictable from Digital Records of Human Behavior' (2013) 110 Proceedings of the National Academy of Sciences 5802; Lawrence Busch, 'A Dozen Ways to Get Lost in Translation: Inherent Challenges in Large-Scale Data Sets' (2014) International Journal of Communication 1727.

over the years.[89] Meanwhile the costs of storing and processing data have decreased. With the rise of the Internet and later the World Wide Web in the early 1990s, the *production* of digital data started to increase exponentially. The creation and sharing of digital information grew and kept rising, as the Internet and digital technologies have become ever more important in daily life. It is difficult to measure all data in the digital domain,[90] but estimates have been made. According to Scandinavian research from 2013, 90% of all the data in the world was generated in the two years preceding the research.[91] Cisco forecasts that annual global IP traffic will exceed a zettabyte[92] per year in 2016.[93] The International Data Corporation estimates that the size of the 'digital universe' is currently over 4.4 zettabytes.[94] This unprecedented increase in the amount of digital data in recent years is fuelled by many contemporary technological and societal developments. The *quantified self*-movement is an example of such a development.[95] Through sensors worn on (or even in) the body, individuals are able to constantly track their physical condition.[96] *Self-trackers* continuously collect and analyse data about, for example, their weight, hours of sleep, heart rate, and calorie intake; data that are also transferred to and used by the providers of the tracking software.[97] Related to the quantified self but broader is the development called the *Internet of things*; objects being online without the mediation of

89. Davey Alba, '50 Years On, Moore's Law Still Pushes Tech to Double Down' (2015) *WIRED* <http://www.wired.com/2015/04/50-years-moores-law-still-pushes-tech-double/> accessed 17 August 2016.
90. David Bounie and Laurent Gille, 'International Production and Dissemination of Information: Results, Methodological Issues, and Statistical Perspectives' (2012) 6 International Journal of Communication 1001.
91. Åse Dragland, 'Big Data, for Better or Worse' <http://www.sintef.no/home/corporate-news/Big-Data--for-better-or-worse, www.sciencedaily.com/releases/2013/05/130522085217.htm> accessed 7 May 2015.
92. A zettabyte is 1021 bytes, or a trillion gigabytes, which equals roughly two billion years of music. *See* '2016: The Year of the Zettabyte' *Daily Infographic* (23 March 2013) <http://www.dailyinfographic.com/2016-the-year-of-the-zettabyte-infographic> accessed 6 May 2016.
93. 'The Zettabyte Era: Trends and Analysis' (Cisco 2014) White Paper 1 <http://www.cisco.com/c/en/us/solutions/collateral/service-provider/visual networking-index-vni/VNI_Hyperconnectivity_WP.pdf> accessed 6 May 2016.
94. Vernon Turner and others, 'The Digital Universe of Opportunities: Rich Data and the Increasing Value of the Internet of Things' (International Data Corporation 2014) White Paper 2 <idcdocserv.com/1678> accessed 6 May 2016.
95. *See* <quantifiedself.com> accessed 12 May 2016.
96. *See* for example tracking wristbands from companies like FitBit and Jawbone, that measure a diverse array of variables and aim to encourage a healthier lifestyle <www.fitbit.com/uk/about> and <jawbone.com> accessed 10 June 2015.
97. J. Dale Prince, 'The Quantified Self: Operationalizing the Quotidien' (2014) 11 Journal of Electronic Resources in Medical Libraries 91.

humans.[98] Through electronics, sensors, and RFID-tags,[99] all kinds of 'things' can be connected to the web, such as household appliances, consumer goods, and even cattle.[100] All these different devices, objects, and sensors transmit continuous flows of data. These data can be related to individuals in society, like the aforementioned health data. But it can also be the data that have nothing to do with individuals or humans, like data measured by sensors in a production process or gathered about certain natural phenomena or in astronomy.[101]

In sum, ever since the beginning of the digital age, the creation of digital data has been increasing, resulting in a volume of data today that had never been anticipated when the first digital computers were made. And this enormous amount of data needs to be stored. Stored information creates possibilities for alternative uses; analysing data and gathering potentially useful knowledge from it. The rise in production and availability of digital data thus incited a new mindset that regards digital data as a resource for insights, to solve problems and improve the efficiency and effectiveness of processes. Both the private and the public sector have recognised the potential value that can be derived from raw data and seek to extract that value.

This new mindset and the accompanying societal changes in, amongst others, data production, spurred the technical innovations that are part of the definition of big data. Conceiving new ideas for making use of and deriving value from data called for new technical solutions for data storage and analysis. To discuss these developments from a technical perspective, big data is usually described by reference to the three Vs: volume, velocity, and variety.[102] Volume refers to the amount of data and thus to the capacity to store and process large quantities of data. There is no fixed definition or minimum number of bits that determine whether data are 'big' or not. It seems to be judged on a case-by-case basis, by exploring whether the dataset

98. Melanie Swan, 'Sensor Mania! The Internet of Things, Wearable Computing, Objective Metrics, and the Quantified Self 2.0' (2012) 1 Journal of Sensor and Actuator Networks 217; Tom Brewster, 'Traffic Lights, Fridges and How They've All Got It in for Us' *The Register* <www.theregister.co.uk/2014/06/23/hold_interthreat> accessed 13 May 2016.
99. RFID (Radio Frequency Identification) tags are very small chips that allow for identification.
100. Duncan Jefferies, 'How the "Internet of Things" Could Radically Change Local Government' *the Guardian* (18 August 2011) <http://www.theguardian.com/local-government-network/2011/aug/18/internet-of-things-local-government> accessed 1 June 2015. RFID (Radio Frequency Identification) tags are very small chips that allow for identification.
101. The different kinds of data in big data and the consequences of this diversity for the legal reflection on big data in subsequent chapters.
102. Sometimes these three Vs are complemented by other Vs, such as value or veracity, yet these Vs seem to be less widely accepted, and arguably proffered for marketing purposes rather than to clarify the technical shifts in data processing.

is too big to be managed by commonly used software tools.[103] Velocity in the big data context refers to speed in all aspects of the process: speed of the incoming data, speed of the output, minimisation of the feedback loop, etc.[104] Variety refers to a variety in data, amongst others, different content, different data formats, and originating from different sources. Dealing with various kinds of (unstructured) data and combining them for analysis creates new challenges for computer science,[105] as do velocity and volume. This demand spurs innovation, for example in the area of distributed computing and cloud computing. As new ways of making use of and deriving value from digital data are devised, new solutions for storage and analysis are called for. And so the circle continues: the cultural phenomena of a great and ever-increasing interest in making use of data and developments in computer science boost each other.

Big data is also described as data that exceeds the storage and processing capacity of conventional database systems,[106] and thus as a problem of data storage and processing that requires new technical solutions. However, this is not a tenable conclusive definition. It refers to a current standard and a technical aspect, which has been a continuous problem in different forms ever since the dawn of capturing information. Likewise, the mere quantity of data that are produced cannot be the defining factor in big data.[107] 'Big' is relative, not absolute;[108] it is an adjective whose meaning is determined by the context in which it is used. Describing big data as a recent or new problem with the storage of large quantities of data is not accurate and neglects the many other, non-technical phenomena associated with the colloquialism 'big data'. For the legal framework and the protection of individual rights and freedoms, important aspects are that personal data are collected and processed and that decisions that impact individuals' lives are taken on the basis of data. Including certain software or methods,[109] or a focus on correlations instead of causality,[110] as part of the definition would limit the scope of this research unnecessarily, as the aim or method of analysis are neither time-proof nor decisive in whether the private life of individuals is affected through the analysis of large quantities of data.

---

103. Note that this explanation of 'volume' is – as are many explanations of big data – somewhat circular; the definition generally refers to the term 'commonly used software tools', which refers to a certain industry standard at a given point in time, which is actually never explained or referred to in the explanation itself.
104. O'Reilly Media, *Big Data Now* (O'Reilly Media 2012) 6–7.
105. *Ibid* 1 9.
106. Manyika and others (n 73) 1.
107. Eric Siegel, *Predictive Analytics: The Power to Predict Who Will Click, Buy, Lie, or Die* (Wiley 2013) 78.
108. *Ibid.*
109. For example Hadoop, *see* above.
110. Mayer-Schönberger and Cukier (n 83) 7, 50–72.

To sum up, big data can be defined in many different ways,[111] but in this research it is considered to be an umbrella term for a socio-technical phenomenon caused by technological developments in computer science. This corresponds with how the term is used in society. Seen through a legal lens, key elements of big data are the view of (personal) data as *raw data,* the intent to keep and collect large quantities of data for multiple and uncertain purposes, and the use of computational analysis as a basis for decisions. Although not a necessary precondition to fit within this definition of big data, this research focuses solely on big data when the data that are collected are *personal* data[112] and/or when the decisions that are made affect individual rights and freedoms. The definition of big data is explained in more detail in subsection 2.4 which contains a further, more in-depth analysis of big data as a process.

2.3 BIG DATA IN PRACTICE: ILLUSTRATIONS

Both the areas in which big data are applied and the data that are used for big data are incredibly diverse. Examples range from foresting and forest preservation, to fraud prevention in retail.[113] This section discusses three sectors in which big data is used: finance, medical research, and online personalisation. They have the twofold aim of illustrating how the theory of the previous sections works in practice, and showing diversity in areas of application and the type of data used in big data. The examples from the finance, health, and general online area are selected because they affect people's individual rights and freedoms differently, and involve the processing of personal data in various ways; they are not meant to be representative of all big data projects.[114] The cases indicate that big data can be regarded as

---

111. Gloria González Fuster, 'Big Data and Smart Devices and Their Impact on Privacy' (European Parliament 2015) Study for the LIBE Committee PE 536.455 11; Article 29 Working Party, 'Opinion 03/2013 on Purpose Limitation' (2013) WP 203 45; European Data Protection Supervisor, 'Meeting the Challenges of Big Data: A Call for Transparency, User Control, Data Protection by Design and Accountability' (2015) 7/2015 7.
112. *See* Chapters 3 and 4.
113. Mike Wheatley, 'Big Data Goes Green: How Data Analytics Is Saving the World's Forests' <siliconangle.com/blog/2013/07/02/big-data-goes-green-how-data-analytics-is-saving-the-worlds-forests> accessed 6 May 2016 and <https://www.globalforest watch.org>, and the solutions offered by IntelliQ <https://www.intelliq.co.uk> accessed 6 May 2016, that provide 'intelligent tools required to assess any area of fraud/process failure, to eliminate false positives, incorporate data from other sources including banking and CCTV, to discover unique anomalies and to drill down to the core of a gift wrapped case' <http://www.intelliq.co.uk/solutions.htm> accessed 6 May 2016.
114. Big data projects do not necessarily process the personal data or individuals. *See* for example on how big data not involving personal data could aid in the prevention of world hunger: Paul Rubens, 'Can Big Data Crunching Help Feed the World?' (*BBC*

a process consisting of different phases. This process view aids big data's legal analysis and is the subject of subsection 2.4. Additionally, they show that different societal interests are at stake in big data and display a range of positive and negative effects that will return in subsection 2.5 on big data's influence on individual rights and freedoms. Under the next three headings the three illustrations of finance and medical research sectors and online personalisation are concisely described, to give three practical examples before the following subsections dive into more detail on the process view and big data's impact on individual rights and freedoms. These three cases also serve as illustrations throughout the book.

2.3.1 Credit in the Financial Services Industry

In the financial services industry, lenders such as banks or credit card companies need to predict who will default on debts and who will not. The better the lender's capability to predict, the less capital is lost and the more competitive the offers that can be made to prospective customers. Lenders can ask about income, outstanding debts, and marital status before deciding on whether to offer an individual a loan or rely on a *credit score* that is assigned to individuals.[115]

Big data creates new opportunities for credit scoring, as 'all data is credit data'.[116] Data about individuals can be gathered from a multitude of sources, e.g., from social media or through apps on mobile phones. More factors can be taken into account in the assessment due to the previously mentioned increases in storage and processing capabilities. Moreover, the credit scoring models can become more sophisticated and detailed through big data. Large datasets can be analysed for (past) correlations between random (combinations) of variables and defaulting on payments. The analysis is not limited to the data of the individual herself; data of others, for example, previous clients or people that are known for having defaulted on loans, can be taken into account. The history and data of other individuals can be used to make more accurate predictions regarding a potential new

---

News) <www.bbc.com/news/business-26424338> accessed 24 April 2015 or on the potential of big data in the oil and gas industry; Robert K. Perrons and Jesse W Jensen, 'Data as an Asset: What the Oil and Gas Sector Can Learn from Other Industries about "Big Data"' (2015) 81 Energy Policy 117.

115. A credit score is a number that represents the applicant's creditworthiness, i.e., the risk that a borrower will default on her debt. The most well-known credit scoring model is the American FICO score, which is based on amongst others payment history, debt burden and types of credit that are used by the individual. *See* for example Kaiser Fung, *Numbers Rule Your World: The Hidden Influence of Probability and Statistics on Everything You Do* (McGraw Hill 2010) 45 61.

116. Mikella Hurley and Julius Adebayo, 'Credit Scoring in the Era of Big Data' (2016) 18 Yale Journal of Law and Technology 148, 151.

customer and predict events further into the future. An address or a combination of seemingly unrelated variables, like the colour of one's car, the preference for a certain brand of shower gel, or the number of hours spent on the Internet on a weekly basis, could lead to a prediction of a high chance of defaulting on a loan, because similar patterns are reflected in the data of previous defaulters. These factors and patterns would in all probability not be found with traditional methods to assess creditworthiness. They classify as correlations, indicating the existence of a link between two variables, such as lesser creditworthiness and individual characteristics. As such, they do not implicate causality, i.e., lesser creditworthiness is not (necessarily) *caused* by these characteristics.

Big data-based credit scoring can have many different effects in practice. Predictions and risk assessments are based on multiple models combined and underlying correlations in large datasets.[117] As more factors and correlations are taken into account, it is possible that individuals that would normally be rejected for a mortgage are accepted because of big data predictions. For example, a person with a college debt might receive a positive credit score because her score is not solely based on the outstanding debt, but on many data points, including correlations found in the datasets preceding the individual's application. Yet the reverse is also possible. People who have an income and no outstanding debts may receive higher interests rate or no loan at all, because factors that seem unrelated to credit risk correlate with defaulting on loans in the future.[118]

Credit offering based on big data is already applied in practice, by companies such as ZestFinance, Kreditech, and Big Data Scoring.[119] ZestFinance uses 'thousands of datapoints and advanced machine learning algorithms' to help customers from the financial services industry make better predictions on who will default on their loans.[120] The data used stem from both the applicants themselves as well as from third parties.[121] The aim is to improve underwriting, through more accurate predictions made possible by big data. To achieve this aim, data are collected from different sources and analysed using advanced data analysis techniques. The yields of the analysis are then applied to people on the basis of the limited information they share with the credit company. These people are not necessarily, and certainly not solely, the sources from which the data were collected. Acquisition of data, analysis of data, and application of the outcomes of analysis can thus be

117. *Ibid* 168–183.
118. *See* subsection 2.5.2 for potentially unfair effects.
119. Marcus Wohlsen, 'Tech's Hot New Market: The Poor' (2013) *WIRED*; Hurley and Adebayo (n 116) ZestFinance <www.zestfinance.com>, Kreditech <www.kreditech.com> and Big Data Scoring <www.bigdatascoring.com> accessed 12 December 2016.
120. 'ZestFinance Introduces Big Data Model For Collections Scoring: New Industry-Specific Models Can Increase Collections by 30%' <https://www.zestfinance.com/pdf/ZestFinance_Collections_Model.pdf> accessed 6 May 2016.
121. *Ibid.*

viewed as separate phases of big data. Each phase has its own effects on individual rights and freedoms, and each phase fits differently within the EU legal privacy and data protection law framework, as we shall see in the coming sections and chapters.

2.3.2 Biobanks in Medical Research

General practitioners see a limited number of patients with diverse medical conditions, specialists see a limited number of patients and focus on particular medical conditions, and researchers usually have a limited number of research subjects. Consequently, each of them has a limited view on the overall population and what factors, such as genetic make-up, use of treatment or other drugs, or lifestyle, influence whether people get diseases or not, and whether a particular treatment is successful. With big data in the form of biobanking, the information on these factors from all these different practitioners and institutions is pooled. This creates a rich resource for the advancement of medical science. Through the combination of data from general practitioners, specialists, and researchers with data from other sources and the use of big data analytics, patterns can be revealed that are not visible in smaller datasets. For example, when a general practitioner prescribes a drug to multiple people, and only one of them experiences serious side effects, usually it is not clear why this particular person has side effects. When large quantities of data are available from every person in a given population that has taken the drug, big data can be used to uncover factors that influence or cause side effects, such as a genetic factor or the interaction with other drugs.[122] When data are collected, updated, and analysed in real-time, it will be possible to discover and respond to patterns quickly, for example to unknown negative effects of drugs that are already on the market.

There are many problems to be solved in health care, ranging from optimal treatment to prevention. Much is expected of big data in terms of improvements and solutions. Big data is believed to advance the research, treatment, and prevention of diseases and to reduce health care costs.[123] One of the means through which these improvements are sought is by means of biobanks. Biobanks are large repositories in which biomaterials and (clinical) data are stored. These data and materials can be linked to other data, for

122. *See* for examples that regard the discovery of side effects Eric Topol, *The Creative Destruction of Medicine: How the Digital Revolution Will Create Better Healthcare* (Basic Books 2012) 216–217.

123. *See* for example Peter Groves and others, 'The "Big Data" Revolution in Healthcare: Accelerating Value and Innovation' (McKinsey&Company 2013) McKinsey Report; Science Europe, 'How to Transform Big Data into Better Health. Envisioning a Health Big Data Ecosystem for Advancing Biomedical Research and Improving Health Outcomes in Europe' (2014) Workshop Report.

example, to administrative registries of the government such as civil registration registers or pathology registers. In Europe, many different biobank initiatives exist. Some of these are national and operated by governmental institutions,[124] others are charities based on voluntary participants,[125] and yet others exist mainly as cooperation between (academic) hospitals.[126] Commercial initiatives of biobanks are also established in the pharmaceuticals and life science industry, for in-company research or other purposes. An example is the personal genomics company 23andMe that offers personal genome tests for consumers.[127] Individuals submit their DNA to the company to receive information on more than 100 health conditions and hereditary traits. At the same time, the company uses the data of individuals to create their own biobank. Third parties can access this biobank when they pay and meet certain conditions.[128] The aims, targeted participants, and collected data thus differ according to each biobank.

The large, diverse datasets in biobanks are also used for research into causes of diseases. With the data about individuals' genetic and physical characteristics, lifestyle, and environmental information, correlations between these variables and specific medical conditions can be discovered. Markers can be identified that, for example, relate to the prevalence of a disease like Alzheimer's or the likelihood of suffering from a particular kind of cancer. These findings spur personalised medicine, medicine that is geared towards (effective) treatment of the individual instead of towards the population at large, which is more cost-efficient and has better results.[129] The kind of knowledge that big data can uncover supports the prevention and treatment of diseases and prevents unnecessary treatments with potentially harmful side effects. Ultimately big data helps society by advancing medical science and decreasing health care costs. Although most applications and outcomes of big data in biobanks will only become known in the long run and will not always be publicly attributed to the biobank, some discoveries have already been made through their use.[130] For example, through the

---

124. Generation Scotland <www.generationscotland.org> and the Danish National Biobank <www.biobankdenmark.dk> accessed 7 May 2016.
125. UK Biobank <www.ukbiobank.ac.uk> accessed 7 May 2016.
126. Parelsnoer Institute <en.parelsnoer.org> accessed 7 May 2016.
127. 23andMe <www.23andme.com> and <www.23andme.com/en-eu> accessed 10 June 2015.
128. Charles Seife, '23andMe Is Terrifying, but Not for the Reasons the FDA Thinks' [2013] *Scientific American* <www.scientificamerican.com/article/23andme-is-terrifying-but-not-for-reasons-fda> accessed 8 June 2015 <www.23andme.com/about/privacy/#Full> and <www.23andme.com/en-eu/about/privacy/#Full> accessed 10 June 2015.
129. Topol (n 122) 22–32.
130. Many of the mentioned biobanks have been established less than a decade, and it takes time for patterns and research results to become known or drugs to be developed and approved for the market. Furthermore many organisations use biobanks as mere resources for research and drug development and there is no obligation to publicly credit the biobank afterwards.

United Kingdom (UK) Biobank discoveries were made regarding the origins and development of the rare Ménière's disease, lifestyle decisions that can reduce breast cancer risk in middle-aged women, and the link between a father's diabetes and low birthweight in infants that indicates a higher risk of developing various conditions later in life.[131]

2.3.3 Online Personalisation

Many people will at some point in their life experience a form of big data as described in the previous two illustrations, but there is one example of big data that already directly affects many Europeans: the personalisation of their online experience. What people see when they are online, whether it be for work, practical matters, or entertainment, is adapted to circumstances such as where they are located, what time it is, what they do, and who they are. There is not *one* Internet which is the same for all users; our online experience is tailored to us in different ways.

A pervasive form of online personalisation based on big data is behavioural advertising. Behavioural advertising, also referred to as behavioural targeting, refers to the practice in which individuals are shown online advertisements that are targeted at their person, based on what is known about them, such as their location, browsing history, known interests, or additional information such as characteristics of the device and browser that are used to view the website.[132] Advertisements on websites are usually not provided by the website itself, but by third parties, like advertising networks or advertising exchanges. These networks collect large amounts of data about individuals, for example, data about web browsing behaviour, webpages visited, demographics, social interactions, and locations, on the basis of which individual profiles and predictions about individuals can be made.[133] When an individual user is identified, generally through a cookie,[134] the advertising network serves an ad that is tailored to the user, based on the data

131. UK Biobank, 'Research Gives New Insights into Ménière's Disease' <http://www.ukbiobank.ac.uk/2014/04/research-gives-new-insights-into-menieres-disease> accessed 10 June 2015; UK Biobank, 'Keeping Active in Middle Age May Help Cut Breast Cancer Risk, Study Shows' <http://www.ukbiobank.ac.uk/2014/11/keeping-active-in-middle-age-may-help-cut-breast-cancer-risk-study-shows/> accessed 10 June 2015; UK Biobank, 'Dad's Influence on Birth Weight Linked to Diabetes Genes' <http://www.ukbiobank.ac.uk/2013/12/dads-influence-on-birth-weight-linked-to-diabetes-genes/> accessed 10 June 2015; Jessica S. Tyrrell and others, 'Parental Diabetes and Birthweight in 236 030 Individuals in the UK Biobank Study' (2013) 42 International Journal of Epidemiology 1714.
132. Frederik Zuiderveen Borgesius, 'Behavioural Targeting', *Improving Privacy Protection in the Area of Behavioural Targeting* (Kluwer Law International 2015) 15–16.
133. Siegel (n 107) 37; Zuiderveen Borgesius, 'Behavioural Targeting' (n 132) 33–41.
134. A cookie is a small piece of data that is stored on an individual's computer for identification purposes. Profiles and other data may be linked to a cookie.

that it has and the predictions it makes about what is effective for this specific individual. Alternatively, real-time bidding can take place to serve the ad. Within a few milliseconds an automated bidding process amongst multiple (competing) advertising networks and other parties is completed, after which the winner gets to serve the ad to the visitor.[135] Except for perhaps mild surprise at seeing the same ad on multiple different websites, or seeing an ad in one's native language instead of in the language of the website that one is visiting, the user will not notice the massive collection, analysis, and further processing that is taking place behind the scenes.

Behavioural advertising across websites is far from the only means of online personalisation that is based on big data. Personal data, models, and predictions are continuously used for optimisation and to adapt what people get to view to individual visitors, to retain their attention, offer them personalised services, and generate bigger revenues. Users often unconsciously end up in online experiments, where they view pages the layout of which differs slightly from that of other visitors, so that the service learns about minor differences that make people click or purchase.[136] Online, we are constantly segmented into different groups that receive different content, as 'individualization trumps universals'.[137] Search engines like Google Search create complex algorithms that take amongst others users' location data and search history into account.[138] Social networks like Facebook personalise what people see in their news feed, which is based on a plethora of data, including data about how users and their network engage with content.[139] Entertainment platforms such as Netflix and web shops like Amazon provide personalised recommendations for next viewings or future purchases,[140] and news websites change their pages depending on who is viewing it.[141] Many people know about phenomena such as behavioural advertising or personalised product suggestions, but the actual personalisation often remains invisible to users, and in our daily Internet use we generally do not dwell on

135. Zuiderveen Borgesius, 'Behavioural Targeting' (n 132) 45–47.
136. Brian Christian, 'Test Everything: Notes on the A/B Revolution' (2012) *WIRED*.
137. Siegel (n 107) 23.
138. Steven Levy, 'How Google's Algorithm Rules the Web' (2010) *WIRED*; Martin Feuz, Matthew Fuller and Felix Stalder, 'Personal Web Searching in the Age of Semantic Capitalism: Diagnosing the Mechanisms of Personalisation' (2011) 16 First Monday.
139. Josh Constine, 'How Facebook News Feed Works' <social.techcrunch.com/2016/09/06/ultimate-guide-to-the-news-feed> accessed 13 December 2016.
140. Xavier Amatriain, 'Big & Personal: Data and Models behind Netflix Recommendations' (2013) Proceedings of the 2nd International Workshop on Big Data, Streams and Heterogeneous Source Mining: Algorithms, Systems, Programming Models and Applications 1; Greg Linden, Brent Smith and Jeremy York, 'Amazon.com Recommendations: Item-to-Item Collaborative Filtering' (2003) 7 IEEE Internet Computing 76.
141. Natali Helberger, 'Merely Facilitating or Actively Stimulating Diverse Media Choices? Public Service Media at the Crossroad' (2015) 9 International Journal of Communication 1324, 1329.

how the information we view differs from the content that other people receive.

In sum, people find themselves in a digital realm that is personalised in a multitude of small ways, based on endless streams of (personal) data. This enables companies to segment and target individuals, saving resources and being more effective. It has advantages for individuals too, serving them content that is likely more interesting to them in an age of informational overload.[142] Personalisation based on big data is here to stay.

2.4 PROCESS VIEW OF BIG DATA

To summarise what has been argued so far: big data is neither sector specific nor it is one specific technique. It is an umbrella term for a cultural phenomenon caused by technological developments, which has become a seemingly endless loop, the extensive publicity surrounding the term spurring the advance of further technical developments, these developments in turn feeding the hype. Big data can be positive or negative, good or bad, depending on the context and aim of the project. But it can never be truly neutral, since there is always someone who determines what is done with the data and with the information it yields. Furthermore, it is important to note that big data does not necessarily involve personal data, and that it is often not interested in individual users.[143]

As a consequence of the previous remarks and of the ambiguous nature of the definition it is very important to see what actually happens in big data, instead of discussing the legal implications of the vague and disputed term as such. This is necessary from a legal and a normative perspective, as it is impossible to formulate definite or general statements regarding the effects or regulation of such an abstract and multi-interpretable term as ‘big data’. Through viewing big data as a process, it becomes possible to see what the problems are, where these problems arise, how the regulatory framework applies to these problems, and which legal instruments are the most appropriate to combat them. From a legal perspective, calling for the regulation of big data as a singular concept ignores the fact that many separate (legal) actions take place in big data processing. These actions raise distinctly different values and fears that in turn merit distinctly different approaches and solutions. For example, big data cannot be merely seen as one concept that can be solved by data protection legislation, since big data can affect the private life of individuals without their personal data being

142. In later sections, notably 2.5, the dark side(s) of online personalisation are considered.
143. In the definition used where the aim of big data is the finding of correlations in large datasets, i.e., gaining general knowledge, not targeted knowledge about one individual. In the ‘application’ phase on the other hand the individual is often the subject or the ‘target’.

collected.[144] In the following subsections the division of big data into three different phases is advanced, with a view to operationalising big data for normative and legal analysis.

2.4.1 The Three-Phase Model of Big Data

A simple schematic representation of the big data process could look like Figure 2.1 (*see* below), dividing big data into acquisition, analysis, and application phases.[145] This schematic representation is not meant as a definitive explanation of how big data works in practice. It is a simplification of a complex iterative process divided into phases that are of particular relevance for the legal dimension of big data. The first phase is the phase in which the data are gathered. In the second phase, the analysis phase, the acquired data are analysed. Something is done with the data, for example through self-learning algorithms,[146] which creates a model or the knowledge sought by big data projects. The final phase is the phase in which the gathered knowledge is applied. In the previous example of big data and credit scoring, the knowledge is applied by assigning a specific score to individuals that apply for a loan and thereby making a decision to provide a loan or reject the application. In the health context it can mean giving an individual a personalised treatment, or the changing of prescription guidelines or medicine instructions on the basis of the research conducted. In the online personalisation example, it is personalising the online information and choices that people receive. However, as mentioned before, the phases in the process overlap. For example, often big data involves a self-learning algorithm that responds to the input of new data. In other words, big data projects are generally continuous and non-static processes, in which certain actions can be distinguished that are summarised in the three-phase model. The three separate phases are explained in the subsections below.

144. *See* Chapter 4 on data protection law.
145. Many different process models for big data and sub or related fields such as data mining or KDD (*see* above) are employed in practice. The phases of the three-phase model as introduced in this chapter can be distilled from those process models, but this simplified three-phase model leaves out many distinctions that are irrelevant from a legal perspective. This schematic representation is a general, abstract example to be able to discuss what is happening instead of discussing abstract terms that are multi-interpretable. It is not meant as a definitive statement of what happens in practice.
146. Self-learning algorithms are algorithms that change – or 'learn' – after the input of new data, changing their predictions.

Figure 2.1 Big Data Process

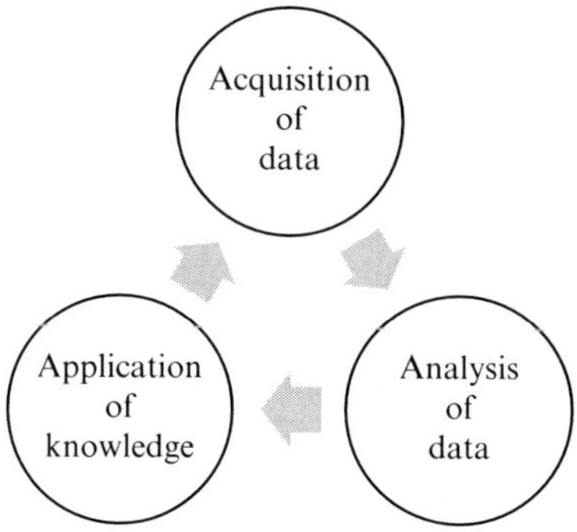

2.4.2 The Acquisition Phase

The acquisition phase is the phase in which data for the big data project are acquired by the person, programme or entity that runs the big data project. Big data projects need data to start with, but data are also gathered throughout the process. In practice, the application phase recurs or is continuous throughout the process. Big data often involves a self-learning algorithm that responds to *inter alia* the input of new data. The data can be collected directly from individuals, like in the credit scoring or biobanking example where individuals are asked to provide the company or a doctor with personal data. Data can also be gathered through sensors that can gather information not only about people but also about things and processes. Obtaining data through buying it from data brokers, companies that collect personal data with the purpose of selling it to third parties,[147] is another possibility for acquiring new data.

New data are not always acquired from individuals, sensors, or intermediaries. Data can also be harvested from publicly available data sources like websites (web scraping) or created by combining existing data sources. Alternatively, inferences and predictions can be made on the basis of existing data, which in turn constitutes new (personal) data. This influences whether the EU data protection law regime is applicable, as we shall *see* in Chapter 4, subsection 4.2 in particular. In sum, the acquisition phase is characterised by the amassing of data, whether personal or non-personal (often a combination of both), as a resource for further analysis.

147. *See* for example Acxiom Corporation <www.acxiom.com> accessed 26 May 2016.

2.4.3 The Analysis Phase

In the second phase, the acquired data are analysed. In this phase, the data are either still linked to individuals or anonymised.[148] As described in subsection 2.2 the processing is done with the aid of database management and data processing software. The analysis phase is interpreted broadly in this work. It covers both storage and processing of the data; both pre-processing techniques to prepare data for analysis, as well as data mining and supporting techniques. These approaches are manifold and are constantly improved and changing.[149] In data mining various methods from fields such as statistics, machine learning, and artificial intelligence are used and created with the aim of discovering useful patterns in large datasets.[150] The current much-used techniques to group data and discover useful patterns are clustering, classification, and pattern mining like regression.[151] In these techniques the data are used to create the hypotheses, contrary to traditional statistical methods employed in, for example, the social sciences that commence with a hypowork before gathering and/or analysing the data.[152] This makes it seem objective, true, and neutral, but big data analysis is far from that. Similar risks of false positives and negatives exist as in traditional statistics,[153] and the risk of overfitting, i.e., mistaking coincidental patterns for patterns that are actually generalisable, is particularly high.[154] Regardless of the size of the dataset, the data used for analysis are always a selection; data can never completely and conclusively encapsulate the actual world. Data can also reflect pre-existing societal biases, for example, discrimination on the basis of gender or race, which is discussed in more detail in subsection 2.5, particularly in subsection 2.5.2.3.[155] Furthermore, the choice of data is

---

148. In general when data are anonymised data protection regulation does not apply (*see* in greater detail Chapter 4). Moreover big data organisations are often interested in patterns in data and not in the particular individual as such, which makes it generally irrelevant whether the data can be linked to an individual in the analysis. Accordingly there is a strong incentive for organisations to anonymise the data. Nevertheless anonymisation does not necessarily happen in practice and can be impossible depending on the data or the purpose of the big data project.
149. Bart Custers, 'Data Dilemmas in the Information Society: Introduction and Overview' in Bart Custers and others (eds), *Discrimination and Privacy in the Information Society: Data Mining and Profiling in Large Databases*, vol. 3 (Springer 2013) 7.
150. Christopher Clifton, 'Data Mining', *Encyclopaedia Britannica* (2014) <http://www.britannica.com/technology/data-mining> accessed 11 June 2015.
151. Toon Calders and Bart Custers, 'What Is Data Mining and How Does It Work?' in Bart Custers and others (eds), *Discrimination and Privacy in the Information Society: Data Mining and Profiling in Large Databases*, vol. 3 (Springer 2013) 31–38.
152. *Ibid* 28.
153. Nassim Taleb, 'Beware the Big Errors of "Big Data"' [2013] *WIRED* <http://www.wired.com/2013/02/big-data-means-big-errors-people> accessed 12 June 2015.
154. Provost and Fawcett (n 77) 111–113.
155. *See also* Kate Crawford, 'The Hidden Biases in Big Data' <https://hbr.org/2013/04/the-hidden-biases-in-big-data> accessed 14 December 2016.

determined by availability and the aims of the organisation, and the effects and representativeness cannot be fully predicted or assessed afterwards. What is even more important is that, as explained in subsections 2.1.1 and 2.2, big data analysis yields information about correlations, not about causal relationships. A link between two variables or events may be purely coincidental;[156] correlations do not imply causation.[157] In the analysis phase, processing may also lead to changes in the data, for example through combining datasets which creates new data, of through stripping them of identifiers or aggregating them, which turns them into 'anonymous' data. This is important for the applicability and protective potential of the EU legal privacy and data protection regime, as we shall see in later chapters. Furthermore, it is important to realise that this analysis is conducted on data acquired from the acquisition phase, and will influence people in the application phase. These are two different groups of people, and even though people may find themselves in both groups, the two groups do not always overlap.

One of the most exemplary and praised examples of big data analytics is Google Flu Trends. In 2009, researchers from Google published a paper that explained how Google's algorithms were able to predict influenza epidemics.[158] Using flu-related queries entered in the Google search engine for finding patterns in the incredible amount of data that Google holds, the company's predictions matched the eventual flu spikes in the US. Initially, Google was even deemed better at predicting the flu than the U.S. Centre for Disease Control and Prevention.[159] But all praise came to a halt in 2013. It turned out that Google's algorithms had been overestimating the flu outbreaks for three years in a row, and had simultaneously missed some major flu outbreaks, amongst which the Mexican swine flu in 2009.[160] Google's query-based predictions were not accurate reflections of actual flu outbreaks for many reasons.[161] Amongst others the selected queries turned out to be very much linked to winter and not to flu as such, and extensive media coverage of flu cases likely influenced search behaviour.[162] Google Flu Trends went from being big data's poster child to the principal example of big data gone wrong. Its capricious predictions illustrate that the analysis

---

156. *See* for many examples <www.tylervigen.com/spurious-correlations> accessed 13 May 2016.
157. Siegel (n 107) 88
158. Jeremy Ginsberg and others, 'Detecting Influenza Epidemics Using Search Engine Query Data' (2009) 457 Nature 1012.
159. Miguel Helft, 'Google Uses Searches to Track Flu's Spread' *The New York Times* (12 November 2008) <http://www.nytimes.com/2008/11/12/technology/internet/12flu.html> accessed 12 June 2015.
160. Decan Butler, 'When Google Got Flu Wrong' (2013) 494 *Nature* 155.
161. David Lazer and others, 'The Parable of Google Flu: Traps in Big Data Analysis' (2014) 343 *Science* 1203.
162. Butler (n 160).

phase is a precarious phase in big data. It is statistics, data science, and algorithms, whose results are dependent on input and selection. Moreover, the input is data, which are always interpretations of reduced parts of reality. The match with real life and effect on reality should always be scrutinised, particularly given the effects emanating from the analysis when the results are applied, as explained in the ensuing subsection.[163]

2.4.4 The Application Phase

In the third phase, the information derived from the analysis of the data, whether it be knowledge, models, or predictions, is applied. This can lead to either general decisions or decisions that target individuals. The former can, for example, constitute finding risk factors for a disease through biobanks, which can lead to new decisions on medical treatment conditions. Using the information to take decisions that target individuals is possible through automated means, or by individuals or entities that make decisions on the basis of the knowledge yielded by the analysis. These decisions can be aimed directly at individuals, but it is also possible that general decisions are made that are not geared towards a particular individual. An example is a decision that certain drugs are not prescribed or reimbursed anymore due to limited effectivity discovered through big data. It is important to note that these decisions are based on data that stem from numerous sources, and not on data derived solely from the individual. As explained in the analysis phase the knowledge is generated through the pooling of large datasets from a wide array of sources. This is the knowledge behind the decision that affects the individual. In most cases a limited amount of information about the individual is necessary to draw conclusions and as a basis for decisions. In the aforementioned situation, where general decisions are taken that affect the private lives of individuals, private life can even be affected without the processing of personal data being necessary.

But also, when decisions are made that are aimed at the individual herself it is still primarily the data from other sources in the analysis phase, combined with limited information in the application phase, that determines the outcome or decision. In behavioural targeting, often only an IP address, MAC address, or cookie is used to offer individuals targeted advertisements on the basis of, amongst others, browsing history. The targeting is based on conclusions drawn about, for example, particular websites in the browsing history of an individual, conclusions that primarily rest on the analysis of historical data from other people in the analysis phase. Names, addresses,

163. Mikkel Krenchel and Christian Madsbjerg, 'Your Big Data Is Worthless If You Don't Bring It Into the Real World' (*WIRED*, 4 November 2014) <http://www.wired.com/2014/04/your-big-data-is-worthless-if-you-dont-bring-it-into-the-real-world/> accessed 10 June 2015.

and other information regarding the individual are not important and generally not collected. It is primarily data from others that determine what decisions are made about the individual. In conclusion, the enormous amounts of data of the analysis phase combined with, often very little, personal information in the application phase is what spurs decisions, predictions, and new information in big data. For a normative and legal analysis, the diversity in applications, as well as in *means* of application, i.e., general decisions or decisions targeted at individuals with or without the use of much personal data, are of significant importance.

2.4.5 Concluding Remarks

Big data projects are complex processes. In this research, they are divided into three phases based on what happens in practice and what is important from a normative and legal perspective. In the acquisition phase, most (personal) data are collected.[164] In the analysis phase the data are processed and analysed, using a diverse array of techniques to distil knowledge from the data. The data may be modified or altered, leading to de-identification which is important for the legal analysis in later chapters. In the application phase, personal data may be used to apply the outcome of the analysis phase to individuals. Although personal data of individuals may be collected in this phase, the primary source of knowledge and information is not always or exclusively the personal data from the individual herself, but data from other sources. This is a key aspect of big data, which is important for the ensuing analysis: the acquisition phase and analysis phase are often disconnected from the application phase.

The schematic representation of phases shows that different types of data processing occur in the process, and that in some phases data processing is key, whereas in others it is of minor significance. This already hints at the idea that in big data different legal regimes govern different parts of the big data process, and that the different phases merit a focus on different legal instruments or solutions. As we shall see in the following section, each of the phases has different effects on individual rights and freedoms. In the ensuing chapters, we shall also see that the different actions in each phase, notably whether and how (personal) data are processed, affect whether the EU legal privacy and data protection regime is applicable, and what other areas of law may be important in protecting individual rights and freedoms in each of the phases. This affirms the necessity and advantage of dividing big data into phases for the normative and legal analysis: big data consists of different actions, to which the legal regime applies in dissimilar ways, and different risks are associated with these actions.

164. Not all big data projects involve personal data, *see* earlier remarks.

2.5 BIG DATA'S INFLUENCE ON INDIVIDUAL RIGHTS AND FREEDOMS

This section discusses the influence big data has or can have on individual rights and freedoms, starting with an outline of the positive potential of big data, after which the focus shifts to the negative influence based on the selected individual rights and freedoms as described in Chapter 1. Often, positive and negative effects occur concurrently in the same process; neither the aim nor the effects of a given big data process can generally be described as inherently good or bad. However, given this work's focus on big data's negative effects on individual rights and freedoms, the positives and negatives are discussed separately, and more attention is allocated to the negatives.

2.5.1 Positive Potential

Big data is seen by many as an extremely promising and positive development. Indeed, it is often heralded as the panacea that will cure the world of many ills, as the possibilities of big data seem endless.[165] Governments, commercial entities, and individuals make decisions on a daily basis and big data can enable better-informed decision-making. Basing decisions on knowledge or information derived from big data usually gives more insight into the policy or business options while simultaneously decreasing the risks associated with the decision. Big data's problem-solving capability is praised, particularly when it is used to find solutions to pressing societal issues such as diseases and the rising health care costs mentioned in the biobanking illustration above, or as an economic enabler in amongst others discussions on the digital single market.[166] As a result, resources can be saved, processes can be made more efficient, fraud can be prevented, profits can be increased, and better decisions can be made.

Data and big data techniques can also provide answers to questions that are difficult, or seemingly impossible, to answer. Big data holds the possibility of providing answers that were previously not within man's reach or that we 'did not know to ask'.[167] The collection and analysis of data from different sources reveal patterns that can be interpreted and thus yield new information. All the aforementioned benefits of big data are amplified by the ever-decreasing costs of storage and processing, which increases the potential and popularity of big data. The examples are countless and more

165. *See* for instance the many examples listed in works like Mayer-Schönberger and Cukier (n 83); Sander Klous and Nard Wielaard, *Wij zijn big data* (Business Contact 2014) and in the technology sections of newspapers like *the Guardian* or magazines like *Wired.*
166. Kuner and others (n 82) 48; González Fuster (n 111) 17.
167. Zarsky (n 80) 4.

applications keep being developed.[168] However, in spite of the numerous ways in which big data is and can be used to improve society, it also negatively affects the lives of individuals, as explained in the following subsection.

2.5.2 Negative Impact on Individual Rights and Freedoms

In spite of the many benefits of big data, there is widespread concern over its possible negative consequences.[169] Amongst others, the large-scale collection and processing of personal data and the increasing reliance on algorithmic decision-making can have far-reaching consequences for individual rights and freedoms. Possible negative consequences are mapped out below, grouped according to the individual rights and freedoms that are affected. In this discussion, the negative effects should be seen as a cascade: small immediate interferences with the rights and freedoms below can multiply or interfere with other rights and freedoms in the long run and have a lasting effect on a person's chances and personal life.[170] Small decisions, such as volunteering data by an individual or categorising a person by a company, influence the future and change its course. In addition to immediate effects or interferences, there are effects that are small but cumulate into more serious results, or decisions and effects that have long-term or evolving consequences.

2.5.2.1 Personal Autonomy

Big data puts personal autonomy at risk, because it hinders individuals' capacity to live a free life without their choices being determined through distorting or manipulative external forces.[171] Personal autonomy can be limited through big data in multiple ways, explained here chiefly through the online personalisation illustration of subsection 2.3.3.

In the first place, the means used to gather individuals' personal data, how the data are processed, and the lack of transparency surrounding it, exert pressure on the personal autonomy and informational self-determination of

168. *See* for example the EU Commission's big data strategy, <https://ec.europa.eu/digital single-market/en/towards-thriving-data-driven-economy> accessed 14 December 2016.
169. *See* in addition to the sources referred to earlier amongst others Article 29 Working Party, 'Opinion 03/2013 on Purpose Limitation' (n 111); European Data Protection Supervisor, 'Meeting the Challenges of Big Data: A Call for Transparency, User Control, Data Protection by Design and Accountability' (n 111); Krasnow Waterman and Paula Bruening, 'Big Data Analytics: Risks and Responsibilities' 4 International Data Privacy Law 89.
170. Frank Pasquale, *The Black Box Society. The Secret Algorithms That Control Money And Information* (Harvard University Press 2015) 32.
171. Cf. Chapter 1, subsection 7.2.1. and Christman (n 11).

the individual.[172] For instance, when consent is sought for the collection of data in the acquisition phase, it is often not clear what the individual consents to, e.g., what happens with the personal data in the analysis phase, what the purpose of the analysis is, and how the acquisition and analysis of her personal data could affect her life or that of others through the application phase. Properly informing individuals can be difficult given the complexity inherent in big data and the uncertainties about future aims and processing that are often present.[173] The limits here reside in the self-determination aspect of personal autonomy; in the difficulty of accepting a decision as being made autonomously when it is based on incomplete or incomprehensible information.

In addition, ubiquitous data processing can create a perception of surveillance, which can inhibit individuals' behaviour.[174] This is generally associated with chilling effects on freedom of speech discussed below, but for personal autonomy it also holds relevance because of its influence on individuals' identity. People are not one-dimensional human beings; different aspects of our identity and personality come to the fore, depending on where we are and who we are with. We present ourselves differently depending on whether we are with family, different (groups of) friends, or colleagues.[175] The more transparent we become to the outside world and feel we are being tracked and watched, the more we curb this diversity in self-representation, as well as our desire to explore, develop, and change over time.[176] In the absence of the possibility to self-present, we keep up appearances for the sake of conforming to a false ideal of a singular identity, to avoid conflicts and social rejection, and become accepted but dulled-down members of a pluralistic society.

In the application phase, more direct techniques are employed to actively influence individuals' behaviour and choices. How (and what) information is presented to individuals, what choices they are given, what information is withheld, and how this differs from what others receive significantly affects or even determines what we choose and believe.[177] Generally, people choose from the options that they are presented with,

---

172. Neil Richards and Jonathan King, 'Three Paradoxes of Big Data' (2013) 66 Stanford Law Review Online 41, 42–43.
173. This issue is discussed in greater detail in subsection 4.4.1 of Chapter 4 on the EU data protection framework.
174. Orla Lynskey, *The Foundations of EU Data Protection Law* (Oxford University Press 2015) 215–218.
175. *Ibid* 219–220.
176. Cf. Ruth Gavison, 'Privacy and the Limits of the Law' in Ferdinand David Schoeman (ed) (Cambridge University Press 1984) 363–369; Jenny L. Davis and Nathan Jurgenson, 'Context Collapse: Theorizing Context Collusions and Collisions' (2014) 17 Information, Communication & Society 476, 476–480.
177. Tristan Harris, 'How Technology Hijacks People's Minds – from a Magician and Google's Design Ethicist' (2016) *Medium*.

without enquiring how these choices are realised, whether they are representative of all options, and what is deliberately left out of the list. As such, online personalisation based on big data exerts pressure on personal autonomy, for example when commercial entities use the effects of the illusion of choice for their own gain. Personalisation may also turn into intentional coercion, persuasion, or manipulation. An infamous and thought-provoking example of what can be achieved is the social network 'emotional contagion' experiment, in which researchers influenced people's moods through deciding what content appeared on their Facebook timeline.[178] Examples of persuasion through personalisation that are currently commonly used for commercial gain are behavioural targeting and website optimisation through A/B testing.[179]

A related concern about personalisation and autonomy is that individuals will end up in filter bubbles.[180] This concern focuses on the individual herself instead of on intentional external pressure. The fear is that personalisation results in filter bubbles, also referred to as information cocoons or echo chambers,[181] in which individuals become isolated in a world that consists of limited information that always confirms their beliefs and opinions, without being exposed to diverging information and viewpoints.[182] Under such circumstances people think they make independent choices and form their opinions autonomously, but they are in fact influenced by the limited and customised information that is offered to them, narrowing their perception of the world.

---

178. Adam Kramer, Jamie Guillory and Jeffrey Hancock, 'Experimental Evidence of Massive-Scale Emotional Contagion Through Social Networks' (2014) 111 Proceedings of the National Academy of Sciences 8788; danah boyd, 'Untangling Research and Practice: What Facebook's 'Emotional Contagion' Study Teaches Us' (2016) 12 Research Ethics 4.
179. For behavioural targeting, *see* subsection 2.3.3. A/B testing here refers to showing groups of users websites that differ slightly from each other in terms of lay-out or content, to see what minor differences, e.g., the colour, size or position of a button, make people click or buy more often. This is automated and happens in real-time, and great numbers of website-visitors (unwittingly) participate in these 'experiments'. The knowledge is used to optimise the website and boost effectiveness. This is much used by for example travel websites, like Booking.com: Erin Weigel, 'A/B Testing – Concept != Excution' <https://blog.booking.com/concept-dne-execution.html> accessed 18 May 2017; *A/B Testing: Test Your Own Hypotheses & Prepare to Be Wrong – Stuart Frisby (Booking.Com)* (2015) <https://www.youtube.com/watch?time_continue=3&v=_sx5LV23hIE> accessed 18 May 2017.
180. Eli Pariser, *The Filter Bubble: What the Internet Is Hiding from You* (Penguin Books 2012).
181. Cass R. Sunstein, *Infotopia* (Oxford University Press 2006); Cass R. Sunstein, *Republic 2.0* (Princeton University Press 2007).
182. Pariser (n 180); However, so far no clear evidence of actual filter bubbles has been found, *see* Frederik Zuiderveen Borgesius and others, 'Should We Worry about Filter Bubbles?' (2016) 5 Internet Policy Review.

Ways in which content and experiences are personalised, and how opinions and behaviour are steered, may be small or trivial in terms of their context. But there does not need to be a large, imminent effect for big data to pose a threat to personal autonomy. Personalisation is rapidly becoming ubiquitous, influencing both our online and offline decisions and lives. The danger lies just as much in small but cumulative derogations of personal autonomy as in big data's potential to shape our lives in high-impact significant ways. The cumulative effect may even be more dangerous in the long run, because of the opacity surrounding it. Small instances of limited autonomy based on the above neither spark outrage nor do people perceive them clearly, because in isolation their effects are as small as to often go unnoticed. And filter bubbles or small instances of limited choice or other external pressure can cause a cascade of effects, changing who people are and how they develop, and what choices and opportunities they get in the long run.

What makes matters worse is that the knowledge gathered through big data is contentious. Big data yields knowledge about correlations that may be mistaken for causal relationships where they are in fact mere coincidences.[183] When these correlations are used as a basis for decisions, this yields false positives and negatives, and errors will be made eventually. Second, the knowledge derived from big data is often deemed to be objective whereas it is not. The design of the analysis and selection of data (sources) influence the outcome and there is rarely only one possible interpretation of the results.[184] No matter how much data is used or how sophisticated the model is, big data will always be a limited reflection of reality. In addition, there is the fear that 'information monopolies' and digital divides aggravate the risks of opacity and manipulation.[185] The largest quantities of digital data in the world are collected and stored by a few large enterprises, such as Google, Facebook, and Amazon.[186] Irrespective of questions regarding rights and ownership, these companies hold considerable power over the data and the individuals that the data belong to, for example because they operate the most-used platforms for a specific category of services and the infrastructure that stores the data.

In sum, big data holds the power to nudge people's behaviour. Aside from the fact that their interests often do not align with those of individuals, this can delude individuals and corrupt their free and informed choices.[187]

---

183. boyd and Crawford (n 81) 665–668. *See also* subsection 2.4.3.
184. *Ibid* 665–671; Busch (n 88).
185. *See* Richards and King (n 85) and in general Frank Pasquale, *The Black Box Society: The Secret Algorithms That Control Money And Information* (Harvard University Press 2015).
186. One could also mention the surveillance capacities of some states here, but government surveillance is explicitly excluded from the scope of this work, *see* Chapter 1.
187. Karen Yeung, '"Hypernudge": Big Data as a Mode of Regulation by Design' (2016) 1 Information, Communication & Society 121–124.

The aforementioned can be extrapolated to the fear that our identities are increasingly formed by external forces, most of these external forces' sole concern being the capitalisation of our personal data and behaviour, and deriving profit from us.[188] Cumulative and ubiquitous influence and reduction of free choice threatens people's personal autonomy and, ultimately, their identity – the possibility to freely become who they are.[189]

2.5.2.2 Privacy and Data Protection

Big data starts with the collection of data, including personal data about individuals. Therefore, big data has the potential to negatively affect the fundamental rights to privacy and data protection.[190] To start with the most obvious, when personal data are collected, the right to data protection is at stake. Certain characteristics of big data, such as the focus on the accumulation of as much personal data as possible for continuous analysis for vague or future aims, are profoundly at odds with the principles of the protection of personal data. These characteristics inherent in big data clash with data protection principles designed to protect the individual, such as the purpose limitation principle that indicates that personal data may only be processed for predetermined specified purposes.[191] Moreover, the collection of data can reveal intimate details about a person's life, and decisions taken in the application phase can also affect the right to privacy. In sum, big data has the potential to infringe people's privacy and data protection in a similar way to any other data-collecting development or technology. Yet a few characteristics of big data, make it particularly pertinent to privacy and data protection.[192]

The first prominent and problematic characteristic of big data is the *quantity* of data that is collected and processed. Collecting more data is generally considered better from the perspective of those engaging in big data, but the more the data are gathered, the more severe the potential interference with a person's private life.[193] More data generally yields deeper knowledge about individuals. As the quantities of data increase, it also

188. Hildebrandt, 'Profiling and the Rule of Law' (n 88) 63; Shoshana Zuboff, 'The Secrets of Surveillance Capitalism' (2016) *Frankfurter Allgemeine Zeitung*.

189. Mireille Hildebrandt, 'Privacy and Identity' in Erik Claes, Anthony Duff and Serge Gutwirth (eds), *Privacy and the Criminal Law* (Insertia 2006) 51–52.

190. Chapter 3 is about how big data fits under the fundamental rights to privacy and data protection.

191. Cf. Article 8 (2) CFREU, Article 5 (b) GDPR, Rubinstein (n 84) 45–46. For big data's compatibility with data protection law, *see* Chapter 4.

192. *See also* International Working Group on Data Protection in Telecommunications, 'Working Paper on Big Data and Privacy: Privacy Principles under Pressure in the Age of Big Data Analytics' (2014) 675.48.12 6 11.

193. Tene and Polonetsky, 'Big Data for All: Privacy and User Control in the Age of Analytics' (n 84) 251–252.

becomes more difficult to protect people's privacy and personal data through securing and anonymising the data.[194] Moreover, it conflicts with data protection law's data minimisation principle, which demands that personal data be 'adequate, relevant and limited to what is necessary in relation to the purposes for which they are processed'.[195] Some question whether data minimisation, in its current form, is even tenable in the context of big data.[196]

Also distinguishing for big data is that data from multiple different sources are combined into one dataset. The combination of data is not a new risk, but increasingly prevalent with unpredictable outcomes. On the basis of the combined data new inferences can be made: the combination of data can 'create' new data about individuals. This combination aspect is also important for a third characteristic of big data that creates new privacy issues: its predictive powers.[197] This is of key importance in the application phase of big data. The predictive modelling and self-learning algorithms as described in the previous subsections can yield personal data that the individual has not volunteered herself; data that might accurately predict details of her future. This creates data protection and privacy issues, because a knowledge gap may come to exist between the individual and others, as others may know more about the individual than she herself does.[198] It can also happen that the individual does not want to have these data uncovered in general, for example, when it concerns (the increased probability of getting) certain incurable diseases. People may have a wish not to know, and others having that knowledge likely interfere with that wish too. In the application phase, many of the risks and negative effects emanate not from the processing of personal data per se but from the application of (the results of) big data to individuals.

2.5.2.3 Non-discrimination

There is widespread acceptance that big data can have discriminatory effects, but how and why discrimination occurs in big data is a complex matter. It can originate from different phases of the big data process, be intentional or unintentional, direct or indirect, translate existing prejudices and inequality to the digital domain, or cause new kinds of discriminatory divisions in society. This subsection examines big data's different discriminatory effects.

---

194. Paul Ohm, 'Broken Promises of Privacy: Responding to the Surprising Failure of Anonymization' (2010) 57 UCLA Law Review 1701; *see also* Chapter 4.
195. Article 5 (c) GDPR.
196. Tene and Polonetsky, 'Big Data for All: Privacy and User Control in the Age of Analytics' (n 84) 259–260.
197. Kate Crawford and Jason Schultz, 'Big Data and Due Process – Toward a Framework to Redress Predictive Privacy Harms' (2014) 55 Boston College Law Review 93, 96–99.
198. Mark Andrejevic, 'The Big Data Divide' (2014) International Journal of Communication 1673, 176.

Big data allows for clustering and detailed categorisation of people, and the customisation of the treatment of individuals. As such it can lead to (intentional or unintentional) discrimination:[199] treating alike people differently in similar situations, on the basis of amongst others characteristics listed in the Convention and the Charter, such as sex, ethnicity, colour, or religion.[200] When it is clear that a big data application uses these variables to make distinctions in the treatment of people, and this is not corrected by those in charge, this counts as direct intentional discrimination. However, in big data discrimination is generally not that obvious, and may not even be intended by those in control.

In addition to discrimination on the basis of prohibited characteristics, big data can cause a more covert kind of discrimination. Certain data may serve as proxies for sensitive data on the basis of which discrimination can take place. For example, there can be a high correlation between postal code and ethnicity, in which case selection on the basis of postal codes masks discrimination on the basis of ethnicity.[201] This example is relatively obvious,[202] but due to the high number of variables processed in big data, discrimination in the application phase can be more covert and indirect. Mere Facebook likes are known to reveal sensitive personal attributes.[203] A combination of seemingly random variables with no apparent link to sensitive attributes may yield discriminatory results in practice. This discriminatory effect will generally be unintended. Moreover, this 'hidden' discrimination is more difficult to uncover than direct discrimination. It may also prove to be difficult to hold people or organisations accountable. Because decisions are based on complex and possibly self-learning algorithms, it is easily claimed that no discriminatory decisions were taken or that discriminatory treatment was unintentional.

An additional fear is that *intentional* discriminatory practices can be masked by big data. Intentional discrimination can be masked in multiple ways, for example, through biasing the sample data used for analysis or by intentionally using proxies for attributes like ethnicity or religion. An

---

199. Oscar Gandy, *The Panoptic Sort: A Political Economy of Personal Information* (Westview Press 1993); David Lyon, 'Surveillance as Social Sorting: Computer Codes and Mobile Bodies' in David Lyon (ed), *Surveillance as Social Sorting: Privacy, Risk and Digital Discrimination* (Routledge 2003); Tene and Polonetsky, 'Judged by the Tin Man: Individual Rights in the Age of Big Data' (n 80) 355–358; Dennis Hirsch, 'That's Unfair! Or Is It? Big Data, Discrimination and the FTC's Unfairness Authority' 103 Kentucky Law Journal 345, 345–346, 352–353.
200. Article 14 European Convention on Human Rights (n 6); Article 21 EU Charter of Fundamental Rights (n 6).
201. Toon Calders and Indrė Žliobaitė, 'Why Unbiased Computational Processes Can Lead to Discriminative Decision Procedures', *Discrimination and Privacy in the Information Society: Data Mining and Profiling in Large Databases*, vol. 3 (Springer 2013) 47.
202. This is referred to as redlining, a practice which is often forbidden. Schermer (n 88) 49; Barocas and Selbst (n 3) 689–690.
203. Kosinski, Stillwell and Graepel (n 88).

example of the latter case is using variables such as music taste, likes, and a network of friends on social media as proxies for race or religion.[204] Such situations look similar to cases of unintentional indirect discrimination described above. The only difference is the intent: this type of discrimination is calculated, instead of it being an accident or by-effect. Unfortunately, it is just as difficult to uncover. Because it is based on (possibly self-learning) algorithms and statistics that are mistakenly believed to be rational and neutral,[205] the blame for sorting and other negative consequences is easily put on the machine.[206]

Unsurprisingly, the credit scoring example described above in the subsection on big data in finance receives much attention in the context of discrimination. Discrimination in personal credit and targeting of vulnerable groups with high interests and other unfavourable conditions increases inequality in society, and is a much-discussed negative effect associated with big data.[207] In addition to the short-term effect of having to pay high-interest rates or not obtaining credit at all, discrimination has long-term consequences. In the case of credit scoring it can reduce an individual's chances in society, for example, because she decides not to study due to difficulties in paying tuition fees.

The risk of discrimination through big data credit scoring is significant for a number of reasons. First of all, the data used for analysis can reflect existing biases in society, contain proxies that mask discrimination, or be over- or under-inclusive with respect to certain groups.[208] More data will not always yield more realistic results, on the contrary: the quality and representativeness of the input data may suffer because of a fixation on quantity of data.[209] And even if there is no bias in the selection of data, many things can go awry in the analysis phase, for example because of poorly defined target variables or spurious correlations that yield discriminatory results.[210] Moreover, in practice, big data credit scoring firms base their analysis on data such as where people shop, where they live, and who their friends are. This amounts to people being judged on the basis of other people's behaviour that can make them 'guilty by association' and can amount to a new kind of (digital) redlining.[211] In essence, people are not only profiled based on past behaviour or ethnicity, which can already lead to

204. Barocas and Selbst (n 3) 712.
205. Calders and Žliobaitė (n 201) 44.
206. Tene and Polonetsky, 'Judged by the Tin Man: Individual Rights in the Age of Big Data' (n 80) 358–360.
207. *See* O'Neil (n 80) amongst others on pp. 47–48, 70–72, 81, 150–155.
208. Calders and Žliobaitė (n 201) 46–51; Crawford (n 155); Crawford (n 80); Kate Crawford, Mary L. Gray and Kate Miltner, 'Critiquing Big Data: Politics, Ethics, Epistemology' (2014) 8 International Journal of Communication 10, 1667.
209. Hurley and Adebayo (n 116) 178.
210. *Ibid* 173, 177.
211. *Ibid* 167.

discrimination, but also on the basis of who they associate with or who they seem akin to, which constitutes an additional and different kind of discrimination.[212] In this context it is extra important to keep in mind that big data predictions are about probabilities: the chance that something will happen in the future, such as a person defaulting on a loan. As a consequence, there will be false positives, in this case people who will not be eligible for credit, based on the past behaviour of others. In big data, past behaviour of groups determines the possibilities and chances that an individual gets. And since discrimination will often be indirect and the outcome of a complex personalised process that, as we shall *see* in Chapter 4, remains largely hidden from the individual, it will be not be easy for the individual to prove that she is being discriminated against.

Some practices may not qualify as discrimination in a strict legal sense.[213] For example, when and whether price discrimination is (and should be) prohibited is open to question.[214] However, given the fairness of practices that rely on personalisation and information asymmetries, and how it may reinforce inequality in society, these harmful effects should be considered discrimination, even if precedents clearly prohibiting such practices are lacking. Future claims of differential treatment resulting from big data, such as price discrimination, can become violations of the right not to be discriminated against. There are also a number of unwanted *effects* of big data that are not discrimination proper, but linked to it, such as social exclusion and stratification.[215] People from certain groups, such as the elderly and the economically disadvantaged, produce less digital data, or their data are less likely to end up in big data projects.[216] As commercial entities and governments make more use of big data, for example when deciding where to open new shops, what new products to make, and to whom to allocate social benefits, or when forecasting housing needs, the interests of these groups are at risk of being overlooked.[217] In conclusion, both inclusion and exclusion can lead big data to reinforce existing inequalities, or create new ones.

---

212. Cf. Oscar Gandy, 'Engaging Rational Discrimination: Exploring Reasons for Placing Regulatory Constraints on Decision Support Systems' (2010) 12 Ethics and Information Technology 29, 29.
213. Tal Zarsky, 'Understanding Discrimination in the Scored Society' (2014) 89 Washington Law Review 1375, 1381–1383.
214. Cf. Joseph Turow, *Niche Envy: Marketing Discrimination in the Digital Age* (MIT Press 2008) 177–192; Mark Armstrong, 'Recent Developments in the Economics of Price Discrimination' in Richard Blundell, Whitney Newey and Torsten Persson, *Advances in Economics and Econometrics: Theory and Applications, Ninth World Congress, Volume II* (2006); Frederik Zuiderveen Borgesius, 'Online Price Discrimination and Data Protection Law' (2015) Amsterdam Law School Research Paper No. 2015-32 1, 9–10, 19.
215. Article 29 Working Party, 'Opinion 03/2013 on Purpose Limitation' (n 111) 45–46.
216. Lerman (n 80).
217. *Ibid.*

2.5.2.4 Freedom of Expression

Big data poses a threat to freedom of expression because it can interfere with the negative rights to receive and impart information, and the right to hold opinions.[218] These interferences are caused primarily by the chilling effects and risk of self-censorship that can be a by-effect of the large-scale processing of personal data, and by big data's possibilities for manipulating people's thoughts and behaviour, and personalising their reality.

In the first place, as already raised under the heading of personal autonomy, big data affects our thinking. Free thinking and freedom of thought can be seen as a precondition for freedom of expression in general and conceivably also as an aspect of the right to hold opinions.[219] Given the limited ways of gaining access to people's thoughts or interfering with them, freedom of thought has been under the radar for many years.[220] However, with big data, things may change. Through the use of digital technologies, our thinking becomes visible and traceable.[221] Our search history, for example, gives insights into the topics we research and how we are led from one topic to another, and, given this information, it also provides information on what we believe and what our opinions are from one moment to the next. With big data analytics, others can discover (new) meaning in it. As our lives increasingly take place online, and we are tracked across all kinds of different platforms, those who have that data are coming ever closer to *accessing* our minds. And it does not stop at access to thoughts. As Richards writes, 'controlling what a person can read is controlling the moral content of their thoughts'.[222] In this sense, personalisation of the information we receive already affects how we think and form our opinions. Big data applications can even be or become capable of influencing our minds, dreams, and thoughts in a way similar to how the emotional contagion experiment referred to earlier influenced people's moods.[223]

---

218. *See* Chapter 1.
219. In its phrasing '*freedom of thought*' corresponds to Article 9 of the Convention on thought, conscience, and religion. Up until now this right has only been referred to in the context of religion or similar coherent beliefs, but one could make the case for new types of interferences with Article 9's freedom of thought in the future, cf. Jean Christoph Bublitz, 'Freedom of Thought in the Age of Neuroscience: A Plea and a Proposal for the Renaissance of a Forgotten Fundamental Right' (2014) 100 Archiv für Rechts- und Sozialphilosophie 1. Nevertheless, given the doctrine and case law of the ECtHR on freedom of expression and Article 9, it is more logical to place these issues and possible interferences under freedom of expression. *See also* the opinion of the ECtHR in *Zana v Turkey* [1997] ECtHR 18954/91 [39].
220. Neil Richards, *Intellectual Privacy: Rethinking Civil Liberties in the Digital Age* (Oxford University Press 2015) 113, 115–116.
221. *Ibid* 119–122.
222. *Ibid* 127.
223. *See* 2.5.2.1.

When it comes to individuals actively searching for information, it is becoming commonly accepted and supported by empirical evidence that surveillance and a lack of privacy can lead people to alter their behaviour and as such may have a chilling effect on freedom of expression.[224] Faced with governmental or corporate surveillance, whether it be the knowledge that it is happening or merely having the feeling that one may be watched, overall people change what they gather and consume in terms of information.[225] In other words, when online behaviour is tracked, individuals may be inhibited from freely seeking information.[226] Certain information will not be sought, for example because of the information's controversial nature, because of an individual's fear of being misrepresented, or because of possible resulting detrimental effects on the individual's daily life. In the first instance, this effect is located in the acquisition phase of big data, since that is where the collection takes place, and the threat of surveillance is often felt by the individual. However, fear for the incomprehensible analysis of data and information and the consequences thereof, i.e., the analysis and application phases, may aggravate these chilling effects. Consciousness about privacy, big data, and the Internet that never forgets may lead to self-censorship, a limitation of freedom of expression. After all, if we are conscious about how data can be used in different contexts at different points in time, and the consequences such traces may have on future decisions, we may choose not to seek or volunteer certain data, information, and opinions.[227] Here, big data affects the freedom both to receive and impart information. The reception of information is affected, because the gathering of information creates personal data that are processed in big data, such as a digital trail of which websites a person visited. The right to impart information is affected principally due to the reuse of data that is typical for big data. Reuse creates uncertainty about what will happen with the information that is imparted, and in which contexts and to what ends it may be used.

Persuasion, personalisation, and manipulation in the application phase of big data can also compromise freedom of expression's rights to hold opinions and freely receive information and ideas. People are included or

224. Solove, 'A Taxonomy of Privacy' (n 34) 513–514, 529–530; Dara Hallinan, 'Effects of Surveillance on Freedom of Assembly, Association and Expression' in David Wright and Reinhard Kreissl (eds), *Surveillance in Europe* (Routledge 2015) 268–271; Tene and Polonetsky, 'Big Data for All: Privacy and User Control in the Age of Analytics' (n 84) 256; Ronald Krotoszynski, *Privacy Revisited: A Global Perspective on the Right to Be Left Alone* (Oxford University Press 2016) 175; Aleecia M McDonald and Lorrie Faith Cranor, 'Beliefs and Behaviors: Internet Users' Understanding of Behavioral Advertising' (2010) 28 <https://ssrn.com/abstract=1989092> accessed 25 May 2017; Penney (n 36).
225. This is the idea of the panopticon as described by Bentham; when one knows one can be watched but cannot see when, one will act as if constantly watched, changing one's regular behaviour.
226. Richards (n 220) 101, 105–106.
227. International Working Group on Data Protection in Telecommunications (n 192) 10–11.

excluded from particular information because certain characteristics place them in groups, on the basis of which the offer of information is personalised. Closely linked to big data's hazards for personal autonomy as described, individuals' opportunities to find (new) information and develop ideas and beliefs can be limited. The impact should not be underestimated if it seems small or even hypothetical, given the prevalence of personalisation and the lack of knowledge about how one's ideas and opinions are formed and freedom of expression is affected. Under the pressure of (opaque) personalisation, people's ideas and opinions may be influenced and morphed in the long run, making future holding of opinions and free reception of information less and less free.[228] The possible harmful effects of big data on freedom of expression and thought thus work in two ways: people self-censor their expression, and their free reception of information and forming of thoughts and ideas is hindered.

2.6 CONCLUSION

However tempting it is to see big data as a singular concept, lumping all big data projects and applications together and regarding it as solution and problem in one, it is impossible. What is happening in practice is simply too diverse and very much determined by the purposes and strategies of organisations. However, for the issues caused by the phenomenon, the legal analysis, and the discussion of possible solutions, big data can be divided into three phases: acquisition, analysis, and application. The negative impact on individual rights and freedoms is different for each of the phases and is summarised in the ensuing paragraphs and Figure 2.2.

In the application phase the biggest concern for individual rights and freedoms is of course the accumulation of personal data. The collection of large amounts of personal data negatively affects personal autonomy in multiple ways. First of all, knowing that one's personal data are collected and online behaviour is tracked creates a sense of surveillance that inhibits individuals' behaviour. Ultimately, when individuals change their behaviour and adhere to perceived societal norms, this can have long-term consequences for how people develop their personal identities. Second, the opacity and complexity of the data collection process and the possible future consequences of processing exert pressure on informational self-determination and the making of autonomous choices. Therefore data

228. Ultimately this also affects democracy and the social value of privacy (*see* for example Sunstein, *Republic 2.0* (n 181); Daniel J. Solove, *Nothing to Hide: The False Tradeoff Between Privacy and Security* (Yale University Press 2011) 47–53; Kirsty Hughes, 'The Social Value of Privacy: The Value of Privacy to Human Rights Discourse' in Beate Rössler and Dorota Mokrosinska (eds), *Social Dimensions of Privacy: Interdisciplinary Perspectives* (Cambridge University Press 2015) 225–230), but these aspects are beyond the scope of this work on individual rights and freedoms.

protection and privacy are also affected by the large-scale collection of personal data, particularly when datasets are combined and new data are created. Lastly, again related to individuals feeling watched as a result of data collection, there can be chilling effects on freedom of expression.

In the analysis phase, the negative effect on individual rights and freedoms seems moderate. The data have already been collected and analysis is done out of sight of the individual, so it does not seem to impact her directly. However, the analysis phase can be seen as the source of many of the negative effects that occur in the application phase. For example, discriminatory models are created in the analysis phase, even though their effect will only become apparent when applied. The foundations for judging people on the behaviour of others, on their past behaviour, and on contentious knowledge are laid in the analysis phase. The analysis contains the core of unfairness, of becoming guilty by association or ending up in vicious loops based potentially on one bad move in the past. And in spite of the grand aims and expectations of big data, the techniques remain based on statistics and a limited amount of data about reality. Even not ending up in the dataset that is analysed could lead to disadvantages in the application phase. Moreover, the risk of false positives and negatives is ever-present. The analysis shows the disconnectedness of the phases: data that have been collected from one group can lead to a model or other type of knowledge that impacts another group of people. The limited control and lack of transparency in the analysis for both the person whose data are collected and then processed in the analysis phase, as well as for the individual to whom the knowledge or model is applied in the application phase, attest to the personal autonomy problem in the analysis phase.

Given that big data is employed to many different ends in many different situations, it comes as no surprise that the application phase harbours the most diverse array of negative effects on individual rights and freedoms. Personal autonomy is at stake, because of the ways in which people can be nudged, coerced, persuaded, and manipulated. The danger lies not only in the possibilities of generating a big impact but also in the cumulative effect: in the countless small ways in which our thoughts, behaviour and opportunities can be steered. A lack of diversity in the reception of information, possibly resulting in filter bubbles, also hinders personal autonomy and individual self-development. Additionally it is a threat to freedom of expression, complemented by the possibility of manipulating people's reception of information, and the risk that they will censor themselves. Obviously, the application phase is also the phase in which the discriminatory effects of big data are almost palpable. Here the cascade of effects is again of additional concern: the potential of big data to reinforce existing inequalities in society, and create new ones. And last but not least, there are a myriad of ways in which the application of big data can interfere with people's private lives.

Figure 2.2 Effect on Individual Rights and Freedoms

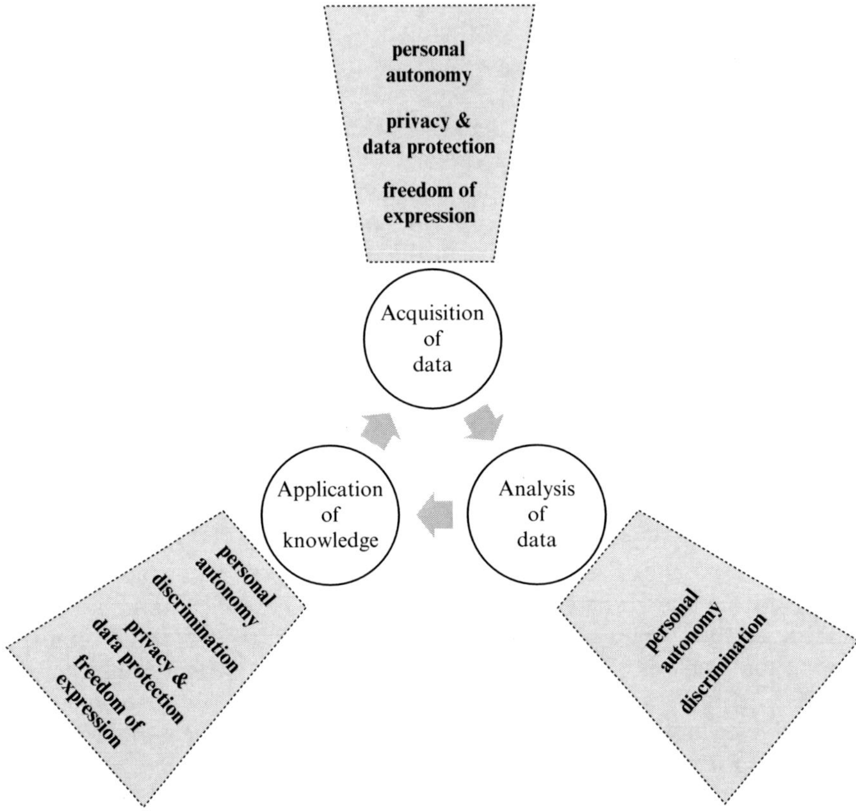

In sum, big data has a negative impact on personal autonomy, privacy and data protection, non-discrimination, and freedom of expression. However, the negative impact differs according to the processing phase; different issues arise in each phase, affecting individual rights and freedoms in multiple ways. Also, the people whose individual rights and freedoms are affected differs according to the phases; the people whose data are used as inputs for the application of the knowledge or models derived from big data, are not necessarily the people affected in the application phase. Yet all the issues come together in the analysis phase, which is based on the data of the first group, and is the source of the negative effects that people of the second group are confronted with in the application phase. This chapter has also shown that when discussing the negative impact of big data, we should not limit ourselves to very visible high-impact effects; there is just as much, or maybe even more, danger in cumulative effects and long-term consequences of big data.

The complex reality of contemporary big data processing is certainly a challenge for the EU framework on privacy and data protection. In any case it is clear that the extent to which it protects individual rights and freedoms is dependent on how it applies in each of the phases of big data. The potential of the EU framework with respect to protection against the negative impact on individual rights and freedoms as described in this chapter is analysed in the following chapter on the fundamental rights to privacy and data protection in the EU, and in Chapter 4 on secondary EU data protection law.

Chapter 3

Big Data and the Fundamental Rights to Privacy and to Data Protection

3.1 INTRODUCTION

Central to this chapter is the question of the scope of the rights to privacy and data protection in relation to the big data process and its potential negative effects.[229] This question is answered on the basis of Article 8 ECHR and Articles 7 and 8 CFREU, since these rights and their interpretation by the Courts create a comprehensive and authoritative interpretation of the normative concepts of individuals' rights to privacy and data protection.[230]

The purpose of the chapter is to develop an understanding of how these fundamental rights apply to big data in the light of the norms, their legal dogmatic and case law, and their scope of protection as stand-alone rights and as enabling rights. In the context of protecting individuals in big data, the

229. Parts of this section will be published as part of Manon Oostveen and Kristina Irion, 'The Golden Age of Personal Data: How to Regulate an Enabling Fundamental Right?' in Mor Bakhoum and others (eds), *Personal Data in Competition, Consumer Protection and IP Law – Towards a Holistic Approach?* (Springer 2018) (forthcoming, with changes).

230. *See* subsection 1.2.5.2 for a more detailed explanation of the selection of these fundamental rights. The most important doctrinal argument is that the interpretation of the CFREU is made dependent on the ECHR by Articles 52 and 53 CFREU.

right to privacy and data protection have both intrinsic value as stand-alone rights, i.e., they protect privacy and data protection itself, as well as instrumental value: they facilitate the protection of other fundamental rights and freedoms. This facilitative function is what the concept of enabling rights refers to. In subsequent chapters, these concepts of privacy and data protection are used to assess what implementation of secondary law is normatively required by the rights to privacy and data protection with respect to big data. In Chapter 4, the protection offered by secondary EU data protection law in the guise of the GDPR is compared with the normative concepts, to assess to what extent the GDPR matches with what they would require in terms of both stand-alone protection of individuals' rights to privacy and data protection, as well as the enabling function of these rights.

The successive comparative analysis of this chapter therefore focuses on the material scope of application of the fundamental rights, deriving the normative scope of the rights with respect to the big data process and its effects primarily from the interpretation by the two Courts. In the legal doctrinal analysis of both jurisdictions, the focus is on cases that are relevant because they concern the activities of one or more big data phases, and the facilitating role of the rights to privacy and data protection for other fundamental rights and freedoms. As the scope of the rights is heavily influenced by procedural particularities and interpretative doctrines of the respective fundamental rights instruments and the Courts, each section commences with a general subsection that provides background information on these aspects and doctrines. A comparison and conceptualisation of the normative concepts follow after the doctrinal analysis of both jurisdictions, at the end of the chapter. The next subsection first positions the chapter in the academic literature on the fundamental rights to privacy and data protection.

3.1.1 Literature Review

There is a great body of literature on privacy and data protection. To begin there is much epistemological literature that focuses on the explanation and scope of the concepts of privacy and data protection, and on their merit.[231] Albeit interesting and possibly illuminating, this branch of privacy literature will not be cited frequently in this chapter, since this work aims to derive the normative concepts of the rights to privacy and data protection from the actual scope of the most important fundamental rights in the EU, i.e., Article 8 ECHR and Articles 7 and 8 CFREU. The key resources for the understanding of privacy and data protection on the fundamental rights level are the legal textbooks or commentaries to the ECHR and the CFREU,

231. For example Schoeman (n 18); Solove, *Understanding Privacy* (n 18); Moore (n 18).

respectively.[232] Privacy, the elder of the two rights, has long been the centre of attention in both textbooks and specific contributions on the scope of rights in articles. In the commentaries, the discussion of private life predominantly follows the development of the case law of the ECtHR, dividing the discussion into the four autonomous concepts of Article 8 ECHR (private life, family life, home, and correspondence). These concepts are then developed as they are in the case law, where the Court has continuously classified new interests and issues under Article 8 over the years. Newly identified interests often serve as the starting point for new strands of case law, further developing these interests under Article 8 of the Convention.[233] In the commentaries, broad divisions are made such as into the categories of personal identity, moral or physical identity, private sphere, collection and use of information, sexual activities, and social life or the enjoyment of relationships.[234] One can also divide the right to privacy according to the topics that the case law deals with, such as security and surveillance, health, or family life topics such as expulsion, marriage, or abortion. For many of these topics, much secondary literature has been published. Often, trends in the literature are sparked by legal or societal trends such as controversial case law or societal developments like the Snowden revelations regarding state-surveillance.

Around and after the time of drafting of the CFREU a new topic emerged in the constitutional literature. The elevation of data protection into the European constitutional legal order led to a surge of works on the fundamental right to data protection, creating a branch in the literature that focuses on the *nature* of the right to data protection.[235] The previous quest for data protection under the right to privacy has evolved into comparison of the rights and debates about the scope of both rights, taking the elevation of the right to data protection and the case law of both Courts into account.[236] Some of these works incorporate extensive case law from the CJEU or from both

---

232. Harris and others (n 38); Rainey, Wicks and Ovey (n 13); Jürgen Meyer and Norbert Bernsdorff, *Charta der Grundrechte der Europäischen Union* (Nomos Verlagsgesellschaft 2011); Steve Peers, Tamara Hervey and Angela Ward, *The EU Charter of Fundamental Rights: A Commentary* (Hart/Beck 2014).
233. Maris Burbergs, 'How the Right to Respect for Private and Family Life, Home and Correspondence Became the Nursery in Which New Rights Are Born: Article 8 ECHR' in Eva Brems and Janneke Gerards (eds), *Shaping Rights in the ECHR: The Role of the European Court of Human Rights in Determining the Scope of Human Rights* (Cambridge University Press 2014) 322–329.
234. Categorisation of Mowbray, *see* Alastair R. Mowbray, *Cases, Materials, and Commentary on the European Convention on Human Rights* (Oxford University Press 2012) 362–372. Other divisions are also possible.
235. *See* for example Tzanou (n 22) 88; González Fuster (n 16); Orla Lynskey, 'Deconstructing Data Protection: The "Added-Value" of a Right to Data Protection in the EU Legal Order' (2014) 63.
236. *See* for example De Hert and Gutwirth (n 27), De Hert and Gutwirth (n 23).

Courts;[237] others focus more on the conceptual differences between privacy and data protection.[238]

Given the big data context, this chapter has a special focus on the so-called *branches* of privacy with respect to personal data and positive obligations.[239] Nevertheless, it also features a more general analysis of the fundamental right to privacy to determine its scope in the application phase, where personal data are not necessarily processed, and to find connections between the right to privacy and the other individual rights and freedoms (personal autonomy, freedom of expression, and non-discrimination). Branches of the case law that are irrelevant for big data, such as those developed from the family life interest, are not taken into account. For the general descriptive subsections, this chapter relies on the constitutional literature as described above. When analysing the scope of the fundamental rights regarding big data, however, almost no such literature is available. These subsections depend primarily on the legislative context of the rights and case law analysis.

3.2 THE COUNCIL OF EUROPE (ECHR)

This subsection analyses the right to privacy under Article 8 of the Convention focusing on aspects that are important for big data. First, general information about the CoE, ECHR, and ECtHR that is of significance for the subsequent analysis is set out. The analysis of the content of Article 8 as explained by the ECtHR follows focusing on the three big data phases and the negative effects on individual rights and freedoms that may occur.

3.2.1 History and Interpretation of Fundamental Rights in the CoE

The ECHR is a fundamental rights treaty created by the Council of Europe (CoE). The CoE was formed in 1949 as an intergovernmental organisation in Europe dedicated to the safeguarding and advancement of fundamental rights, democracy, and European cooperation. The drafting of the ECHR drew inspiration from the Universal Declaration of Human Rights that was adopted two years earlier.[240] Yet in creating a treaty that binds the states that signed and ratified the Convention (the 'Contracting States'), the European

237. De Hert and Gutwirth (n 23).
238. Gellert and Gutwirth (n 25).
239. *See* for example Bygrave, 'Data Protection Pursuant to the Right to Privacy in Human Rights Treaties' (n 57).
240. Oliver Diggelmann and Maria Nicole Cleis, 'How the Right to Privacy Became a Human Right' (2014) 14 Human Rights Law Review 441, 452.

States went further than the Declaration in effectively protecting fundamental rights. The primary explanations for this vigour are the experiences of the European States with the atrocities of the Second World War on their own territory, as well as the post-war tensions in Europe between the West and (communist) East.[241] In 1950 the CoE opened the ECHR for signature, and on 3 September 1953 it entered into force. The Convention established the ECtHR,[242] which interprets and enforces the ECHR against the Contracting States.

Both Contracting States and individuals can lodge applications alleging that a Contracting State has breached the Convention.[243] Applications by individuals to the Court are only admissible when all national remedies have been exhausted.[244] Complaints can only be made against a Contracting State, which means that complaints against private entities are inadmissible *rationae personae*.[245] This is in line with the traditional conception of fundamental rights as rights that protect individuals against abuse of power by the state. Correspondingly, most rights of the ECHR are formulated as negative obligations that require states to refrain from interfering with these rights. In constitutional law, this vertical effect is common, but it means that the findings of this chapter are not directly applicable to the situations in which big data processing is taking place. As explained above, this is why this research takes the normative content of the rights as the starting point for further analysis.[246] There are, however, ways in which the ECHR can affect private parties.

Based on the *practical and effective* doctrine and Article 1 ECHR that requires states to secure individuals' enjoyment of the rights of the ECHR, the Court has decided that states may have positive obligations with respect to Convention rights.[247] Positive obligations require the state to take action, even though the state itself does not directly interfere with the rights of the Convention.[248] The typical positive obligation is the case in which the state is responsible for failing to protect an individual's fundamental right that is

241. Ed Bates, 'The Birth of the European Convention on Human Rights – and the European Court of Human Rights' in Jonas Christoffersen and Mikael Rask Madsen (eds), *The European Court of Human Rights: Between Law and Politics* (Oxford University Press 2011) 18; Rainey, Wicks and Ovey (n 13) 4.
242. Article 19 ECHR.
243. Articles 33 and 34 ECHR.
244. Article 35 ECHR.
245. Articles 33 and 34 ECHR.
246. Subsection 1.2.5.2.
247. *Marckx v Belgium* [1979] ECtHR 6833/74; Laurens Lavrysen, 'The Scope of Rights and the Scope of Obligations: Positive Obligations' in Eva Brems and Janneke Gerards (eds), *Shaping Rights in the ECHR: The Role of the European Court of Human Rights in Determining the Scope of Human Rights* (Cambridge University Press 2014) 162.
248. Rainey, Wicks and Ovey (n 13) 102.

violated by a private party.[249] The Court first asserted that states may be obliged to take positive action to comply with Article 8 ECHR in the landmark case of *Marckx v Belgium*.[250] Positive obligations are significant for the assessment of the right to privacy in the context of big data, since in big data the actors are often private parties instead of states. Through positive obligations, states can be forced to take measures to protect the rights under the Convention, thereby affecting private parties. In this way, even though private entities cannot be defendants before the Court, the decisions of the ECtHR can have a direct effect on their actions.

But positive obligations are not described or limited in the rights of the Convention: they are determined by the Court. The Court has stated that this determination depends on a fair balance and whether the effective exercise of a right is prevented or the essence of a right is destroyed, but it has not set any general fixed limits to describe the boundaries of the possible positive obligations.[251] The Court has held that the principles applicable to negative and positive obligations are similar,[252] but it has not developed a full theory of positive obligations.[253] It decides on alleged infringements of the state's positive obligations on a case-by-case basis.[254] Consequently the scope of positive obligations under Article 8 can only be assessed on the basis of existing case law, and generalisations are difficult to make. Moreover, the case law regarding positive obligations is not as structured as when negative obligations are at stake.

There are currently no cases that give clear indications regarding positive obligations in the area of big data. Although states have been ordered to comply with the positive obligation to give access to information and prevent unwarranted access or publication of personal data, these obligations were accepted under exceptional circumstances (danger to health and paternity issues) and often concerned semi-governmental institutions for which the state was held responsible. Therefore, the conclusions of these cases cannot be directly applied to the big data process in general, as the actors in big data are usually independent private parties. In general, big data is not an area devoid of (national or European) regulation, as is elucidated in later chapters of this research, which will make it difficult to accuse the state

249. An example is the case of *X and Y v the Netherlands*, where the Court decided that the Dutch Government had violated Article 8 ECHR, because there were no adequate provisions in the Dutch Criminal Code that a mentally handicapped girl could appeal to after she had been sexually abused, *X and Y v the Netherlands* [1985] ECtHR 8978/80.
250. *Marckx v Belgium* (n 247) [31].
251. *Appleby v UK* [2003] ECtHR 44306/98 [40, 47]; Dimitris Xenos, *The Positive Obligations of the State under the European Convention of Human Rights* (Routledge 2012) 4.
252. *Verein gegen Tierfabriken v Switzerland (No 2)* [2009] ECtHR 32772/02 [82]; *Von Hannover v Germany (No 2)* [2012] ECtHR 40660/08, 60641/08 [99].
253. *Ärzte für das Leben v Austria* [1988] ECHR 10126/82 [31].
254. Lavrysen (n 247) 162.

of passivity in relation to big data. In light of existing secondary legislation, the fair balance test, and the margin of appreciation of states as elucidated below, it does not seem likely that the Court will be quick to accept new substantive positive obligations in this area.

The normative concept of the right to privacy under the ECHR is also dependent on the interpretative rules and doctrines of the ECHR, as these give indications about the current and future application and confines of the concepts. The interpretation of the ECHR is first and foremost bound by the rules of the Vienna Convention on the Law of Treaties.[255] Hence its terms must be interpreted in accordance with their ordinary meaning in context and in accordance with the object and purpose of the ECHR. 'Context' includes the CoE's Convention 108 as an 'instrument relating to the treaty'. It must therefore be taken into account when interpreting Article 8 ECHR. Additional interpretative principles flow from the judgments of the ECtHR itself. One of the Court's most important methods is the *living instrument* doctrine.[256] Throughout its case law, starting with *Tyrer v UK*,[257] the Court has determined that the Convention is a *living instrument* and that the rights in the Convention must therefore be interpreted in the context of 'present-day conditions'.[258] This means that the Court can take contemporary standards and contextual factors into account in its judgments. Through the doctrine the Court can consider matters that did not exist at the time of drafting of the Convention. An example is email, which did not exist in the 1950s but is now deemed covered by 'correspondence'.[259] In other words, the interpretation of the Convention rights is not set in stone; the Court may adapt its reasoning or even reverse its earlier case law when it deems that present-day conditions so require.[260] Finally, regarding the rights of the ECHR the Court has made it clear that the Convention protects rights that are 'practical and effective' instead of 'theoretical and illusory'.[261] The *practical and effective* doctrine increases the interpretation of rights in the light of the Convention's object and purpose.[262] It provides an extra measure of protection of individuals under the Convention and can oblige states to act instead of remaining passive.[263] All this enables the Court to take new technological developments and changes in society into account, which is of particular importance in the

255. Vienna Convention on the Law of Treaties (n 62); *Golder v UK* (n 62) [29]. *See also* section 1.2.5 of Chapter 1 on methodology and the Vienna Convention.
256. George Letsas, 'The ECHR as a Living Instrument: Its Meaning and Legitimacy', *Constituting Europe: The European Court of Human Rights in a National, European and Global Context* (Cambridge University Press 2013).
257. *Tyrer v UK* [1978] ECtHR 5856/72.
258. *Ibid* 31.
259. *Copland v UK* [2007] ECtHR 62617/00 [41].
260. *Goodwin v UK* [2002] ECtHR 28957/95 [74].
261. *Airey v Ireland* [1979] ECtHR 6289/73 [24].
262. Rainey, Wicks and Ovey (n 13) 73.
263. Alastair R. Mowbray, 'The Creativity of the European Court of Human Rights' (2005) 5 Human Rights Law Review 78.

context of big data, and makes sense from the perspective of protection. What may on the other hand limit the protection of individuals under the Convention is the *margin of appreciation* doctrine.[264] The doctrine allows the Court to take the non-uniformity of the cultures and interpretations of fundamental rights amongst the Contracting States into account in its judgments.[265] Under the margin of appreciation doctrine, Contracting States are offered a range of discretion in the area of Convention rights. The scope of the margin of appreciation depends amongst others on which right is at stake and on the level of consensus about the interpretation amongst the Contracting States. Generally the margin of appreciation that states have when Article 8 ECHR is applied is deemed quite wide by the Court.[266] These interpretative doctrines recur in the analysis of the ECHR's right to privacy in the following subsection.

3.2.2 The Right to Privacy (Article 8 ECHR)

At the time when the ECHR was drafted, European national constitutions did not contain a general right to privacy. Only specific interests, such as the right to privacy of the home or confidentiality of correspondence, were covered.[267] Nevertheless drafters of the Convention created a broad, general right to privacy in Article 8 (1) ECHR, by explicitly enshrining a right to respect for 'private life' in the Convention, in addition to incorporating key elements that were protected by national constitutions preceding the Convention:

> Everyone has the right to respect for his private and family life, his home and his correspondence.

The second paragraph of Article 8 enumerates the criteria that justify an interference with the right. It reads as follows:

> There shall be no interference by a public authority with the exercise of this right except such as is in accordance with the law and is necessary in a democratic society in the interests of national security, public safety or the economic well-being of the country, for the prevention of disorder or crime, for the protection of health or morals, or for the protection of the rights and freedoms of others.

When the ECtHR decides a case on Article 8, it follows the structure of the article by conducting a fundamental rights test that consists of three separate steps, except when cases involve positive obligations. To determine whether a positive obligation exists, the Court usually assesses whether a fair

264. *Handyside v UK* [1976] ECtHR 5493/72 [48–50].
265. Harris and others (n 38) 14–17.
266. Rainey, Wicks and Ovey (n 13) 80.
267. Diggelmann and Cleis (n 240) 448.

balance has been struck between the rights of the community and the rights of the individual.[268] The conditions of Article 8 (2) may be of relevance in this fair balance test, but a full tripartite fundamental rights test is not conducted.[269] In the general tripartite fundamental rights test, the Court first decides whether an issue falls under the *scope of application* of the right to privacy, i.e., whether the subject matter of the case is covered by Article 8. If the issue falls under the scope of application, the Court establishes whether the right is *interfered* with or not. If an interference is found, the Court assesses whether the interference can be *justified*. The interference with the right to privacy can only be justified if it meets the criteria enumerated in the second paragraph of Article 8 (in accordance with the law, legitimate aim, necessary in a democratic society). If the interference cannot be justified, there is a violation of the right to privacy under the Convention. The analysis below is divided according to the tripartite fundamental rights test.

3.2.2.1 Scope of Application

Article 8 (1) ECHR covers four spheres: private life, family life, home, and correspondence, which are autonomous but partially overlapping.[270] The Convention does not contain definitions of these four concepts; their subject matter and delineation have to be determined on the basis of the ECtHR's case law. Yet the Court also refrains from providing fixed definitions in its judgments. It does not always specify which particular concept is at stake; often spheres are discussed conjointly.[271] Nevertheless, particular strands of case law can be recognised under each sphere and certain aspects of privacy can be classified under a singular interest. The 'private life' interest is a broad umbrella term under which many aspects related to big data fit, including personal data.[272] The right to respect for family life primarily governs relationships between (potential) members of a family and their legal recognition. It is not likely to address core issues of (personal) data processing, so it is not discussed any further in this section. The concept of 'home' primarily governs issues that involve access to the physical place where the individual resides. Although this interest has not yet been of major importance for big data in the case law of the Court, there is a possibility that this might change in the future. Issues related to big data can also fall within the interest of 'correspondence'. Therefore, the following analysis of the

---

268. *Rees v UK* [1986] ECtHR 9532/81 [37].
269. Alastair R. Mowbray, *The Development of Positive Obligations under the European Convention on Human Rights by the European Court of Human Rights* (Hart Publishing 2004) 186; *see* for example *Babylonová v Slovakia* [2006] ECtHR 69146/01 [51].
270. Article 8 (1) ECHR.
271. Harris and others (n 38) 524.
272. *Ibid* 522–526.

scope of application broadly follows Article 8 ECHR's division insofar as is relevant for big data.

3.2.2.1.1 Private Life

Of the four interests, private life is the most difficult to describe and delineate. The ECtHR itself regularly states that private life is a broad term, and that an exhaustive definition of the concept cannot be given.[273] The private life interest is interpreted on a non-restrictive case-by-case basis. Over the years the ECtHR has applied the concept in a wide array of cases, ranging from the storage of fingerprints and DNA profiles in databases[274] to receiving records of one's upbringing in foster care (personal identity),[275] and decisions about reproduction and adoption.[276] The right to privacy encompasses a right to identity and personal development, and to the establishment and development of relationships with others.[277] More recently the Court has also included an individual's ethnic and social identity, information about her health, and means of personal identification in its enumeration of important elements.[278] The Court has also stated that gender identification, name, and sexual life are important elements of Article 8.[279] Mowbray classifies these private-life cases in six categories: personal identity, moral or physical identity, private sphere, collection and use of information, sexual activities, and social life or the enjoyment of relationships.[280] Although this categorisation is neither fixed nor directly employed by the ECtHR, it illustrates the broad coverage of the concept of private life. The application of big data can interfere with all of these spheres.

The ECtHR does not generally refer to the enabling function of the right to privacy for other fundamental rights and freedoms that are part of this research (personal autonomy, data protection, non-discrimination, freedom of expression), save for two exceptions. The first is personal data, discussed below, and the second is personal autonomy. The Court has frequently referred to personal autonomy as an underlying principle influencing the interpretation of the ECHR's right to respect for private life and puts it on par

273. *P.G. and J.H. v UK* (n 30) [56]; *Peck v UK* [2003] ECtHR 44647/98 [57]; *Perry v UK* [2003] ECtHR 637337/00 [36].
274. *S. and Marper v UK* (n 30).
275. *Gaskin v UK* [1989] ECtHR 10454/83.
276. *Tysiac v Poland* [2007] ECtHR 5410/03; *Evans v UK* [2007] ECtHR 6339/05; *E.B. v France* [2008] ECtHR 43546/02.
277. *P.G. and J.H. v UK* (n 30) [56].
278. *S. and Marper v UK* (n 30) [66].
279. *P.G. and J.H. v UK* (n 30) [56].
280. Mowbray, *Cases, Materials, and Commentary on the European Convention on Human Rights* (n 234) 364–376.

with self-determination.[281] Moreover, it has even stated that there is a right to personal autonomy included in Article 8 ECHR, making personal autonomy part of privacy's scope of protection, instead of it being solely a meta-value behind the fundamental right.[282] As explained in the first chapter, personal autonomy is not a separate Convention right, but a value underlying many rights and freedoms, receiving particular attention in the context of privacy.[283] This explains the frequency of references to personal autonomy compared with the other rights and freedoms. The other rights and freedoms, save for personal autonomy and data protection, are stand-alone fundamental rights with which an interference can be claimed. The Court assesses these cases separately, occasionally discussing them conjointly, but judging them on their own merit instead of as one being the facilitator of the other.[284] Still, in one case the right to privacy has also been deemed to cover certain practices that are closely related to discrimination, such as the negative stereotyping of certain groups.[285]

3.2.2.1.2 Personal Data under the Right to Privacy

Article 8 has been applied to protect a broad array of personal data and uses thereof, predominantly under the interest of private life, and can therefore cover many parts of the big data process. The ECtHR established the general principle on the scope of application of Article 8 regarding personal data in *Leander v Sweden.*[286] In the *Leander* case the Court stated that the storage and release of information relating to private life fall under the scope of the right to respect for private life.[287] This principle has been affirmed by subsequent case law.[288] According to the Court, its interpretation of data related to private life corresponds to the definition of personal data of Convention 108.[289] Convention 108 defines personal data as 'any information relating to an identified or identifiable individual'.[290] The Court has emphasised this link between personal data and data related to private life on multiple occasions.[291]

281. *Pretty v UK* (n 12) [61]; *Goodwin v UK* (n 260) [90]; *Reklos and Davourlis v Greece* [2009] ECtHR 1234/05 [39]; *Ciubotaru v Moldova* [2010] ECtHR 27138/04 [49].
282. *Evans v UK* (n 276) [71]; *Tysiac v Poland* (n 276) [107]; *Kalacheva v Russia* [2009] ECtHR 3451/05 [27].
283. Koffeman (n 12) 6–7, 62–64; Rainey, Wicks and Ovey (n 13) 383.
284. *See* for example *E.B. v France* (n 276).
285. *Aksu v Turkey* [2012] ECtHR 4149/04 and 41029/04 [58].
286. *Leander v Sweden* [1987] ECtHR 9248/81
287. *Ibid* 48.
288. *See* for example *Rotaru v Romania* (n 30) [43]; *S. and Marper v UK* (n 30) [67].
289. *Amann v Switzerland* [2000] ECtHR 27798/95 [65].
290. Article 2 (a) Convention 108.
291. *Rotaru v Romania* (n 30) [43]; *P.G. and J.H. v UK* (n 30) [57]; *Uzun v Germany* [2010] ECtHR 35623/05 [46].

Although it is possible in theory that the Court would deem information related to individuals outside the scope of Article 8 ECHR, the Court's current interpretation of 'data related to private life' in connection with the definition of personal data of Convention 108 seems sufficiently broad to include personal data in general.[292] For example, in *Amann* the Court held that short statements written on a card regarding an individual's contact with a third party and a link to his business 'undeniably' fell within the scope of the right to respect for private life.[293] Data that are in a file about an individual, for example in medical records or police registers, are covered by Article 8 because they directly relate to an identified individual. In addition to written information, fingerprints,[294] DNA samples,[295] photographs,[296] and voice[297] or video recordings[298] can be within the scope of Article 8. Moreover, the Court concluded that personal information relating to e-mail and Internet usage are also within the scope of application of Article 8.[299] In *Rotaru v Romania* the Court decided that when public information is 'systematically collected and stored in files held by the authorities', it can fall within the scope of the right to respect to private life.[300] Consequently, information about an individual that is collected in a public space or that constitutes public (or published) information can be covered by Article 8.[301]

The previous cases concerned information that directly relates to an individual, but Article 8 ECHR also covers data that have a weaker link with the individual's identity. In *Malone* the Court considered that metering records are covered by Article 8.[302] The metering records in question were telephone records that disclosed the duration of calls as well as which numbers were dialled at which date and time. The records essentially contained telephony metadata.[303] The acceptance of metadata within the scope of Article 8 was continued in the Court's case law after *Malone*.[304] In *Copland* Article 8 was applied to metadata regarding Internet use, e-mail,

292. De Hert and Gutwirth (n 23) 24–25. *See also* subsection 3.2.2.2 on interferences with Article 8 ECHR.
293. *Amann v Switzerland* (n 289) [66–67].
294. *S. and Marper v UK* (n 30).
295. *Ibid.*
296. *Von Hannover v Germany* [2004] ECtHR 59320/00.
297. *P.G. and J.H. v UK* (n 30).
298. *Peck v UK* (n 273).
299. *Copland v UK* (n 259) [44].
300. *Rotaru v Romania* (n 30) [43].
301. However compared to private data the Court adopts a much stricter test for public data when establishing an interference in the second step of the fundamental rights test. This will be discussed in subsection 3.2.2.2 on interferences with Article 8.
302. *Malone v UK* [1984] ECtHR 8691/79 [83–84].
303. Metadata is '*data about data*'. In the context of communications it means that it does not concern the content of the communications, but data about the communication as such. Examples are the previously mentioned traffic data that indicate amongst others the origin, destination, and duration of the communication.
304. *P.G. and J.H. v UK* (n 30); *Copland v UK* (n 259).

and telephony.[305] Metadata on Internet usage includes data about which websites are visited at what time and for how long, and metadata about e-mails such as sender, receiver, date, and time.[306] In the *Uzun* case, location data acquired through GPS were deemed to fall within the scope of private life.[307] Accordingly Article 8 covers a broad array of metadata.[308]

In sum, data related to private life are within the scope of Article 8 ECHR. In principle, there is no quantitative requirement regarding the scope of application, nor is it necessary that the data are truly private or unpublished. In addition to being covered by the private life interest, personal data can also be covered by Article 8 through the right to respect for home and correspondence.

3.2.2.1.3 Home

The 'home' interest does not seem to have immediate relevance for the big data context. Although home is a broad concept that may include business premises,[309] the home cases dealt with by the ECtHR are usually about issues like eviction or the enjoyment of property.[310] However, as it flows from this case law that the interest requires broad interpretation of a physical place of residence, home may become of future relevance in the big data context.[311] Modern households are increasingly filled with smart devices. Many devices are physically connected to the house and collect data about the home and its inhabitants. For example, smart electricity meters and thermostats allow for real-time registering of energy consumption and accessory data in homes. These data are collected for remote reporting to companies but can also be transmitted to smartphones of the home's inhabitants. Smart security systems offer remote monitoring of the home through amongst others alarms and cameras. Data are transmitted to smartphones but storage and collection of data is often offered by the company that supplies the security system. All of these data can be used for big data purposes, and the future likely sees a rise in similar applications of smart devices in our home.[312] These appliances, but also the data flows of these devices and the application of big data in houses, are inextricably linked to the home. It is conceivable that issues regarding these devices or data collected through them, for example regarding the

305. *Copland v UK* (n 259) [39–42].
306. *Ibid* 11, 13.
307. *Uzun v Germany* (n 291) [44–46].
308. All these cases concern targeted surveillance; additional data was processed through which the individuals were identifiable.
309. *Niemietz v Germany* [1992] ECtHR 13710/88.
310. Rainey, Wicks and Ovey (n 13) 405–406.
311. Harris and others (n 38) 528–530.
312. *See* for a vision of the future and the legal implications Mireille Hildebrandt and Bert-Jaap Koops, 'The Challenges of Ambient Law and Legal Protection in the Profiling Era' (2010) The Modern Law Review 428.

ability of the user to control and switch off the devices or the use of the data transmitted through them by the government or insurance companies, will fall under the right to respect for the home.[313]

3.2.2.1.4 Correspondence

The right to respect for correspondence protects private communications: the right to communicate without government interruption or interception. Over the course of time the Court's interpretation of the concept gradually evolved from pertaining purely to written communications to also include other forms of communication like telephony and email, both at the time of communication and when stored.[314] In 2012 the Court seemed to step away from the casuistic approach to correspondence in the case of *Michaud v France*, declaring that Article 8 ECHR protects the *confidentiality* of private *communications*, regardless of content and format.[315] Furthermore, the Court stated that 'the confidentiality of all the exchanges in which individuals may engage for the purposes of communication' is protected.[316] The Court's reasoning implies that the content of chat sessions or other digital message services may fall under correspondence, whereas the content of public websites does not, due to the lack of confidentiality.[317] For example, private conversations through messenger services such as WhatsApp will be covered, provided the service is not public but offers confidential communication. On the other hand, messages on microblogging websites such as Twitter, or social networks such as Facebook, will in all probability not fall within the scope of 'correspondence', as they lack a confidential nature.

Under *correspondence,* it is possible for information to be covered by Article 8 even though the interest of private life is not at stake. In *Bernh Larsen* case a server belonging to a commercial entity was at issue.[318] The case was lodged by a commercial entity and there was no additional private life complaint by an individual. In the absence of a complaint by an individual the Court deemed it unnecessary to examine the issue under the interest of private life.[319] Instead, the access to and copying of the data on the server were deemed to fall within the scope of the interests of home and correspondence.[320] The case shows that personal data do not necessarily have to fall under the interest of private life to be protected by Article 8. However

313. This type of data may also be covered under the interest of private life, *see* above.
314. *Halford v UK* [1997] ECtHR 20605/92 [44]; *Amann v Switzerland* (n 289) [43]; *Copland v UK* (n 259) [41]; *Niemietz v Germany* (n 309) [32].
315. *Michaud v France* [2012] ECtHR 12323/11 [90].
316. *Ibid.*
317. *See also* Christoph Grabenwarter, *European Convention on Human Rights: Commentary* (CH Beck; Hart; Nomos; Helbing Lichtenhahn 2014) 198.
318. *Bernh Larsen Holding AS and others v Norway* [2013] ECtHR 24117/08.
319. *Ibid* 107.
320. *Ibid* 104–106; *Niemietz v Germany* (n 309).

other criteria may apply, for example, the condition that communications need to be confidential to fall within the scope of correspondence, and many confidential communications will constitute personal data anyway.

3.2.2.2 Interferences with the Right to Privacy

Although the scope of application of Article 8 is very broad and consequently covers numerous aspects of the big data process, many actions regarding this subject matter will not constitute an actual interference with the right to privacy. This subsection discusses interferences with Article 8 ECHR insofar as relevant for the context of big data. As mentioned in the context of the scope of application, it is important to note that the cases on which the analysis is based deal with interferences by the state. This does not only mean that they concern vertical relationships, it also means that crime and surveillance are frequently part of the context of the case, and that individuals usually did not consent to the processing of their personal data.

The right to privacy is interfered with when there is a limitation on the enjoyment of the right. Although the Court has never explicitly stated it in its judgments, processing of data related to private life, and thus of personal data, will generally constitute an interference (*see* above). The Court has established that the mere storage of data relating to private life can constitute an interference with Article 8.[321] Subsequent uses of the data constitute stand-alone interferences that are separately assessed by the Court.[322] Whether and how the data are subsequently used does not affect the infringing nature of the initial storage.[323] This means that, for example, the storage of information, the subsequent use of it, and the refusal of a chance to refute it constitute separate interferences with the right to privacy.[324] Also when the data are not sensitive and have probably never been consulted, its inclusion in a file can constitute an interference.[325] Interferences with personal autonomy have not been explicitly identified by the Court.

Nevertheless, not all processing of personal data necessarily constitutes an interference with the right to respect for private life. Particularly when the data are of a public or published nature, such as photographs taken in public spaces, special criteria apply to determine whether there is an interference.[326] The Court decides on the basis of the context in which the information has been collected and stored, the kind of record that is made from the

321. *Leander v Sweden* (n 286) [48].
322. *See* as an example, including the ECtHR's explanation of this approach, *Z. v Finland* [1997] ECtHR 22009/93 [100]
323. *Amann v Switzerland* (n 289) [69]; *Kopp v Switzerland* [1998] ECtHR 23224/94 [53].
324. *Rotaru v Romania* (n 30) [45–46].
325. *Amann v Switzerland* (n 289) [70].
326. *Peck v UK* (n 273) [59]; *S. and Marper v UK* (n 30) [66–67].

information, how the information is processed, to whom it will be disseminated, and to what results this might lead.[327] Whether the individual had a reasonable expectation of privacy can also be of relevance.[328] Additionally, the Court may take into account whether data have been gathered specifically on one individual, whether and how the data have been subsequently processed, and whether there has been publication of the information that goes beyond what is normally foreseeable.[329] Even when systematically collected and stored public information is concerned, additional criteria apply. In this context, the Court has deemed it relevant whether the information relates to the individual's distant past, contains errors or inaccuracies or is expected to harm the reputation of the individual, in which case the information is more likely to interfere with Article 8.[330]

As regards other criteria to determine whether there is an interference, in the context of secret surveillance by the authorities the Court decided that it is not necessary to prove that an act that would constitute an interference actually took place.[331] Belonging to a group of persons that is 'potentially liable to be directly affected' by the act is sufficient to constitute an interference.[332] In the same vein, the concern of an individual about possible future uses of the information that cannot fully be anticipated at the time has been accepted by the Court as relevant for establishing an interference.[333] The fact that information is encoded and/or is only intelligible to a specific category of people has not prevented the Court from finding an interference either.[334] Nor is the individual's consent decisive; even after agreeing to public disclosure the individual is not necessarily deprived of the protection of Article 8.[335] Similarly, whether information about an individual is gathered from the individual herself or from a third party, for example through a GPS on the third party's car or a tap on a third party's telephone line, is not important for the establishment of an interference.[336]

In sum, not all processing of personal data constitutes an interference; additional criteria apply particularly in the context of public data, where the severity of the consequences and expectations of the individual play a big role. Nevertheless, the scope of interferences with privacy through the processing of personal data is broad, and each instance of collecting or processing is deemed a separate interference by the Court.

---

327. *S. and Marper v UK* (n 30) [67]; *Von Hannover v Germany* (n 296) [52].
328. *P.G. and J.H. v UK* (n 30) [57]; *Copland v UK* (n 259) [42].
329. *Uzun v Germany* (n 291) [45].
330. *Rotaru v Romania* (n 30) [43–44].
331. *Zakharov v Russia* [2015] ECtHR 47143/06 [164–179].
332. *Malone v UK* (n 302) [86]; *Weber and Saravia v Germany* [2006] ECtHR 54934/00 [78–79].
333. *S. and Marper v UK* (n 30) [71].
334. *Ibid* 75, 84.
335. *M.M. v UK* [2012] ECtHR 24029/07 [189].
336. *Uzun v Germany* (n 291) [49]; *Lambert v France* [1998] ECtHR 23618/94 [21].

3.2.2.3 Justification of Interferences with the Right to Privacy

When certain acts have triggered the application of Article 8 and an interference has been found, the behaviour of the state is a violation of the right to respect for private life unless the criteria of the second paragraph of Article 8 are met. This last part of the Court's tripartite fundamental rights test consists of the three cumulative main criteria of the second paragraph of Article 8 that justify a limitation of the right to respect for private life. A limitation of the right to privacy must (1) be in *accordance with the law*,[337] (2) have a *legitimate aim*,[338] and (3) be *necessary in a democratic society*.[339] These criteria are well developed in the case law of the ECtHR. Their relevance in the big data context is limited, save for one aspect of the Court's reasoning under the justification test.

When judging whether an interference that consists of data processing is justified, which is often the case in (covert) surveillance cases where the Court is extra strict regarding the quality of the law, the Court often refers to the necessity of safeguards related to the data processing.[340] In cases on surveillance measures consisting of data processing, the Court has specified that there must be minimum safeguards at each stage in the collection, storage, and use of the data, and that these safeguards should be appropriate safeguards and 'reflect the principles of data protection instruments'.[341] Of particular importance for the big data context is that the Court has emphasised, by reference to Convention 108, that when data are processed automatically, more safeguards are required.[342] Furthermore, the greater the scope of collection and storage of data becomes, the more important the

337. This means that there must be a basis in national law that authorises the interference and that the relevant rule is complied with. The legal basis has to meet the criteria of being accessible to individuals as well as foreseeable, meaning that it is sufficiently precise for the individual to regulate her conduct (if need be with appropriate advice), the so-called quality of the law. *See Cemalettin Canli v Turkey* [2008] ECtHR 22427/04 [42]; *Silver and others v UK* [1983] ECtHR 5947/72; 6205/73; 7052/75; 7061/75; 7107/75; 7113/75; 7136/75 [86].
338. This list of aims enumerated in Article 8 (2) ECHR is limitative but the aims are broadly formulated. The requirement is relatively straightforward and rarely triggers extensive discussion by the ECtHR. *See* Harris and others (n 38) 509–510.
339. 'Necessary in a democratic society' means that the interference corresponds to a pressing social need, and that the limitation of the right of the individual must be proportionate to the aim pursued by the state. A fair balance has to be struck between the interests of the individual and the interests of the community. Is the decisive part of most judgments under Article 8 in which a fair balance has to be struck and in which the margin of appreciation doctrine, discussed in subsection 3.2.1, is of key importance. *See* Rainey, Wicks and Ovey (n 13) 333; *Silver and others v UK* (n 337) 97; *S. and Marper v UK* (n 30) 101, 118, 125.
340. *Malone v UK* (n 302) [67–68]; *Uzun v Germany* (n 291) [61].
341. *M.M. v UK* (n 335) [195].
342. *Gardel v France* [2009] ECtHR 16428/05 [62]; *S. and Marper v UK* (n 30) [103]. The ECtHR occasionally uses 'the Data Protection Convention' to refer to Convention 108.

safeguards implemented at different stages in the processing.[343] Strict safeguards are also necessary when the data that are processed are of a sensitive nature, for example when they include data about the genetic constitution or health of individuals.[344]

3.2.3 Conclusion: Article 8 ECHR Applied to Big Data

In this conclusion the right to privacy as described in the previous subsections is applied to the big data process as explained in Chapter 2, with the aim of clarifying what parts of big data are protected by the concept of privacy derived from the ECHR and the ECtHR's case law.[345]

In the first phase of the big data process, the *acquisition* phase, (personal) data are acquired and stored. The general principle that applies to the acquisition phase is that data related to the private lives of individuals are within the scope of the right to respect for private life. Data should be read in a broad sense, covering video recordings and photographs, as well as potential conduits for personal information, such as DNA profiles. The content of telephony and email communications is also covered. For the applicability of Article 8 ECHR it is irrelevant whether the communications are collected when they are transmitted or whether stored communication is used; both trigger the applicability of the communications and/or private life interest. Furthermore, the collection and storage of metadata (including location data) is within the scope of Article 8.[346]

All personal data are presumably within the scope of the right to privacy.[347] However, the processing of personal data does not automatically interfere with Article 8 ECHR. When sensitive data are processed, there will generally be an interference (that may or may not be justified), but particularly when public data are processed, additional conditions apply. Whether people had a reasonable expectation of privacy is important, and the systematic collection and storage of public data generally create an interference.[348] When the data that are gathered in the acquisition phase do not qualify as personal data or data related to private life, the acquisition phase is most likely not governed by the right to privacy. Each instance of

343. *M.M. v UK* (n 335) [200].
344. *S. and Marper v UK* (n 30) [103]; *Z. v Finland* (n 322) [95]; *M.S. v Sweden* [1997] ECtHR 20837/92 [41]; *L.L. v Finland* [2006] ECtHR 7508/02 [44].
345. The following conclusions thus give an overview of the concept of privacy with respect to big data and not of the actual scope of protection offered by the Convention; the general caveat regarding context and horizontal applicability applies.
346. *Copland v UK* (n 259) [39–42]; *Uzun v Germany* (n 291) [44–46].
347. *Leander v Sweden* (n 286) [48].
348. *Halford v UK* (n 314) [42–46]; *Rotaru v Romania* (n 30) [43].

processing should be judged individually, on its own merits, and consent does not necessarily block the applicability of the right to privacy.[349]

The processing of personal data in the *analysis* phase of the big data process is also within the scope of the right to privacy. The Court has stressed that the collection of data as well as its subsequent use may constitute separate infringements; the analysis phase is therefore individually covered, irrespective of the acquisition phase. The Court has shown reluctance to consider interferences with Article 8 ECHR justified when sensitive data are processed, when data are processed automatically, and when the scope of processing increases. In these cases, it has emphasised the necessity of a high level of protection against abuse, and that adequate safeguards must be in place. These obligations only exist with respect to the processing of *personal* data. Both the concept of personal data and the measures that have to be taken are linked to Convention 108.[350]

In the *application* phase the same principles as above apply when personal data are processed: personal data processing in the application phase is covered but does not always constitute an interference. In addition, the concepts of private life and home can extend to the application phase even when no or very limited personal data are used, because notwithstanding the processing of personal data, the respect for private life or the home can be interfered with. Aspects of the right to respect for private life regarding the private sphere, personal identity, or the construction of social relationships can apply when knowledge gathered through big data is applied to individuals or has an influence on these aspects of their private life. For example, if a municipality were to use big data in the creation of the zoning plan of a city, and place a chemical plant close to a person's home, there may be serious implications for the individual's health. In such cases Article 8 ECHR may be violated, without personal data being processed.[351] Accordingly, the right to private life may also be of importance during the application phase of big data in which knowledge is applied and decisions are made without these being directed at identifiable individuals. As the applications of big data are legion, it is impossible to explain in this conclusion exactly when and how the right to privacy would apply to big data applications in practice. In general, when a big data application can be expected to affect one of the broad interests of private, home or family life, and correspondence as interpreted by the ECtHR, the scope of the concept of privacy under the ECHR includes the application phase of that big data process. The next section assesses the right to privacy and the right to data protection of the CFREU in a similar manner to Article 8 ECHR of this section, after which the results are compared in subsection 3.4.

349. *Z. v Finland* (n 322) [100]; *M.M. v UK* (n 335) [189].
350. *Amann v Switzerland* (n 289) [65]; *M.M. v UK* (n 335) [195].
351. Cf. *Taşkın v Turkey* [2004] ECtHR 46117/99; *Fadeyeva v Russia* [2005] ECtHR 55723/00; *Giacomelli v Italy* [2006] ECtHR 59909/00.

3.3 THE EUROPEAN UNION (CFREU)

This section examines the scope of Articles 7 and 8 CFREU with respect to big data. It starts with an overview of the history and interpretation of fundamental rights in the EU. The section continues with an analysis of the scope of application of Article 7 (private life), divided into the scope of application and the interferences with the right. The ensuing subsection on Article 8 (data protection) follows the same structure. The possible justifications for interferences with both articles are discussed in the penultimate subsection, after which this section closes with a conclusion on Articles 7 and 8 CFREU in the context of big data.

3.3.1 History and Interpretation of Fundamental Rights in the EU

This subsection provides a general introduction to the Charter. The subsection starts with a short overview of the legislative background of the development of fundamental rights protection in the EU. An explanation of the legal effect and application of the Charter follows this overview. The analysis then turns to the key interpretative rules of the Charter, including their (current) relationship with the ECHR.

The EU has its direct origin in the increased cooperation between European States to ensure peace after the Second World War.[352] At its core are the European communities of atomic energy, coal and steel, and economic cooperation, established in the 1960s.[353] After years of developments in Europe, the Maastricht Treaty was signed in 1992, creating the EU.[354] These treaties founding the predecessors of the EU in the 1950s did not contain any provision or reference to fundamental rights. The European Court of Justice did not make any references to fundamental rights either, in the first years after its establishment.[355] Arguments based on fundamental rights were consistently rejected by the Court, until the *Stauder* case in 1969.[356] In this case the Court referred to 'fundamental human rights enshrined in the general principles of Community law and protected by the Court', thereby establishing the protection of fundamental rights as part of the EU legal order.[357] This approach was elaborated in later case law, when the Court stated that the protection of fundamental rights must be ensured in

352. Paul Craig and Gráinne De Búrca, *EU Law: Text, Cases, and Materials* (Oxford University Press 2011) 14–15.
353. The European Coal and Steel Community (ECSC), European Economic Community (EEC) and European Atomic Energy Community (Euratom).
354. Treaty on European Union (Maastricht) 1992; Craig and De Búrca (n 352) 3–7.
355. Craig and De Búrca (n 352) 364.
356. *Stauder* [1969] CJEU 29/69.
357. Craig and De Búrca (n 352) 109.

the Community and that possible infringements have to be assessed by the Court.[358] Constitutional traditions of the Member States and international human rights treaties were given as the two main sources of inspiration.[359]

After these three cases, the Court increasingly referred to fundamental rights. The ECHR became the main source of inspiration for fundamental rights protection as part of the general principles of EU law, with direct references to the ECtHR's decisions becoming ever more frequent.[360] The practice of the Court was codified in European law with the adoption of the Maastricht Treaty, which referred to ECHR and the national constitutional traditions of the Member States and classified the respect for fundamental rights as a general principle of EU law.[361] Through the incorporation of the Convention in the case law of the Court, the ECHR exerted considerable influence inside the EU jurisdiction. In parallel to these developments, a number of policy documents on fundamental rights were drafted.[362] The aforementioned documents emerged from EU institutions, which shows that the protection of fundamental rights in the EU prior to the Charter was not an individual undertaking of the Court.[363] In the run-up to the Charter both EU institutions and Member States clearly assigned importance to the development of European fundamental rights protection.

The drafting and adoption of the Charter of Fundamental Rights marked a new phase in the protection of fundamental rights in the EU. The initiative to create a European charter of fundamental rights was taken in 1999. The intention behind the push for an EU fundamental rights instrument was to consolidate the fundamental rights that already applied to the EU and to make their importance more visible to the general public.[364] The Charter was drafted within a year and solemnly proclaimed in 2000. However, the legal status of the Charter remained unclear for many years thereafter.[365] Only with the Lisbon Treaty of 2009 did the Charter enter fully into force for the EU including its Member States.[366] Through Article 6 TEU the Charter acquired the same legal status as the other EU treaties.[367]

---

358. *Internationale Handelsgesellschaft* [1970] CJEU C-11/70 [4].
359. *Nold* [1974] CJEU 4/73 [13].
360. Craig and De Búrca (n 352) 366–367.
361. Article 6 (2) TEU. The Treaty has since then been amended.
362. Joint Declaration by the European Parliament, Council and the Commission concerning the protection of fundamental rights and the ECHR 1977 (OJ C103/1); Resolution of the European Parliament adopting the Declaration of Fundamental Rights 1989 (OJ C120/51); *see* further Paul Craig, 'Rights, Legality, and Legitimacy', *The Lisbon Treaty, Revised Edition: Law, Politics, and Treaty Reform* (Oxford University Press 2013).
363. Craig (n 362) 195.
364. *Ibid* 196–197.
365. *Ibid* 197, 199.
366. Treaty of Lisbon amending the Treaty on European Union and the Treaty establishing the European Community 2007 (OJ C306/01).
367. Consolidated versions of the Treaty on European Union and the Treaty on the Functioning of the European Union 2012 (OJ C326/01).

When looking at the articles of the Charter, its scope of application seems limited. According to Article 51 CFREU it only extends to actions of EU institutions and the Member States when they are *implementing* Union law. Although Member States and EU bodies should 'promote' the rights of the Charter, this should remain within the limits of the powers conferred to the EU; the Charter does not create any new competencies for the EU or modify existing powers.[368] However, the CJEU maintains a broad understanding of Article 51 CFREU, in line with the Explanations to the Charter, interpreting 'implementing EU law' as (also) meaning 'situations governed by EU law'.[369] Accordingly Article 51 (1) should not be interpreted restrictively; its scope of application extends to all situations that are governed by EU law, even when the primary rule at stake has a national origin.[370]

When a situation falls within the scope of application of the Charter as described in the previous subsection, a complaint can be lodged with the CJEU. Complaints can be filed by EU bodies, Member States, natural or legal persons, and national courts, provided that specific requirements are met.[371] Natural or legal persons must amongst others be 'directly concerned' by the regulatory act against which they institute proceedings.[372] Complaints can be made against the EU (generally the Commission) or against Member States. Whether or to what extent the Charter has horizontal effect is currently undecided and frequently discussed in the literature, but in any case private parties cannot be defendants before the CJEU.[373] There can, however, be effects on disputes between private parties, as the EU or the Member States may be required to take positive action to protect the rights of the Charter.[374] Furthermore, the Charter can affect private parties through preliminary procedures, in which national courts submit questions of interpretation of EU law to the CJEU. These questions can involve the interpretation of the Charter, or the interpretation of secondary law through the scope of the Charter.[375] The CJEU has a history of referring to provisions from Treaties, 'general principles of EU law', and the Charter.[376] Through

368. Article 51 (1) and 52 (7) CFREU and Explanations Relating to the Charter of Fundamental Rights (n 67); Craig and De Búrca (n 352) 397.
369. *Åkerberg Fransson* [2013] CJEU C-617/10 [18–19]; Explanations Relating to the Charter of Fundamental Rights (n 67).
370. *Åkerberg Fransson* (n 369) [19 and 24–31].
371. *See* amongst others Articles 258, 263, 265 and 267 TFEU. National courts can ask preliminary questions, *see* below.
372. Article 263 TFEU.
373. Koen Lenaerts and José Antonio Gutiérrez-Fons, 'The Place of the Charter in the EU Constitutional Edifice', *The EU Charter of Fundamental Rights: A Commentary* (Hart/Beck 2014) 1593; Jacqué (n 50).
374. Craig (n 362) 219–220. *See also* sections 3.2.1.1–3.2.1.2.
375. *See* for example *Google Spain* (n 50).
376. Sonya Walkila, *Horizontal Effect of Fundamental Rights in EU Law* (Europa Law Publishing 2016) 33–42, 62–69.

this procedure the CJEU's case law affects (national disputes between) private parties, when the national courts incorporate the CJEU's decisions in their judgments. Examples of these procedures will be cited frequently in the subsections analysing the scope of Articles 7 and 8 CFREU below.

The Charter has to be interpreted following the rules of the Vienna Convention.[377] For the interpretation of the rights to privacy and data protection of the Charter this means amongst others the Explanations to the Charter and secondary legislation like the GDPR are part of the interpretative context.[378] In addition, the ECHR and its interpretation are of paramount importance for the interpretation of the Charter. According to Articles 52 (3) and 53 CFREU, Charter rights that correspond to ECHR rights should have the same meaning and scope as those rights, except where the Charter would provide a higher level of protection.[379] Consequently, the interpretation of the Charter is inextricably linked to the ECHR and the ECtHR.

3.3.2 The Right to Privacy (Article 7 CFREU)

Article 7 of the Charter is titled 'respect for private and family life' and reads:

> Everyone has the right to respect for his or her private and family life, home and communications.

Article 52 (1) CFREU contains a general limitation clause for all Charter rights:

> Any limitation on the exercise of the rights and freedoms recognised by this Charter must be provided for by law and respect the essence of those rights and freedoms. Subject to the principle of proportionality, limitations may be made only if they are necessary and genuinely meet objectives of general interest recognised by the Union or the need to protect the rights and freedoms of others.

Article 7 is a 'corresponding right' in the sense of Article 52 (3) CFREU; it has to be interpreted with Article 8 ECHR including accompanying case law, save when the Charter or its interpretation by the CJEU offers a broader scope of protection.[380] An assessment of Article 7 CFREU can in principle be divided into three parts, based on Articles 7 and 52 (1) CFREU: scope of application of the article, interference, and justification. The following subsections will stick to the established fundamental rights

377. Vienna Convention on the Law of Treaties (n 62); *Golder v UK* (n 62) [29]. *See* subsection 1.2.5.2 of Chapter 1 for a more detailed explanation.
378. Sorel and Boré Eveno (n 67) 825.
379. Cf. subsection 1.2.5.2 of Chapter 1.
380. Explanations Relating to the Charter of Fundamental Rights (n 67).

doctrine and the wording of the Article and divide the analysis of Article 7 CFREU accordingly.[381]

As a corresponding right, much of what has been discussed regarding Article 8 ECHR under subsection 3.2.2 equally applies to Article 7 CFREU. Article 7 CFREU mirrors the interconnectedness of the individual concepts as well as the broad scope of application of the right to privacy under the ECtHR.[382] To avoid repetition, the analysis below focuses on instances where Article 7 CFREU and its interpretation by the CJEU deviate from Article 8 as interpreted by the ECtHR.

3.3.2.1 Scope of Application

The scope of application of the right to respect for private life of Article 7 CFREU corresponds to the right to respect for private life under Article 8 ECHR. Consequently private life is a broad, overarching term that covers many aspects of the personal sphere; from the physical integrity of the person to the collection of personal data or the legal recognition of family ties.[383] Personal data have received much attention from the Court under Article 7 CFREU. Before the Charter, the CJEU had already decided that the protection of personal data is important for the right to privacy by reference to Article 8 ECHR and the ECtHR's case law.[384] After the CFREU was created, the CJEU started to take the Charter's rights into account when deciding on the scope of applicability regarding personal data, even before the Charter officially entered into force for the Member States.[385] In the context of personal data the CJEU refers to the Charter in two distinct ways. First of all the CJEU can assess whether there has been an interference with the rights, using the three-step fundamental rights test.[386] Second, the CJEU refers to the Charter rights in preliminary rulings when deciding on questions regarding the interpretation of secondary EU law, in which case the tripartite structure is not followed.[387] Instead the Court refers to the fundamental rights and explains them in the context of the case and the secondary law under discussion. In both cases the Court takes the same approach to personal data under the right to privacy.

The CJEU frequently uses a special approach in privacy cases where the subject matter is personal data. It combines Article 7 with the right to data

---

381. The Court may stick to this tripartite division, cf. *Schwarz* [2013] CJEU C-291/12; *Trabelsi* [2013] CJEU T-187/11, but often, particularly in preliminary questions on the interpretation of EU law, it does not.
382. Jens Vested-Hansen, 'Article 7 (Private Life, Home, and Communications)', *The EU Charter of Fundamental Rights: A Commentary* (Hart/Beck 2014) 182.
383. *See* subsection 3.2.2.1.
384. *Österreichischer Rundfunk* [2003] CJEU C-465/00, C-138/01 and C-139/01 [73].
385. *Promusicae* [2008] CJEU C-275/06 [64–65].
386. *See* for example *Schwarz* (n 381).
387. *See* for example *Google Spain* (n 50).

protection of Article 8 CFREU, referring to 'the right to respect for private life with regard to the processing of personal data'.[388] In the context of this combined right the Court also refers to Article 8 ECHR and landmark privacy cases of the ECtHR.[389] The right concerns information on identified or identifiable individuals and its limitations correspond to those that apply to Article 8 ECHR.[390] Many different kinds of personal data are covered by this construction of the right to respect for private life regarding the processing of personal data. The CJEU has accepted that amongst others data on the individual's identity and address,[391] tax and income data,[392] fingerprints,[393] and metadata on electronic communications[394] are within its scope of application. In addition, the CJEU has deemed search engine results pages with hyperlinks corresponding to a search on an individual's name a matter of personal data under the right to respect for private life.[395] In conclusion the scope of application of the right to privacy with respect to personal data is linked to both Article 8 ECHR and Article 8 CFREU, and the subject matter covered is broad; all personal data are covered.

There is no case law from the CJEU that has been specifically decided on the basis of the 'home' interest that is of immediate relevance to the big data context. Regarding the fourth sphere of Article 7 CFREU: instead of the ECHR's 'correspondence', the Charter's right to privacy contains 'communications' as the protected sphere. According to the Explanations to the Charter this was done to keep pace with technological developments.[396] This does not create difficulties with the corresponding rights obligation, as communications is a broader term than correspondence. In fact, it matches with the broad interpretation of correspondence by the ECtHR under the living instrument doctrine.[397] Communications should thus be interpreted in line with the established case law of the ECtHR regarding the concept of correspondence.[398] There is no case law by the CJEU that has been specifically decided on the basis of the 'communications' sphere of Article 7 that is of immediate relevance to the big data context, nor on the 'home' sphere. Therefore the ECtHR's case law is the primary point of reference for the relevance and interpretation of the home interest under the Charter.[399]

---

388. *Volker und Markus Schecke and Eifert* (n 32) [52].
389. *Ibid*; *Amann v Switzerland* (n 289); *Rotaru v Romania* (n 30).
390. *Volker und Markus Schecke and Eifert* (n 32) [52].
391. *Promusicae* (n 385); *Runevič-Vardyn* [2011] CJEU C-391/09.
392. *Satamedia* [2008] CJEU C-73/07; *Volker und Markus Schecke and Eifert* (n 32).
393. *Schwarz* (n 381).
394. *Digital Rights Ireland* (n 32).
395. *Google Spain* (n 50) [80–81].
396. Explanations Relating to the Charter of Fundamental Rights (n 67).
397. *Michaud v France* (n 315) [90].
398. *See* the conclusion of paragraph 2.2.1.3.
399. Rainey, Wicks and Ovey (n 13) 405–406.

In its case law, the CJEU does not commonly refer to the facilitative function of the right to privacy (including the right to privacy with respect to personal data) for other fundamental rights and freedoms. There is, however, one noteworthy exception: the CJEU's recent references to freedom of expression in the context of privacy and data protection. In *Digital Rights Ireland,* the Court carefully stated that it was 'not inconceivable' that the retention of personal data could have an effect on the exercise of freedom of expression; corporate or government surveillance has a potentially chilling effect.[400] In the *Tele2 Sweden* case, the Court takes it one step further, by explicitly recognising that the feeling of constant surveillance affects freedom of expression, eventually invalidating a national (blanket) data retention rule on the basis of Articles 7, 8 and 11 read in conjunction.[401] Through acknowledging the function of privacy with respect to personal data in the context of chilling effects on freedom of expression through surveillance involving personal data collection, the CJEU recognised the facilitative function of privacy (with respect to personal data) for freedom of expression under the scope of Article(s) 7 (and 8) CFREU.

3.3.2.2 Interference with the Right to Privacy

This section discusses aspects of establishing interference with the right to respect for privacy under the Charter in the context of big data. Like the scope of application, interferences with the right to privacy under the Charter as interpreted by the CJEU matches the ECtHR's case law.

The Luxembourg Court has on numerous occasions confirmed that the processing of data relating to individuals can be an interference with the individual's right to privacy. Although theoretically the right to privacy can be applicable without personal data being at stake and vice versa, an interference with the right to personal data usually triggers the applicability of the right to privacy.[402] This does not mean that all data processing constitutes an interference with the right to privacy.[403] Interferences under the CFREU match the ECtHR's interpretation of Article 8 ECHR. Collecting personal data with the intention of disseminating it to third parties constitutes an interference, even when the data are not sensitive and when nobody has been 'inconvenienced' by the processing.[404]

The CJEU makes distinctions between types of interference. In addition to 'regular' interferences, the Court has found 'serious interferences' such as in the *Digital Rights Ireland* case.[405] The Court does not give a precise

400. *Digital Rights Ireland* (n 32) [28, 37].
401. *Tele2 Sverige* [2016] CJEU C-203/15 and C-698/15 [101–102, 112].
402. De Hert and Gutwirth (n 23) 24–26; Gellert and Gutwirth (n 25) 524–526.
403. *See* for example *Österreichischer Rundfunk* (n 384) [74].
404. *Ibid* 75.
405. *Digital Rights Ireland* (n 32).

description of what a serious interference is, yet the scale and duration of the collection and use of data and the potential for abuse seem to be of significant importance.[406] Classification as a serious interference triggers 'strict scrutiny' by the Court at the justifications level.[407] If an interference compromises the 'essence' of the fundamental right, it unjustifiably violates the fundamental right.[408] Not only the scale and duration of the interference but also the possibilities for profiling are relevant for establishing the seriousness of an interference.[409] Blanket access to communications content has been deemed to compromise the essence of the right to privacy.[410] Blanket retention of metadata has not, but it constitutes a serious interference.[411] The collection and use of metadata are thus, possibly mistakenly, considered as less harmful for privacy than knowledge about the content of communications.[412] This classification influences how strictly the Court assesses the interference in the justification part of the fundamental rights test, which is the subject of the following subsection.

3.3.2.3 Justification of Interferences with the Right to Privacy

This subsection briefly sets out the general aspects and criteria of the justified interferences with Article 7 CFREU, after which it focuses on aspects that are relevant for the normative concept of the right to privacy in the context of big data.[413] The Charter contains one general limitation clause that applies to all rights of the Charter that are derogable in Article 52 (1) CFREU.[414] This limitation clause consists of a procedural rule ('provided for by law'),[415] a justification ('objectives of general interest' or the protection of the rights and

406. Marie-Pierre Granger and Kristina Irion, 'The Court of Justice and the Data Retention Directive in Digital Rights Ireland: Telling off the EU Legislator and Teaching a Lesson in Privacy and Data Protection' (2014) European Law Review 835, 846.
407. *See* the ensuing subsection for an explanation.
408. Maja Brkan, 'In Search of the Concept of Essence of EU Fundamental Rights through the Prism of Data Privacy' (2017) No 2017-01 Maastricht Faculty of Law Working Paper 2, 17.
409. *Digital Rights Ireland* (n 32) 37, by reference to the Advocate General's opinion.
410. *Schrems* (n 32) [35].
411. *Digital Rights Ireland* (n 32) [39].
412. Granger and Irion (n 406) 847.
413. Where the right to privacy and the right to data processing are treated conjointly by the Court in a personal data case, as in for example the *Schecke* case, the limitation of the right is discussed under the next paragraph regarding the right to data protection.
414. Steve Peers and Sasha Prechal, 'Article 52 – Scope and Interpretation of Rights and Principles' in Steve Peers, Tamara Hervey and Angela Ward (eds), *The EU Charter of Fundamental Rights: A Commentary* (Hart/Beck 2014) 1469–1470.
415. The CJEU has not yet explicitly elucidated its stance on the criterion in its judgments; in many judgments the test is not directly applied or discussed. *Ibid* 1474.

freedom of others)[416] and a balancing test.[417] This final test consists of three elements: the interference must be *proportionate* and *necessary* and *respect the essence of the rights and freedoms* of the Charter. The elements are often considered together, although each can be individually identified.[418] The requirement that an interference respects the essence of the right means that the interference is not justified if it 'undermines the very substance of the right'.[419]

The assessment of interferences with the right to privacy is based on the criteria enumerated above. The CJEU refers to the ECtHR and states that with respect to privacy and the processing of personal data the limitations of the right to privacy under Article(s) 7 (and 8) of the Charter correspond to those of Article 8 ECtHR.[420] For its review of whether the interference meets the proportionality test, relevant factors are the area concerned, the 'nature and seriousness of the interference', and the aim behind the interference, by reference to the ECtHR's case law.[421] As explained, the Court distinguishes between interferences. Blanket access to content is deemed to compromise the essence of the right to privacy, and is therefore an unjustifiable violation.[422] With respect to the retention of metadata the Court has established that this does not impede the *essence* of the right to privacy, as it is not the content of communications that is acquired.[423] When the CJEU finds a *serious* interference, it conducts a more thorough assessment of proportionality. In such cases, there is *strict scrutiny* of the interference.[424] The absence of limits on access, use and retention of personal data, blanket and indiscriminate approaches to collection, and the lack of procedural safeguards are considered particularly problematic in this assessment.[425] In conclusion, in its case law the CJEU links the gravity of the interference with the precautions that have to be taken.

---

416. 'Objectives' refers to amongst others the broadly formulated aims elucidated in Article 3 TEU, and objectives of other EU treaties: Explanations Relating to the Charter of Fundamental Rights (n 67).
417. Peers and Prechal (n 414) 1470.
418. *Ibid* 1480.
419. According to the Explanations to the Charter this is based on the Karlsson case, *Karlsson* [2000] CJEU C-292/97 [45]; the cited paragraph itself cites the older Wachauf case, *Wachauf* [1989] CJEU C-5/88 [18].
420. *Volker und Markus Schecke and Eifert* (n 32) [52]. *See* subsection 3.2.2.3 on justifications for interferences with Article 8 ECHR.
421. *Digital Rights Ireland* (n 32) [47]; *S. and Marper v UK* (n 30) [102].
422. *Schrems* (n 32) [94].
423. *Digital Rights Ireland* (n 32) [39].
424. Granger and Irion (n 406) 845–846.
425. *Digital Rights Ireland* (n 32) [57–64]; Granger and Irion (n 406) 843.

3.3.3 The Right to Data Protection (Article 8 CFREU)

This subsection discusses the right to the protection of personal data as enshrined in Article 8 CFREU. It starts by setting out the legislative background of Article 8 CFREU, discussing its official sources and links with other legal instruments. The section then homes in on the details and scope of the Article.

Article 8 of the Charter is titled 'protection of personal data'. It is divided into three paragraphs and reads as follows:

1. Everyone has the right to the protection of personal data concerning him or her.
2. Such data must be processed fairly for specified purposes and on the basis of the consent of the person concerned or some other legitimate basis laid down by law. Everyone has the right of access to data which has been collected concerning him or her, and the right to have it rectified.
3. Compliance with these rules shall be subject to control by an independent authority.

The right to data protection of the CFREU is a stand-alone fundamental right, next to privacy. There is no provision in the ECHR or any other general international fundamental rights instrument preceding the Charter that is similar; the CFREU is the first fundamental rights treaty that includes a fundamental right to the protection of personal data.[426] It is not a corresponding right in the sense of Article 52 (3) CFREU. However, in the case law of the CJEU, Articles 7 and 8 CFREU are often not entirely separated, but jointly discussed as the 'right to respect for private life with regard to the processing of personal data'.[427] This makes separate discussions of the scope of application and justifiable interferences of Articles 7 and 8 difficult. Yet given its wording and its status as a stand-alone fundamental right, it is clear that the scope of the right to privacy and the right to personal data protection are not identical, even though there is overlap.[428]

The drafting history of the Charter does not give a clear image of what the right to data protection was originally intended to be. Many different suggestions and articles have been proposed in the drafting process. They

426. The link between Article 8 CFREU and international instruments (amongst which Convention 108 on the automatic processing of personal data) and secondary European legislation will be discussed in the next section regarding the legislative background of the Article.
427. *Volker und Markus Schecke und Eifert* (n 32) [52].
428. The differences and similarities between the scope of the right to privacy and the right to data protection are discussed in detail in section 3.4 of this chapter.

range from concise single-paragraph affirmations of a right to the protection of personal data for the individual, to a mere reference to data protection under the right to privacy.[429] The Explanations to the Charter on the other hand are clear on the sources of the right to data protection.[430] The Explanations name the European sources first: Article 16 TFEU and Article 39 TEU that concern data protection and the competences of the EU, and Directive 95/46/EC on the processing of personal data. Article 8 ECHR and the CoE's Convention 108 are then mentioned, and further references are made to Regulation 45/2001 that governs data processing by EU bodies and to Directive 95/46/EC as containing 'conditions and limitations for the exercise of the right to the protection of personal data'.[431] The link with the Data Protection Directive and Convention 108 is strengthened by the wording of Article 8 CFREU, which uses terms and describes rights and obligations that can be directly traced back to the provisions of the aforementioned instruments, particularly the Data Protection Directive and GDPR.[432] Based on the foregoing (and also chronologically) it seems clear that the drafters of the Charter have drawn inspiration for Article 8 CFREU from pre-existing secondary legislation and non-EU instruments regarding data protection.[433] Nevertheless, the Charter is a constitutional instrument that has the same legal value as the EU Treaties.[434] Consequently although Article 8 may be inspired by the regulatory substance of the Data Protection Directive and the other instruments, which may thus offer interpretative guidance, the regulatory substance does not as such define the boundaries of the fundamental right to data protection. Neither can it be concluded that through Article 8 CFREU the full content of the Data Protection Directive is elevated to fundamental rights level, even though this would make the difference between the right to privacy and the right to data protection much clearer (and arguably more valuable).[435] Due to its juvenility there is not such an elaborate body of case law as under Article 8 ECHR on which to base the interpretation of the right. To date, the exact content of Article 8 CFREU,

429. González Fuster (n 16) 193–198.
430. Explanations Relating to the Charter of Fundamental Rights (n 67).
431. *Ibid*; Regulation (EC) No 45/2001 of the European Parliament and of the Council on the protection of individuals with regard to the processing of personal data by the Community institutions and bodies and on the free movement of such data 2001 (OJ L8/01).
432. *See* Articles 2, 6 (1) under a and b, 7, 12 under a and b and 28 (1) Directive 95/46/EC, also implemented in the GDPR that replaces the Directive. The majority of the principles can also be found in Convention 108 (except for the notion of consent).
433. González Fuster (n 16) 204.
434. Craig (n 362) 229.
435. Lynskey, 'Deconstructing Data Protection: The "Added-Value" of a Right to Data Protection in the EU Legal Order' (n 235) 586–587.

particularly vis-á-vis Articles 7 CFREU and 8 ECHR, remains unclear, but the following subsection clarifies its subject matter.[436]

3.3.3.1 Scope of Application

Article 8 CFREU contains three paragraphs. The first paragraph describes the right to the protection of personal data. The second paragraph sets out the condition of fair processing on legitimate grounds and the rights of access and rectification. The final paragraph of the Article contains the requirement for an independent authority. The following analysis is divided into three subsections consistent with the structure of the Article.[437]

3.3.3.1.1 Right to the Protection of Personal Data (Article 8 (1) CFREU)

The first paragraph of Article 8 establishes the general overarching right to data protection, by stating that 'everyone has the right to the protection of personal data concerning him or her'. It is a non-absolute right, which contains the term 'personal data' as the subject of protection.[438] The CJEU's interpretation of Article 8 is inspired by Convention 108 and the Data Protection Directive for its interpretation of the concept of personal data.[439] The concept of personal data in Article 8 (1) CFREU refers to data through which individuals can be identified, which must in principle be understood as all data related to an identified or identifiable natural person.[440] Furthermore, Article 8 is neither restricted to data of a particular sensitive nature[441] nor is it necessary that there is a private life element present.[442] It is also irrelevant whether personal data are public or private; even personal data that has been publicly available is protected subject matter.[443]

---

436. González Fuster (n 16) 199–200; Orla Lynskey, 'The Data Retention Directive Is Incompatible with the Rights to Privacy and Data Protection and Is Invalid in Its Entirety: Digital Rights Ireland' (2014) 51 Common Market Law Review 1789, 1807–1809.
437. The CJEU does not necessarily distinguish between these three paragraphs when it discusses Article 8 CFREU.
438. *Volker und Markus Schecke and Eifert* (n 32) [48–51].
439. Kokott and Sobotta (n 29) 225.
440. *Volker und Markus Schecke and Eifert* (n 32) [52–53]; *Scarlet/SABAM* [2011] CJEU C-70/10 [51]; *SABAM/Netlog* (n 29) [49].
441. *See* amongst others Norbert Bernsdorff, 'Artikel 8: Schutz Personenbezogener Daten', *Charta der Grundrechte der Europäischen Union* (Nomos Verlagsgesellschaft 2011) 220–221.
442. González Fuster (n 16) 205.
443. *Satamedia* (n 392) [37].

The right to the protection of personal data is often referred to in conjunction with the right to private life by the Court.[444] In cases in which reference is made to this right the issues fall under both privacy and data protection.[445] It is also possible that only the right to data protection is at stake. The Court has referred to Article 8 in isolation in cases concerning the filtering of Internet traffic.[446] In these cases the Court decided that the identification, systematic analysis, and processing of data by Internet service providers and (social network platform) hosting providers is covered by Article 8, because it allows for the identification of individuals.[447] The Court also stated that IP addresses are personal data because they allow for the precise identification of individuals.[448] In these cases Article 7 CFREU was not mentioned in the Court's analysis. In conclusion, a difference between the right to data protection in isolation and the right to privacy is that data protection covers data processing irrespective of the context of the processing, although the difference is subtle and can be difficult to recognise.[449]

3.3.3.1.2 Fair Processing on Legitimate Grounds; Access and Rectification Rights (Article 8 (2) CFREU)

The second paragraph of Article 8 CFREU refers back to the protection of personal data in the first paragraph of the Article and enumerates a number of particular aspects of this right. The paragraph consists of two sentences that refer to processing conditions and to the rights of the individual, respectively. The first sentence states that data must be processed fairly, for specified purposes, and on the basis of consent or another legitimate basis. The second sentence of Article 8 CFREU states that individuals have a right of access to, and a right of rectification of, their personal data. These elements can also be found in a wider list of instruments, amongst others the GDPR and Convention 108.[450]

There is discussion in the literature as to the exact meaning of the second paragraph of Article 8 CFREU. There are two main possible readings; one that focuses on the *rights* and the other that focuses on *limitations* of the right to data protection in conjunction with Article 52 (1) CFREU.[451] In the first reading, the paragraph is regarded as adding elements to substantiate

---

444. *See* for example *Volker und Markus Schecke and Eifert* (n 32) [52].
445. *See* subsection 3.3.2.1.
446. *Scarlet/SABAM* (n 440) [50]; *SABAM/Netlog* (n 29) [48].
447. *Scarlet/SABAM* (n 440) [49]; *SABAM/Netlog* (n 29) [50–52].
448. *Scarlet/SABAM* (n 440) [51] The scope of application of Article 8 with respect to IP addresses is not entirely clear. The Federal Court of Justice of Germany referred questions concerning dynamic IP addresses to the CJEU on 28 October 2014.
449. Lynskey, 'Deconstructing Data Protection: The "Added-Value" of a Right to Data Protection in the EU Legal Order' (n 235) 584–586.
450. Cf. Articles 5 under (a) and (b), 6 (1), 15, and 16 GDPR.
451. González Fuster (n 16) 203–205.

the general right to data protection as enshrined in Article 8 (1) CFREU. The obligations are seen as specific conditions that always have to be met under the right to the protection of personal data. This reading of Article 8 (2) is in line with the general structure of the Charter, containing rights in the individual Articles and a general limitation clause applicable to these rights in Article 52 (1) CFREU.[452] However, the paragraph could also be seen as *restricting* the right to data protection of the first paragraph. According to this theory processing is authorised when the conditions of the second paragraph are met.[453]

In general, the Court has remarked that the right to data protection is not absolute, but that it 'must be considered in relation to its function in society'.[454] But the Court's language on the nature of Article 8 (2) CFREU is not clear.[455] It follows from the Court's analyses, however, that if the processing of personal data can be based on one of the legitimate grounds (including consent) and the rights of access and rectification are respected, it is in principle allowed, but this does not mean that Article 8 CFREU cannot be violated anymore.[456] For example, the Court has stated that Article 8 CFREU requires effective protection against risk of abuse, unlawful use, and access; data protection aspects that are not mentioned in the Article.[457] In sum, notwithstanding the ambiguities regarding its classification, Article 8 (2) CFREU contains principles that are part of the scope of the right to data protection.

3.3.3.1.3 Independent Authority

The third paragraph of Article 8 states that there shall be an independent authority that oversees compliance with the rules of the previous paragraphs. The paragraph is linked to the 'supervisory authority' (usually referred to as 'Data Protection Authority') that every Member State must have and to institutions like the European Data Protection Supervisor (EDPS) that oversees data processing by EU institutions.[458] The Commission has started multiple proceedings questioning the independence of national data protection authorities before the CJEU. Article 8 (3) CFREU has not always been

---

452. *Ibid* 204.
453. *Ibid* 203; Birte Siemen, *Datenschutz als Europäisches Grundrecht* (Duncker & Humblot 2006) 283
454. *Volker und Markus Schecke and Eifert* (n 32) [48].
455. It has stated that Article 8 (2) CFREU 'authorises the processing' and because of it, read in conjunction with Article 52 (1) CFREU, certain limits on the rights to privacy and data protection may be imposed, but it has also categorised it as a specification of Article 8 (1) CFREU, *ASNEF* [2011] CJEU C-468/10 and C-469/10 [42]; *Deutsche Telekom* [2011] CJEU C-543/09 [52]; *Google Spain* (n 50) [69].
456. *Volker und Markus Schecke and Eifert* (n 32) [49].
457. *Digital Rights Ireland* (n 32) [66].
458. Article 28 Directive 95/46/EC.

cited, but in most (and in particular recent) cases on the independence of supervisory authorities it has been the essence of the case.[459] Furthermore, depending on circumstances such as the type of personal data, this provision may require the data to remain under the supervision of these authorities; transferring retention-data to a state beyond the control of EU supervisory authorities violates the right to data protection.[460]

3.3.3.2 Interferences with the Right to Data Protection

Several actions can interfere with the right to data protection, based on the language of Article 8 CFREU. First of all, the mere processing of personal data, data relating to identified or identifiable natural persons, constitutes an interference.[461] The collection, transmission, and making available to a wider audience of personal data can each constitute a separate interference, as can processing without consent or another legitimate basis, or not being able to access or rectify one's personal data.[462] In the discussion of personal data under Article 7 CFREU above, the Court's approach to interferences with 'the right to respect for private life with regard to the processing of personal data' has been discussed, i.e., with Articles 7 and 8 CFREU, and this is generally the case when personal data are processed.[463] However, it is also possible that personal data are processed without private life being at stake.[464] Additionally, the right to data protection can be interfered with if there is no independent authority that oversees compliance with data protection rules, or when the data are removed from its supervision.[465]

3.3.3.3 Justification of Interferences with the Right to Data Protection

An interference with the right to data protection can only be justified if the conditions of Article 52 (1) as elucidated above are met. The justification of limitations on the right to data protection holds limited relevance for big data. However, like the ECtHR, the CJEU has made some remarks in relation to the scope of obligations with respect to the processing of personal data. Summarised and elaborated in the *Digital Rights Ireland* case concerning a

459. Cf. *Commission v Germany* [2010] CJEU C-518/07 (not mentioned); *Commission v Austria* [2012] CJEU C-614/10 [36] (mentioned); *Commission v Hungary* (n 29) [47] (mentioned).
460. *Digital Rights Ireland* (n 32) [68].
461. *Ibid* 36.
462. *Ibid* 35; *Schwarz* (n 381) [30]; Article 8 (2) CFREU.
463. These cases have been discussed in section 3.3.2.2 on the possible interferences with the right to privacy and will not be discussed in further detail in this subsection.
464. Cf. subsection 3.3.3.1 and *Scarlet/SABAM* (n 440); *SABAM/Netlog* (n 29).
465. Article 8 (3) CFREU.

'serious interference', the Court identified relevant limitations through its assessment of a violation: restrictions on data gathering, procedures and safeguards regarding the access to and use of the data, and limits on the retention time of the data.[466] Moreover the CJEU decided that Article 8 requires effective protection of personal data against the (risk of) abuse, and unlawful access and use.[467] These considerations thus become part of the normative scope of Article(s) 8 (and 7) CFREU.

3.3.4 Conclusion: Articles 7 and 8 CFREU Applied to Big Data

The EU has a long tradition of fundamental rights protection, although the rights have not always been recorded in Treaties or other fundamental rights instruments. This has changed with the Charter, which codified established practices regarding the right to privacy and added a new right to the existing catalogue: the right to the protection of personal data. The protection of fundamental rights in the EU is influenced by the ECHR and the case law of the ECtHR, both before and after the creation of the Charter, but its application to big data has its own scope and effects. It must also be noted that the attention of the CJEU for the privacy and data protection matters has increased steadily over the past years, strengthening the protection of the fundamental rights to privacy and data protection.[468] This trend can be expected to continue the coming years.

In the *acquisition* phase of the big data process, personal data are covered by the right to privacy of Article 7 CFREU, although the CFREU's decisions differ in minor aspects and incorporate different characteristics, particularly through the combination of Article 7 with Article 8 CFREU ('the right to respect for private life with regard to the processing of personal data').[469] Amongst others, the CJEU specified that it takes blanket collection and retention of metadata very seriously, even though the collection of metadata is considered a lesser privacy risk than the collection of the content of communications itself.[470] It can be distilled from the case law of the CJEU that when the scope of collection, storage, and retention gets larger, the interference becomes more serious, leading to closer scrutiny by the Court.[471] The large-scale collection of personal data, including metadata, is thus without a doubt part of the concept of privacy in the EU. Additionally,

466. *Digital Rights Ireland* (n 32) [59–64]; Granger and Irion (n 406).
467. *Digital Rights Ireland* (n 32) [66].
468. Kristina Irion, 'A Special Regard. The Court of Justice and the Fundamental Rights to Privacy and Data Protection' in Ulrich Faber and others (eds), *Gesellschaftliche Bewegungen – Recht unter Beobachtung und in Aktion: Festschrift für Wolfhard Kohte* (Nomos Verlagsgesellschaft, 2016) 878–882, 886–887.
469. *Volker und Markus Schecke and Eifert* (n 32) [52].
470. Cf. subsection 3.3.2.2
471. *Digital Rights Ireland* (n 32).

removing personal data from EU supervision can interfere with Article 8 CFREU.[472] The same applies to the *analysis* phase, with the addition that a lack of safeguards against abuse and unlawful access can amount to an infringement under Articles 7 and 8 of the Charter. These aspects are explicitly covered in the judgments of the CJEU.[473] When data are anonymised before they are analysed, the data will not be covered by Articles 7 and 8 CFREU, as the definition is linked to the concept of identified or identifiable individuals.

When the knowledge gathered from big data analysis is *applied* to individuals, the right to respect for private life with regard to the processing of personal data can apply when personal data are processed. It is also possible that only the application of Article 8 is triggered when personal data are processed in this phase, even though Article 7 might not be directly applicable. A third possibility is the reverse: knowledge may be gathered from big data which is never directly applied to individual cases, although it does influence individuals' private lives. The right to data protection will not apply to these situations, but the right to respect for private life might. The measures that need to be taken are dependent on the seriousness of the interference, for which the possibilities that people can be profiled are a criterion.

In conclusion, the scope of the rights of the Charter is broad. Applied to big data, the different actions in the acquisition phase and application phase are often within the scope of Article 8 in isolation or combined with Article 7 because personal data will be processed. In the analysis phase, it depends on how the analysis is done. As to the enabling function, the Court has acknowledged the enabling function of the rights to privacy and data protection for freedom of expression. The next section compares the outcomes of the analyses of Article 8 ECHR and Articles 7 and 8 CFREU.

3.4 COMPARISON

In this section, the rights of the two jurisdictions are compared, broadly following the structure of the tripartite fundamental rights test. This comparison serves as the basis for the normative conceptualisation in the ensuing section below.

Comparing the previous subsections on the content of the rights to privacy and data protection gives a clear image, but only after a few disclaimers have been made. It is difficult to come to a general understanding of the ECHR's and CFREU's rights to privacy and data protection, because the contexts of the cases that the ECtHR and the CJEU decide are very specific. For example, almost all of the ECtHR cases deal with interferences

472. *Schrems* (n 32).
473. *Digital Rights Ireland* (n 32) [66].

by the state, and often surveillance measures or sensitive data are at stake. Detailed contextual factors are incorporated in the assessments and can play a big role in the eventual outcome, which makes comparison within and between the two jurisdictions difficult. Moreover, the Courts do not discuss previous case law in a detailed way, and a method or structured approach for the CJEU to use the ECtHR's case law seems to be lacking.[474]

When comparing the scope of protection of the Charter to that of the ECHR, the first conclusion is that everything that is covered under Article 8 ECHR is also covered by Article 7 CFREU (sometimes read in conjunction with Article 8 CFREU), because the Charter cannot offer a lower level of protection than the Convention due to Article 52 (3) and 53 CFREU. This means that for the right to privacy the ECHR and its interpretation by the ECtHR are the floor, or minimum level of protection, to which the CFREU and CJEU add specifics.

In terms of its scope of application, the ECHR already offers a vast scope of protection. Article 8 ECHR covers a profoundly diverse array of interests and aspects of private and family life, home, and correspondence, including personal data. Regarding the scope of application with respect to personal data, the ECtHR has included (private and public) personal data, metadata, and location data within its scope. No criteria on the amount or sensitivity apply. In terms of the right to privacy's subject matter, Article 7 CFREU and its interpretation do not have much to add to this broad concept. However, when it comes to acknowledging the facilitative role that privacy can have for the protection of other fundamental rights and freedoms, the ECtHR has recognised personal autonomy, whereas the CJEU has referred to freedom of speech in relation to surveillance and potential chilling effects.

When looking at what constitutes an interference with the right, there are also differences between the ECHR and CFREU. Interferences with Article 8 ECHR can often be considered 'high-impact' intrusions, and specific contextual factors generally determine whether or not a right is interfered with. For example, when public or previously published personal data are at stake, the ECtHR makes an assessment of whether there has been an interference on the basis of criteria that it developed in its case law. The CJEU does not seem to attach weight to the difference between public and private personal data. Personal data's public nature is not emphasised, and its processing usually leads to what the CJEU refers to as an interference with the 'right to respect for private life with regard to the processing of personal data'. A second difference in the treatment of interferences, is that the CJEU distinguishes between the different types of interference according to their gravity, which influences how strict the Court's assessment is under the justification test. The ECtHR also links the severity of the interference with

474. Sionaidh Douglas-Scott, 'A Tale of Two Courts: Luxembourg, Strasbourg and the Growing European Human Rights Acquis' 43 Common Market Law Review 629, 652, 656–658.

the justification, yet it is much more implicit and diverse in its case law. Both Courts, however, distinguish between content and metadata, with interferences with content being of a more serious character. The severity or type of interference determines which minimum standards have to be observed regarding *inter alia* retention, storage, and security. The Courts link this to data protection instruments, thereby incorporating part of these non-constitutional instruments into the scope of the right to privacy.

What adds even more to the constitutional protection of personal data, is Article 8 CFREU. Although it may seem as if personal data are broadly covered in the case law on Article 8 ECHR, or through the CJEU that includes Article 7 CFREU in its assessment as standard when personal data are at stake, the Charter's right to data protection does offer additional protection as a stand-alone right. Setting aside the influence it may have had on the CJEU's 'right to respect for private life with regard to the processing of personal data', which we cannot ascertain, its text adds principles that have not (yet) been accepted as part of the right to privacy as interpreted by both Courts. Personal data processing that is not based on consent or a legitimate ground or that does not grant individuals rights of access and rectification, interferes with Article 8 (2) CFREU. And if there is a lack of independent oversight or if personal data are removed from that oversight, Article 8 (3) CFREU can be breached. In this respect, Article 8 CFREU mirrors Articles 8 ECHR and 7 CFREU, because its scope is narrower in terms of content, but due to its detail the bar for interferences seems lower. An interference with this detailed right seems more easily established than an interference with the right to privacy as such, and in a few cases the CJEU has found a violation of the right to data protection, without referring to Article 7 CFREU or Article 8 ECtHR. However, given the (more recent) broad interpretation of Article 7 CFREU by the CJEU, it might be an overstatement to say that the latter has proper added value.

3.5 NORMATIVE CONCEPTUALISATION OF THE RIGHTS TO PRIVACY AND TO DATA PROTECTION

The purpose of this chapter is to develop an understanding of how the rights to privacy and data protection apply in the context of big data. Following a comparative analysis of the constitutional dogmatic and case law in the CoE and EU jurisdictions, this section conceptualises the normative content of the rights to privacy and data protection in the EU with respect to the phases of big data and its negative effects, thus as stand-alone and as enabling rights. First, a general elaboration of the normative concept is set out, after which the application to big data is discussed, followed by special attention for the enabling function of the rights to privacy and data protection.

The previous section already showed that a relatively coherent image results from comparing the rights as explained by both Courts insofar as relevant to big data. Since both jurisdictions are relevant to the EU and the highest level of protection offered is the level that should be achieved in practice, the normative concepts keep up this high level of protection.[475] This means that in general the normative constitutional concept of the rights to privacy and data protection encompasses all big data phases when personal data are processed, and the application phase if there is a significant detrimental effect to (one of the protected spheres or interests of) the right to privacy, even if no personal data are processed.

The following is a more detailed explanation of the normative concept in the light of the big data phases. Large-scale processing of personal data (including metadata) in the acquisition and analysis phases is within the scope of the normative concept. When no personal data are processed in the acquisition phase, this is not the case. Similarly, when the data that are used for analysis do not relate to identified or identifiable individuals, for example when the data are aggregated or anonymised before the analysis, the analysis phase is beyond the concept's scope. When personal data are processed, the rights to privacy and data protection apply in a similar manner as in the acquisition phase. In both phases, minimum standards need to be implemented, regarding for example limits on access and retention times, and principles regarding security and prevention of abuse. Also, personal data processing must be based on consent or a legitimate ground, and individuals must be granted rights of access and rectification. When the scope of collection and processing increase or data of a sensitive nature are processed, interferences are likely, and more is required in terms of these safeguards.

In the application phase, multiple scenarios are possible. Because there are legion potential applications of big data, giving a definitive answer on when and how the rights apply to the application phase is impossible. However, the possible scenarios can be divided roughly into three groups. In the first scenario, personal data are processed and there is a clear impact on the right to privacy. These cases fit under the normative concept.

In the second group, personal data are processed but this does not infringe the right to privacy, in which case only the right to data protection can be at stake.[476] In the third group no or limited personal data are processed in the application phase. These cases are not covered by the right to data protection, but the applicability of the right to privacy is not fully excluded.[477] It depends on how the knowledge, models, or profiles are applied

475. Cf. subsection 1.2.5.2 of Chapter 1.

476. As explained this scenario is primarily theoretical and not very plausible in practice, given the broad scope of protection offered to personal data under the two respective jurisdictions.

477. Because no personal data are processed, the right is not triggered. For a more detailed explanation, *see* the second section of the next chapter.

and what influence this application has on the private life of the individual. As explained, the scope of privacy is broad, but the scope of interference more restricted. Private life can be affected, but this must be judged on a case-by-case basis based on the circumstances of the case, notably the severity of the interference, as the applications of big data are simply too diverse to give a comprehensive answer. In sum, the conclusion regarding the concepts of the fundamental rights to privacy and data protection is that together they cover the processing of personal data in big data projects, and have the potential to apply to all phases of the big data project, even when no personal data are processed. In the acquisition and analysis phase the concept of privacy primarily covers the large-scale collection, storage, and processing of their data. In the application phase it does the same, but it also involves interferences with their personal sphere when the processing of personal data is of minor relevance.

In sum, the stand-alone value of the rights to privacy and data protection is considerable; the normative concept covers all big data phases (to a greater or lesser extent), covering a broad array of privacy interferences and adding specific demands with respect to the protection of personal data. The instrumental value, however, receives less attention on a constitutional level in the EU jurisdictions. Therefore, the following paragraphs explain the background and context of the enabling function.

The instrumental value of privacy and data protection receives attention in the literature, but the extent to which it is developed differs greatly. European legal literature, while sometimes making references to *inter alia* personal autonomy, has not produced many genuine conceptual contributions on the enabling function of the rights to privacy and data protection.[478] This may be due to the strong constitutional protection in place and the shift of scholarly attention to judicial interpretations of the fundamental rights and the application of data protection law to a variety of diverse activities involving the processing of personal data. In the social sciences academics are more inclined to interrogate privacy rights as an enabling right, for example in relation to personal autonomy.[479] Conversely, US legal scholarship continues to argue privacy's important contribution to other individual rights and societal values, resulting in a more profound exploration of the relationship between privacy and other rights and values. Solove rejects the idea that privacy has a unitary value, and instead regards it as a concept that protects a plurality of activities, and is therefore of pluralistic value.[480] In his taxonomy of privacy, Solove touches upon many rights and values that privacy affects, ranging from personal autonomy, to freedom of speech, to

478. There are notable exceptions, *see* for example Bernal (n 14).
479. For example Rössler (n 14).
480. Solove, *Understanding Privacy* (n 18) 98–100.

non-discrimination.[481] Richards and Krotoszynski deem privacy indispensable to freedom of speech. Krotoszynski argues that privacy is a precondition for freedom of speech, which makes it also a precondition for democratic self-government.[482] Richards argues the case for intellectual privacy, i.e., the protection of a 'zone to make up our minds freely', which precedes the actual public expression of ideas and opinions.[483] Roberts takes another angle, by focusing on how privacy facilitates non-discrimination, primarily through obscuring the information necessary to discriminate.[484] In sum, the general enabling effect of privacy and data protection is acknowledged in the literature.

The fact that the two Courts do not often mention other fundamental rights and freedoms is not surprising and does not refute the statements about the enabling function. These rights are also stand-alone rights; claims of interferences with freedom of expression and non-discrimination are brought under their respective Articles (Articles 10 and 14 ECHR; Articles 11 and 21 CFREU) and assessed accordingly by the Court. But as mentioned above, there are exceptions. Personal autonomy is considered part of the right to privacy; on the basis of the ECtHR's case law privacy is deemed to encapsulate the protection of self-determination. Freedom of expression is regarded as potentially chilled when the individual's privacy is violated by the CJEU, therefore the protection of privacy has instrumental value for the safeguarding of freedom of expression. With respect to the latter a similar trend may appear under the ECHR, as there are multiple cases pending before the ECtHR in which both Articles 8 and 10 ECHR are claimed to have been violated in the context of mass surveillance.[485] Accordingly, from the literature and partially also from the case law on the fundamental rights to privacy and data protection in the EU emanates the idea of their potential for the protection of other rights and freedoms. But it is clear that for most of the individual rights and freedoms affected by big data, the enabling function should be seen as an effect, not as a goal or criterion under the normative concept of the EU right to privacy and data protection.

3.6 CONCLUSION

This chapter answers the question of what the normative scope of the rights to privacy and data protection is regarding the big data process and its

481. Solove, 'A Taxonomy of Privacy' (n 34) 513–514 and 529–530.
482. Krotoszynski (n 224) 175.
483. Richards (n 220) 95.
484. Jessica L. Roberts, 'Protecting Privacy to Prevent Discrimination' (2015) 56 William and Mary Law Review 2097.
485. *Tretter and Others v Austria* [2010] ECtHR (application no. 3599/10); *Big Brother Watch and Others v UK* [2013] ECtHR (application no. 58170/13); *10 Human Rights Organisations and Others v UK* [2015] ECtHR (application no. 24960/15).

potential negative effects, focusing on the stand-alone value of these rights and their enabling function for the protection of the other individual rights and freedoms. As the fundamental rights to privacy and data protection are addressed to states, they cannot be enforced in disputes between private parties. It is unlikely that the rights will acquire full horizontal effect, even though there are many arguments in favour, and ways in which they have an effect on private parties.[486] Nevertheless, the normative content of the right is essential for the level of protection that secondary law should achieve. The implementation on the secondary legislative level should match with the scope of the normative concepts. The conclusions on the content of the rights as interpreted by the two Courts below maps out the normative concept of the EU rights to privacy and data protection, focusing on their general scope and their application to big data.

The question on the conceptual scope of the fundamental rights to privacy and data protection has proven to be a difficult one, because of the context and casuistic nature of the case law, particularly regarding privacy. Still, in sum and in general, the normative scope of the fundamental rights to privacy and data protection is very broad. What occurs in big data as described in Chapter 2 generally fits under their scope of application, as long as personal data are processed or there is an effect on private life. Although conceptually privacy and data protection encompass much of what happens in big data, this does not mean that such processing or taking decisions should be necessarily prohibited through the implementation of the normative concepts on the secondary legislative level.

The normative scope of the EU rights to privacy and data protection requires the protection of all personal data. Personal data is a broad concept, linked to its interpretation as information that relates to identified or identifiable individuals of amongst others Convention 108. This interpretation also encompasses metadata and location data. Personal data may only be processed when there is a legitimate processing ground, and when the individual's rights to access and rectification are secured. Furthermore, there is a duty to make sure that retention times and other interferences stay limited. Personal data need to be secured, and measures must be taken to protect them against illegitimate access and abuse. At all times, there must be

486. Arguments include: (1) fundamental rights embody universal values, hence erga omnes effect is justified, (2) globalisation, because of which multinationals have come to wield great power and the application of different national (constitutional) norms in cross-border conflicts has become difficult, (3) the impossibility of separating the public sphere from the private sphere. William Wade, 'Horizons of Horizontality' (2000) Law Quarterly Review 217, 224; Walter Leisner, *Grundrechte und Privatrecht* (Beck 1960) 333; Remco Nehmelman and Cornelis Willem Noorlander, *Horizontale werking van grondrechten: over een leerstuk in ontwikkeling* (Kluwer 2013] 66; Andrew Clapham, *Human Rights in the Private Sphere* (Clarendon Press 1993) 93ff, 124ff. Fundamental rights have effects on private parties amongst others through positive obligations and preliminary rulings, as elucidated above.

an independent authority that supervises the compliance with these obligations. Different kinds of personal data collection and storage, as well as monitoring, wiretapping, and sharing of personal data with third parties are deemed within the scope of protection, and under the living instrument doctrine this may extend to new types of personal data processing.

If no personal data are processed, situations may still fall under the normative concept of the right to privacy and aspects of privacy may require safeguarding. Whether this is the case will depend on the context and particular circumstances of a situation. As the applications of both the right to privacy and big data are highly diverse, a detailed conclusive overview cannot be given. However, it may be the case particularly when the application of big data interferes with home, correspondence, or one of the interests under private life that can be categorised as protecting personal identity, moral or physical identity, the private sphere, sexual activities and social life, or the enjoyment of relationships. An example of a situation where private life may be at stake without personal data being necessary is when the big data-based building of a chemical plant would have detrimental effects on the health of people living in the vicinity.[487] The normative concept of private life should not be interpreted restrictively, particularly as the living instrument doctrine may create space for new interests and interferences, as a result of which collection of data from the home, or application of big data in the home, could find application under the 'home' interests of the concept of privacy.

As regards the enabling function of privacy and data protection for other individual rights and freedoms: it is recognised in the literature, particularly in work from the US, but the normative concepts of the rights to privacy and data protection do not encompass a general duty to protect other fundamental rights. References by the Courts to freedom of expression or non-discrimination under an analysis of alleged violation of privacy and/or data protection are rare, likely because of the coexistence of privacy, data protection, freedom of expression, and non-discrimination in the fundamental rights treaties. An exception is personal autonomy, which has been recognised as an underlying principle as well as an aspect of the right to privacy under the ECHR, and therefore is a part of privacy in the EU jurisdiction. As violations of this specific aspect of privacy have not (yet) been found in previous case law, the exact scope of the concept of personal autonomy under the right to privacy remains unclear. In addition to personal autonomy, freedom of expression has also been mentioned in recent case law finding a violation of the rights to privacy and data protection.[488] However, this reference confirmed the link between the three, and did not establish a relationship based on (one-way) dependency. The enabling function of privacy and data protection on the constitutional level thus primarily

487. Cf. subsection 3.2.3.
488. *Tele2 Sverige* (n 401).

functions through the proxy of personal data: when personal data are covered by privacy or data protection, the protective effects trickle down to personal autonomy, freedom of expression, and non-discrimination. There is no direct duty under the normative concepts, but there are obviously many positive by-effects. The ensuing chapter maps out how the secondary legislative level matches these normative concepts of the right to privacy and data protection.

Chapter 4
Big Data and EU Data Protection Law

4.1 INTRODUCTION

This chapter explores the potential and limitations of EU data protection law for protecting individual rights and freedoms, i.e., to what extent EU data protection law can protect against the negative effects of big data on personal autonomy, privacy and data protection, non-discrimination, and freedom of expression.

Data protection law regulates the processing of personal data and has the dual objectives of protecting the fundamental rights and freedoms of individuals, particularly the right to privacy with respect to personal data, and enabling the free flow of data between the EU Member States.[489] It gives individuals a number of rights to exert control over their personal data and restricts its use, which has the potential to strengthen their personal autonomy and prevent discrimination, amongst others. The enabling function of the right to data protection is thus partially secondary EU data protection law's objective and effect. In legal circles, big data is often regarded through a data protection lens. Experts' point of departure in the big data discussion is generally a complex and nuanced version of a statement that can be summarised as: big data is about personal data, so data protection law applies

489. Article 1 Regulation (EU) 2016/679 of the European Parliament and of the Council of 27 April 2016 on the protection of natural persons with regard to the processing of personal data and on the free movement of such data, and repealing Directive 95/46/EC (General Data Protection Regulation) 2016 (OJ L 119/1).

to big data, and should be the solution to big data's issues.[490] In this line of thinking, the Data Protection Directive currently protects personal data, and the new GDPR will or should solve what is wrong with the present-day protection of individuals.

Although data protection law alleviates some big data issues, blind trust in data protection as a solution to big data's negative impact on individual rights and freedoms is unwise. Data protection law does not generally apply to the entire big data process; parts of the acquisition, analysis, and application phases of big data are beyond its scope of protection, as will be shown below. And the extent to which the negative impact on individual rights and freedoms can be mitigated by substantive data protection norms is limited, for various reasons elucidated below. This chapter scrutinises where data protection law can be of assistance in the protection of individuals in the context of big data, and which aspects make it unfit as the *sole* solution to counter the detrimental impact of big data on individual rights and freedoms. The method and structure of the analysis are mapped out below.

4.1.1 Literature Review

EU data protection law is a tremendously popular topic in legal research, a popularity that has developed alongside the development and increasing reliance on (personal) data-intensive technologies during the past decades. The body of literature can be divided in different ways, but for this chapter a division in terms of generality and specificity is key: a division in general literature on specific legal provisions, principles or mechanisms, writings that focus on data protection law and big data in particular, and (critical) analyses of data protection law's underlying mechanisms or values. General literature on specific legal provisions or data protection principles is used for the interpretation and explanation of the legal provisions reviewed in this chapter and analyses of the potential and flaws thereof.[491] Articles that focus on big data and data protection law are used to highlight specific issues with the application of EU data protection law in the context of big data, and support insights into its potential and limitations in this context.[492] With

490. Article 29 Working Party, 'Statement of the WP29 on the Impact of the Development of Big Data on the Protection of Individuals with Regard to the Processing of Their Personal Data in the EU' (2014) WP 221 2.

491. Gabriela Zanfir, 'The Right to Data Portability in the Context of the EU Data Protection Reform' (2012) 2 International Data Privacy Law 149; For example Eleni Kosta, *Consent in European Data Protection Law* (Martinus Nijhoff Publishers 2013) on the consent; Giovanni Sartor, 'The Right to Be Forgotten in the Draft Data Protection Regulation' (2015) 5 International Data Privacy Law 64 on the right to be forgotten.

492. Cate and Mayer-Schönberger (n 82); Solon Barocas and Helen Nissenbaum, 'Big Data's End Run Around Anonymity and Consent' in Julia Lane and others (eds), *Privacy, Big Data, and the Public Good: Frameworks for Engagement* (1 edition, Cambridge

respect to this branch of data protection law, the same disclaimer as made in the literature review of Chapter 2 on big data applies: there is a tendency to refer to 'big data' in literature, without devoting attention to big data-related issues at all, so some literature of this type has limited relevance in this context. Closely linked to much of the valuable data protection law and big data literature is the last category: (critical) analyses of mechanisms and values underlying data protection law.[493] This type of literature is mostly used to analyse the potential and limitation of EU data protection law to a level that transcends the particularities of the specific GDPR provisions. It shows where the potential and limitations lie not so much in the legal provisions but in the data protection law approach to big data, which constitutes an important foundation for the exploration of possible alternative solutions in Chapter 5.

For the interpretation of EU data protection legislation there is another important source in addition to the historical development of the law and academic literature: the opinions of the Article 29 Working Party (Working Party). The Working Party, named after its establishing article in the Data Protection Directive, is an independent advisory body consisting of representatives from the national supervisory authorities/data protection authorities (DPAs), the EDPS, and the European Commission.[494] When the Regulation enters into force, the Article 29 Working Party shall be succeeded by the European Data Protection Board (EDPB, Articles 68 and 94 GDPR). One of the tasks of the Working Party, and of the future EDPB, is to advise on data protection, which it does amongst others through issuing (non-binding) opinions. The Working Party publishes multiple documents each year about the interpretation of data protection rules and contemporary societal developments. While these opinions are not binding, they are an authoritative source for the interpretation of EU data protection law.[495] Additionally, as the Working Party mainly consists of amongst others representatives of national DPAs, its opinions give an indication as to how the law will be enforced, and they contain detailed and well-argued interpretations of legal concepts. Although they are based on the Data Protection Directive instead of on the Regulation, the Working Party's

---

University Press 2014); Guiseppe D'Acquisto and others, 'Privacy by Design in Big Data – An Overview of Privacy Enhancing Technologies in the Era of Big Data Analytics' (European Union Agency For Network And Information Security (ENISA) 2015).

493. For example Daniel Solove, 'Privacy Self Management and the Consent Dilemma' (2013) 126 Harvard Law Review 1180; Bert-Jaap Koops, 'The Trouble with European Data Protection Law' (2014) 4 International Data Privacy Law 250; Hazel Grant and Hannah Crowther, 'How Effective Are Fines in Enforcing Privacy?' in David Wright and Paul de Hert (eds), *Enforcing Privacy: Regulatory, Legal and Technological Approaches* (Springer International Publishing 2016).

494. Article 29 Directive 95/46/EC.

495. Christopher Kuner, *European Data Privacy Law and Online Business* (Oxford University Press 2003) 9–10.

opinions continue to be an important interpretative source under the Regulation, because of their history and the interpretative role they have played under the Directive, and because many concepts and rules from the Directive are also in the Regulation. Possible dissimilarities between the Working Party's opinions and the new rules of the Regulation are discussed where relevant. The opinions are also of added importance, as there is not much case law on data protection, even though the number of data protection cases has been rising over the past few years. Due to this lack of primary sources and because of the particular nature of the Working Party, subsection 4.3 of this chapter in particular makes much use of the Working Party's opinions, in addition to *inter alia* academic literature.

In this chapter, the link between EU data protection and individual rights and freedoms is discussed, before turning the attention towards the GDPR. The analysis of the GDPR is divided into a part on the material scope of application, the substantive norms, and enforcement. The concluding part analyses the lacunae in the protective framework. These lacunae are compared to the normative concept of the rights to privacy and data protection of Chapter 3, to supplement the conclusions on the potential and limitations of EU data protection law with an explanation of where it does not meet the standards of the normative concept. This chapter frequently refers to the concepts 'data subject' and 'controller'. A data subject is someone whose personal data are processed (Article 4 (1) GDPR), which is generally the individual in the big data process. The data subject is also referred to as the 'individual' in this work. A controller is the person or legal entity who determines the means and purposes of the processing (Article 4 (7) GDPR), the 'big data entity' who makes use of big data.

4.2 DATA PROTECTION LAW AND ITS LINK WITH INDIVIDUAL RIGHTS AND FREEDOMS

There is a strong link between data protection law and individual rights and freedoms, that has not received much explicit attention in the legal literature. However, this link is of particular importance in big data, where the processing of personal data can be regulated by data protection law, but other rights and freedoms (personal autonomy, privacy, freedom of expression, and non-discrimination) are affected. Data protection here functions as an 'enabling right', as a legislative extension of the fundamental rights' enabling functions at the constitutional level explained in the previous chapter. Before analysing the GDPR to determine its potential and limitations for the protection of individual rights and freedoms in big data, this section first traces the doctrinal link between data protection and these other rights and freedoms.

In Europe, data protection legislation was often conceived with the enabling function for individuals' fundamental rights and freedoms in mind.[496] Statutory data protection laws explicitly aim to protect a number of individuals' fundamental rights and freedoms. In Germany, the Federal Data Protection Law adopted in 1976, also the first national statute of its kind in Europe, broadly aims to protect against the impairment of individual interests through protecting personal data against being abused in the course of its processing.[497] The protected individual interests ('schutzwürdige Belange des Betroffenen') certainly include personal integrity and the private sphere, but also other constitutionally protected individual rights and freedoms, namely freedom of expression, freedom of assembly and association, and freedom of religion.[498] Thus, the formulation of the protected subject matter has been kept deliberately open for interpretation depending on the circumstances of the processing of personal data.

Similarly, the first French law on the protection of personal data from 1978, refers to human rights, private life, and individual or public liberties (*'droits de l'homme, […] vie privée, […] libertés individuelles ou publiques'*) as its objects of protection.[499] The French law took much inspiration from the 1975 *Rapport de la Commission Informatique et Libertés* (*'Le Rapport Tricot'*) which emphasised the close connection between private life and other individual freedoms.[500]

When adopting the 1995 Data Protection Directive, the EU legislator acknowledged that the directive aims to protect 'fundamental rights and freedoms of natural persons, and in particular their right to privacy, with respect to the processing of personal data'.[501] As Dammann and Simitis observe, this creates a functional link between the protection of personal data and fundamental rights and freedoms in general, instead of narrowing its object of protection down to the private sphere.[502] They mention the right to freedom of expression, the right to property, and the freedom of profession as individual rights and freedoms that data protection law promotes. Following their commentary, Recital 2 of the Data Protection Directive underscores this general objective when providing:

> Whereas data-processing systems are designed to serve man; whereas they must, whatever the nationality or residence of natural persons,

496. This section has been published before as part of Oostveen and Irion (n 229) (with changes).
497. Article 1 Bundesdatenschutzgesetz BDSG (n 23).
498. Hans-Joachim Reh, 'Kommentar zum Bundesdatenschutzgesetz' in Spiros Simitis and others (eds), *Kommentar zum Bundesdatenschutzgesetz* (Nomos Verlagsgesellschaft 1978) paras 1–6.
499. Article 1 Loi informatique et libertés (n 23); Ulrich Dammann and Spiros Simitis, *EG-Datenschutzrichtlinie: Kommentar* (Nomos Verlagsgesellschaft 1997) 102.
500. 'Rapport de La Commission Informatique et Libertés I (Le Rapport Tricot)' (1975) 19f.
501. Article 1 Directive 95/46/EC. *See also* the recurring references to '(fundamental) rights and freedoms' and 'the right to privacy' as separate concepts in the recitals to the Directive.
502. Dammann and Simitis (n 499) 101.

> respect their fundamental rights and freedoms, notably the right to privacy, and contribute to economic and social progress, trade expansion and the well-being of individuals.

The GDPR, which will succeed the Data Protection Directive, will enter into force in May 2018. Despite repeating certain elements of the paragraph above, there is, however, a shift of connotation in Recital (4):

> The processing of personal data should be designed to serve mankind. The right to the protection of personal data is not an absolute right; it must be considered in relation to its function in society and be balanced against other fundamental rights, in accordance with the principle of proportionality. This Regulation respects all fundamental rights and observes the freedoms and principles recognised in the Charter as enshrined in the Treaties […].

Whereas in the Data Protection Directive it was the data-processing systems which had to respect individuals' fundamental rights and freedoms, it is now the regulation itself which has to respect all fundamental rights and observe freedoms and principles of the Charter. This would be alarming were the preamble of EU legislation to have binding legal force, which it does not.[503] The GDPR maintains as a broad objective that '[t]his regulation protects fundamental rights and freedoms of natural persons' but replaces the particular reference to the fundamental right to privacy with reference to the right to the protection of personal data (Article 1 (2) GDPR). Hence, the European legal culture on the protection of individuals' privacy and personal data has always pursued the facilitation of other fundamental rights and freedoms. The following section sets out to explain how this enabling function is recognised in EU law.

Recognising the enabling function of the fundamental rights to privacy and personal data protection was close to visionary in the early 1980s, but in the light of big data developments, it deserves renewed attention. The previous chapters have already hinted at it, but this chapter makes it even clearer: personal data are a proxy for intervention in big data. Regulating personal data can protect other fundamental rights and freedoms, and this section has shown that this has been one of the intentions of legislators from the start of EU data protection law. However, the extent to which data protection law is capable of fulfilling this function in big data, depends on how the current rules work in practice. The following sections analyse the potential and limitations of EU data protection law to protect privacy and data protection, personal autonomy, freedom of expression, and non-discrimination.

503. *Nilsson and Others* [1998] CJEU C-162/97 [54]; *Inuit Tapiriit Kanatami* [2013] CJEU C-583/11 P 64.

4.3 DATA PROTECTION LAW'S MATERIAL SCOPE

When enquiring into the protective potential of data protection for individual rights and freedoms, the first question that needs an answer is whether current EU data protection law applies to big data.[504] As indicated in the introduction to this chapter, there is an issue here. Because of the criteria that delineate the material scope of data protection law, notably the concept of identifiability that is part of the broader concept of personal data, certain activities in big data are beyond the scope of data protection law. This section sets out the criteria that determine the material scope of the GDPR, followed by an evaluation of which parts of the big data process are within data protection law's scope and which are not. Concluding remarks at the end of the section link the scope of application to data protection law's protective potential against the negative impact of big data on individual rights and freedoms.

4.3.1 Criteria: The Concept of Personal Data

Article 2 of the Data Protection Regulation states that the Regulation is applicable to 'the processing of personal data wholly or partly by automated means'.[505] The substantive scope of data protection therefore depends on *personal data* that are *processed.* Article 4 (2) GDPR explains processing as any operation that is performed upon personal data, and enumerates examples such as collection, storage, consultation, use, disclosure, and destruction. Processing is thus a broad concept which is easily met. The concept of personal data is also broad, but less easily met. From its definition in Article 4 (1) GDPR, four elements can be deduced: it is (1) *any information* (2) *relating to* (3) an *identified or identifiable* (4) *natural person.* The Regulation does not explain these elements and there is limited guidance to be gathered from the judgments of the CJEU. Therefore, even though they are not binding, the opinions of the Working Party are an indispensable additional source of interpretation in this section.[506]

504. This section is a modified version of an article published in International Data Privacy Law: Manon Oostveen, 'Identifiability and the Applicability of Data Protection to Big Data' (2016) International Data Privacy Law.

505. Article 2 states that the Regulation is also applicable 'to the processing otherwise than by automatic means of personal data which form part of a filing system or are intended to form part of a filing system'. In the context of big data this latter part is irrelevant, as big data concerns digital data which falls under the category of processing by 'automatic means'.

506. *See* section 4.1.1 of Chapter 4. The opinions are used even though they are based on the Data Protection Directive instead of on the Regulation, because the concept of personal data consists of the same elements in the Regulation. Possible dissimilarities are discussed where relevant.

The first element of the personal data definition, *any information,* is uncontroversial and does not necessitate thorough analysis. It indicates that broad categories of (digital) data are covered, regardless of the data's content or format. Similarly, the *natural person* element does not trigger much discussion. The element emphasises the personal nature of data protection and excludes certain types of data from the scope of application of the Regulation, such as data that are solely about companies or deceased people.[507] The meaning of *relating to* is less self-explanatory. The Working Party discusses this element in detail in its opinion on the concept of personal data.[508] It considers data to be related to an individual when the data are *about* that individual, which can be in the guise of a *content, purpose,* or *result* element.[509] This means that the *relating to* criterion is met when data reveal information about an individual, when the data are used with the purpose of influencing her behaviour or status or to evaluate her, or when the data have an impact on her rights and interests or lead to her being treated differently from others.[510]

The remaining element of the personal data definition refers to *identified or identifiable* individuals. This is referred to as the *identifiability* element in this research, because identifiability is the lower threshold for application of data protection, compared to 'identified' individuals. Article 4 (1) GDPR indicates that people can be identified through names, online identifiers, identification numbers, and location data, or by reference to factors that are 'specific to the physical, physiological, genetic, mental, economic, cultural or social identity' of a person. Previously, the CJEU has decided that combinations of identifiers can make people identifiable.[511] It has also accepted that in addition to names and addresses,[512] other data such as phone numbers,[513] information about work and hobbies,[514] and (dynamic) IP addresses[515] can constitute personal

---

507. *See* Recital 14 of the General Data Protection Regulation. Under the e-Privacy Directive, legal persons are protected, Directive 2002/58/EC of the European Parliament and of the Council of 12 July 2002 concerning the processing of personal data and the protection of privacy in the electronic communications sector (Directive on privacy and electronic communications) 2002 (OJ L201/37).
508. Article 29 Working Party, 'Opinion 4/2007 on the Concept of Personal Data' (2007) WP 136 9–12.
509. *Ibid* 9–10.
510. *Ibid* 10–11.
511. *Lindqvist* [2003] CJEU C-101/01 [27]. *See also* Chapter 3.
512. *Österreichischer Rundfunk* (n 384) [64]; *Satamedia* (n 392) [35].
513. *Lindqvist* (n 511) [27].
514. *Ibid.*
515. *Scarlet Extended* [2011] CJEU C-70/10 [51]; *Digital Rights Ireland* (n 32) [25, 29]; *Breyer* [2016] CJEU C-582/14 [49]. In these cases the IP addresses were held by providers that had additional data that would make identification possible, or by online media service providers for whom it would be possible to acquire additional identifying information through judicial procedures. The CJEU has not decided whether an IP

data.[516] Recital 26 of the Regulation explains that 'all means reasonably likely to be used, such as singling out' should be taken into account to determine whether a person can be identified 'directly or indirectly'. 'Singling out' was not mentioned in the Data Protection Directive, but it can be linked back to the Working Party's opinion on the concept of personal data, in which identifiability is equated with the possibility to single someone out.[517] The Working Party distinguishes between *directly identifiable*, when information immediately singles out a specific individual (usually through a name) and *indirectly identifiable*, when a person is singled out through a unique combination of data.[518] According to the Working Party, singling out is context-dependent; it refers to singling out in a group.[519] As an example: information about a woman with red hair is not personal data in general; however, it is personal data when the context is an office in which there is only one woman with this hair colour. This interpretation has been criticised as being overly broad, unworkable in practice, and detrimental to the protective value of data protection law.[520] Also, what one needs to be able to do or what one needs to know about an individual to deem that individual identified or identifiable, is unclear even with the singling-out explanation.[521] In conclusion, despite the Working Party's interpretation of the concept of personal data, there is room for diverging interpretations and opinions.[522] Yet

---

address constitutes personal data per se; additional personal data seem to be required. However, it is clear that it is not necessary to be able to track a person down in real life to meet the identifiability criterion.

516. Not all of these categories are mentioned in Directive 95/46/EC's definition of personal data, but they are now in the definition of personal data of the Regulation. The cited case law of the CJEU precedes the Regulation.
517. Article 29 Working Party, 'Opinion 4/2007 on the Concept of Personal Data' (n 508) 13–14.
518. *Ibid* 12–13.
519. *Ibid* 13.
520. *See* amongst others Kuan Hon, Christopher Millard and Ian Walden, 'The Problem of "Personal Data" in Cloud Computing: What Information Is Regulated? The Cloud of Unknowing' (2011) 1 International Data Privacy Law 211; Colette Cuijpers and Paul Marcelis, 'Oprekking van het concept persoonsgegevens beperking van privacybescherming?' (2012) Computerrecht 339; Gerrit-Jan Zwenne, 'De verwaterde privacywet' (inaugural lecture, Leiden, the Netherlands, 12 April 2013); for an overview of arguments pro and contra Frederik Zuiderveen Borgesius, 'Singling out People without Knowing Their Names – Behavioral Targeting, Pseudonymous Data, and the New Data Protection Regulation' (2016) Computer Law & Security Review 12–15.
521. This point and Recital 26 are discussed in greater detail below.
522. It was expected that the preliminary questions of the German Bundesgerichtshof in the case on dynamic IP addresses would provide some conclusive answers on this matter, but the CJEU passed over the opportunity by interpreting the case narrowly, *see Breyer* (n 515) [37, 49]. The Court answered the dynamic IP addresses question only for an online media services provider with the specific circumstances that an internet service provider holds additional data that can be acquired through judicial procedures. The Court did not express its opinion on any other data held by the online media services provider itself or by third parties other than the internet service provider.

there is sufficient support to take the Working Party's interpretation of the concept of personal data as the reference point in the coming analysis, considering amongst others the fact that the Regulation's recitals and provisions mirror the wording of the Working Party's opinion on personal data.

On the basis of the *identifiability* element, four different categories of data can be distinguished.[523] These categories can be divided into two groups: data that have the potential to identify an individual, referred to as *identifiable data* here, and data through which an individual cannot be identified, here called *non-identifiable data.* This division determines the material scope of application of the Regulation: *identifiable data* are covered by data protection law, *non-identifiable data* are not. Since all four categories of data are processed in big data, this paragraph describes all four categories consecutively. The first category is *directly identifiable data* (to use the language of the Working Party). This means data through which an individual is immediately identified, such as a person's first and last name. The second category is *indirectly identifiable data*, which refers to a combination of data through which an individual is identified or identifiable, such as a zip code in combination with birthdate and gender. Pseudonymous data that can be attributed to individuals with the use of additional information are considered personal data in the Regulation and fall in the latter category.[524] *Directly identifiable data* and *indirectly identifiable data* together make up the group of *identifiable data*. The third category of data is *de-identified data*, which refers to data that are about individuals or were personal data, but have been de-identified to an extent that makes identification of individuals unreasonably difficult.[525] An example of de-identified data is personal data that are aggregated, consolidated, or summarised on the

523. Different categorisations are possible, *see* for example the division between raw, pseudo anonymous and non-personal data, that broadly corresponds to the Working Party's division, in Frederik Zuiderveen Borgesius, Mireille van Eechoud and Jonathan Gray, 'Open Data, Privacy, and Fair Information Principles: Towards a Balancing Framework' (2015) 30 Berkely Technology Law Journal 2074, 2077; In this article the Working Party's categorisation is maintained, because it is based on one of its well-researched and authoritative European opinions, and based on the concept of personal data as enshrined in Directive 95/46/EC and the General Data Protection Regulation. The categorisation broadly corresponds to risk levels, *see* Sarah Spiekermann and Lorrie Faith Cranor, 'Engineering Privacy' (2009) 35 IEEE Transactions on Software Engineering 67, 75.

524. Article 4 (1) and (5) and Recital 26 General Data Protection Regulation.

525. De-identified data is frequently referred to as anonymous data, as the opposite of identifiable data in legal terms. However, the technical possibility of completely anonymising data, and therefore the term anonymous data, is contested. *See* for example Arvind Narayanan and Vitaly Shmatikov, 'Robust De-Anonymization of Large Sparse Datasets', *IEEE Symposium on Security and Privacy, 2008. SP 2008* (2008); Ohm (n 194) and the work of Latanya Sweeney on identifiability of de-identified data. This article refers to de-identified data rather than anonymous data to reflect this debate and the difficulty of anonymisation, even though 'anonymous' is used in the Regulation. Note that technical difficulties of anonymising data do not automatically make all data

basis of a variable, so that the data give information about an aspect of a group of people instead of being identifiable data related to the individuals within that group. The fourth category is *non-personal data*, which means data that have never been personal and do not relate to individuals at all, such as data from sensors in fully automated production processes in factories, climatological data, or astronomical data. *De-identified data* and *non-personal data* together make up the group of *non-identifiable data*, to which data protection does not apply.[526]

Precisely at the disjunction between data that are within the scope of protection and data that are not, between *identifiable data* and *non-identifiable data*, lies the most challenging and unclear distinction: the distinction between *indirectly identifiable data* and *de-identified data*. Identifiability is a difficult term because it is unclear what the exact meaning of 'identified' is, in part because identifiability is highly context-dependent. A case study in a journal article about an anonymous person with a certain disease is generally not identifiable information, unless the disease or case is extremely rare and other researchers in the field that have worked with the same patient immediately recognise her identity. Data that are not identifiable for one person may very well be identifiable for another because the latter has information or knowledge that the first person does not. An example is dynamic IP addresses, which can be personal data in the hands of those who can legitimately acquire additional data to identify a person, but do not constitute personal data for those who cannot access such additional data.[527] Data can also become identifiable through combination with other datasets, through the addition of non-identifiable data to datasets containing personal data, or because the addition of more data makes people indirectly identifiable. Considering the amount of publicly available digital information and the flourishing trade in data, identifiability seems a broad category indeed, depending on how much effort must be deemed 'reasonable'. Moreover, recent technical and social developments have made categorisation of data into one of the two groups more difficult. The creation and dissemination of (public) information keeps increasing, open data initiatives spur the availability of government information, and the processing power of computers continues to increase.[528] This makes the processing and combination of different datasets easier. At the same time, the technical possibility of (non-reversible) anonymisation is heavily debated, in some cases deemed impossible, and often refuted.[529]

---

identifiable under the law, as the legal standard for anonymity/non-identifiability corresponds to Recital 26 of the Regulation (explained below) and not to the technical notion of anonymity.

526. Articles 2 (1), 4 (1) and Recital 26 General Data Protection Regulation.
527. *Breyer* (n 515) [31–49].
528. Alba (n 89).
529. *See* for example the literature cited under (n 26), Article 29 Working Party, 'Opinion 5/2014 on Anonymisation Techniques' (2014) WP 261; Yves-Alexandre de Montjoye

In conclusion, the elements *any information, relating to, identifiable,* and *natural person* together with the *processing* criterion form the essence of the material scope of data protection. In the context of big data and the protection of individuals, it is usually not difficult to determine whether *any information* and *natural person* elements are present. *Relating to* is ancillary to *identifiable* in the sense that as soon as an individual is identifiable, the *relating to* element will typically be present. The *identifiability* element is thus the benchmark, raising an *identifiability threshold* for the applicability of data protection in big data. If data are assumed to lack the potential to identify individuals, they are beyond the scope of the Regulation, which creates a dichotomy between identifiable data (data that have the potential to identify an individual) and non-identifiable data (data through which an individual cannot be identified). Either the data are in or they are out; the distinction between identifiable and non-identifiable is the demarcation of the material scope of data protection. The difficulty of this identifiable/non-identifiable dichotomy is the uncertainty about the boundary between these two categories. There is no universal, accepted, and detailed demarcation that provides legal certainty and is workable in practical situations. For these reasons identifiability is the focus of the following section on the applicability of data protection to big data.

4.3.2 Applicability of Data Protection Law in the Big Data Process

In each of the three phases of big data (*acquisition, analysis,* and *application*) different categories of data (*directly identifiable, indirectly identifiable, de-identified,* and *non-personal)* are processed. This section maps out which data can be processed in each phase, to show when data protection law applies and when it does not.

The first kind of data that can be gathered in the acquisition phase is pure, directly identifiable personal data. In the credit scoring case, for example, data of previous customers are processed, such as names and addresses connected to financial information, gender, and age. This type of input is fully subject to data protection law, triggering the Regulation's application of the principles and limitations on processing. Such data are often stripped of identifiers such as names, which makes it indirectly identifiable data. Indirectly identifiable data can also be acquired immediately. For example, in behavioural targeting the collected data are often not connected to people's names, but to identifiers such as cookies, IP addresses, or other pseudonyms. In this case individuals are not identified but can be

and others, 'Unique in the Crowd: The Privacy Bounds of Human Mobility' (2013) 3 Scientific Reports 1376, other research by Latanya Sweeney and Arvind Narayanan, and the debates between Naranyanan and Felten and Cavoukian and Castro.

identified through the pseudonyms or through the combined data. The Regulation applies to both types of data in the acquisition phase.

It is also likely that de-identified data are acquired in the acquisition phase. Personal data that have been gathered by, for example, a data broker can be anonymised by this company and subsequently sold to the company that provides credit. Although there must be a legal basis for the initial acquisition of the personal data and the anonymisation,[530] the Regulation no longer applies to the data once they are de-identified. This means that the initial collector of the data can sell them to third parties, who can then process the data without having to comply with data protection rules.

As explained in the previous section, the division between identifiable data and de-identified data is unclear and uncertain. The Working Party favours a broad interpretation of personal data, through its notion of singling out and its extensive interpretation of 'all means likely reasonable to be used' to identify persons. However, in practice, companies regularly maintain that they process non-identifiable data, to try to keep outside the scope of data protection law so they do not have to comply with its rules.[531] When one maintains the Working Party's broad definition of identifiability this seems unlikely, but the categorisation of data as identifiable or non-identifiable is a self-assessment by the controller; the controller determines how the data are categorised and treated.[532] Given the uncertainty about the exact definition and the impossibility for the supervisory authorities to check how every company or individual that processes data interprets identifiability, whether these interpretations are within the limits of the law, and whether they correspond to the Working Party's opinion, it cannot be expected that the interpretation of the Working Party is always maintained in practice. After all, its interpretation is strict, makes many processing actions difficult or impossible, has not yet been fully confirmed in court, and is not conclusive for all the different cases of personal data processing. It is likely that data processing companies try to keep data outside the scope of data protection law in practice. This means that for data processing entities there is an incentive to de-identify the data as much as possible, and to label data as

530. Anonymising data is processing of personal data and therefore requires a legitimate ground for processing, *see* Articles 4 (2) and 6 Regulation 2016/679 and Article 29 Working Party, 'Opinion 5/2014 on Anonymisation Techniques' (n 529) 6–7.

531. *See* for example 'Onderzoek CBP Naar de Verwerking van Persoonsgegevens Met Cookies Door de Publieke Omroep (NPO)' (College Bescherming Persoonsgegevens (Dutch DPA) 2014) 17, 35–37, 54–58; 'Onderzoek CBP Naar de Verwerking van Persoonsgegevens Door Snappet – Bijlage 1: Zienswijze Snappet, Met de Reactie Daarop van Het CBP' (College Bescherming Persoonsgegevens (Dutch DPA) 2014) 1–5; 'Onderzoek CBP Naar de Verwerking van Persoonsgegevens Met Cookies Door de Publieke Omroep (NPO)' 14, 46–50; 'KPN En XS4ALL – Onderzoek Naar de Verwerking van Persoonsgegevens via Interactieve Televisie van XS4ALL' (Autoriteit Persoonsgegevens (Dutch DPA) 2016).

532. Unless eventually proven otherwise in enforcement. *See also* subsection 4.5.

being de-identified or 'anonymous'.[533] This holds true not only for the acquisition phase but also for the analysis and application phases.

Lastly, in the acquisition phase data can be gathered that have no link to an individual whatsoever. Examples are meteorological data, and data about traffic flows, e.g., the number of cars that pass a bridge within a given timespan. In the medical research case examples are purely statistical for instance data on drug sales, or air quality measurements. Data protection law does not apply to this type of data. Nevertheless, through its combination with other datasets (identifiable or non-identifiable), non-personal data can provide information about individuals, which creates new personal data. For example, non-personal data about environmental pollution can be combined with data about postal code areas and the companies and individuals that reside in them, identifying possible polluters and people who run higher health risks.[534] These data can be used for research in the health sector, but also for instance by insurance companies to differentiate between the levels of health insurance premiums that people have to pay. The collection of non-personal data can thus indirectly affect the private life of individuals.

The same types of data that are acquired in the acquisition phase (directly identifiable, indirectly identifiable, de-identified, and non-personal) can be used in the analysis phase. Identifiable data can be processed, but this need not be the case. Big data organisations are often interested in patterns and categories in data and not in a particular individual as such. De-identification can also be a possibility, or maybe even a necessity, to comply with the controller's obligations regarding data protection by design and default of Article 25 GDPR, which is discussed in greater detail in subsection 4.4.3.2 below. Without an interest in processing data linked to an individual, and with a strong incentive to de-identify because it relieves the organisation of the burden of compliance with data protection law, it is likely that personal data are often de-identified before or at the beginning of the analysis phase. But the reverse is also possible. Data that have been acquired as non-identifiable (de-identified or non-personal data) can become identifiable in the analysis phase, due to the combination of different datasets, such as in the earlier example of environmental pollution data. When different (separate) non-identifiable datasets are combined with identifiable datasets or other non-identifiable datasets, new identifiable data may be generated that are within data protection law's material scope.

In the application phase, the knowledge or model derived from the analysis phase is applied. The individuals to whom the model is applied are not necessarily the people whose data have been processed in the first two

533. *See* remark on label of de-identified versus anonymous in (n 525).
534. Zuiderveen Borgesius, van Eechoud and Gray (n 523) 39.

phases.[535] The data in the first two phases are used to *learn*, the data in the last phase are used to *apply*. The acquisition phase and analysis phase use the same data (possibly supplemented by newly generated data in the analysis phase), but the data in the application phase are not necessarily linked to the data of the first two phases. This *disconnectedness* of the phases of big data is not only important for the material scope of protection; it is also paramount for the protective potential of substantive data protection norms. It returns in ensuing sections on *inter alia* consent and automated individual decision-making. One of the novelties of big data resulting from this disconnectedness of the phases is that the treatment of one individual can hinge on data volunteered by other people, or on data that do not relate to identifiable individuals at all.[536] Depending on the big data project, the personal data of the individual can be inside the data pool of the first two phases, but her personal data are not the main source for the knowledge or the model that is applied to her in the application phase.[537] Personal data of millions of others can be used to create knowledge or models that determine how people's online experience is personalised, or whether they are eligible for credit.

A model derived from big data does not constitute personal data as such, and does not always require personal data to be applied.[538] But personal data may be necessary to apply a model or knowledge to individuals. Often a small amount of personal data, like an IP address and cookie in the case of behavioural targeting, is enough to single someone out, but companies might not regard this as personal data.[539] The Working Party

535. If personal data were processed in those phases at all, as it is possible that the first two phases use non-identifiable data as the sole resource, for example when traffic flows are analysed to change the zoning plan of a city, affecting an inhabitant of the city in the application phase.
536. Dubbed the 'tyranny of the minority' by Barocas and Nissenbaum: Solon Barocas and Helen Nissenbaum, 'Big Data's End Run Around Procedural Privacy Protections: Recognizing the Inherent Limitations of Consent and Anonymity' (2014) 57 Communications of the ACM 31, 32; Barocas and Nissenbaum (n 492) 61–63.
537. If a prediction is made about an identifiable individual, this prediction becomes personal data according to the Working Party's interpretation of personal data. Accordingly new data may be created in the application phase.
538. *See* by analogy *YS* [2014] CJEU C141/12, C-372/12. The CJEU decided that a minute regarding a residence permit contained personal data, but that the legal analysis as such did not constitute personal data. Wim Schreurs and others, 'Cogitas, Ergo Sum. The Role of Data Protection Law and Non Discrimination Law in Group Profiling in the Private Sector' in Mireille Hildebrandt and Serge Gutwirth (eds), *Profiling the European Citizen: Cross-Disciplinary Perspectives* (Springer 2008) 249; *See also* Frederik Zuiderveen Borgesius, *Improving Privacy Protection in the Area of Behavioural Targeting* (Kluwer Law International 2015) 124.
539. According to the WP, an IP address and cookie constitute personal data because they make it possible to single someone out, *see* Article 29 Working Party, 'Opinion 2/2010 on Online Behavioural Advertising' (2010) WP 171 9. According to the CJEU, IP addresses can be personal data, but as the Court adopted a relative approach (or 'subjective' criterion) to personal data, it depends on the circumstances of the case and

is of the opinion that if the *purpose* of the processing is to identify individuals and treat them in a certain way, the data should be deemed identifiable because the controller will make an effort to identify individuals.[540] Still, this does not make all data used for profiling identifiable data. It is possible too that the application of big data uses shared characteristics that make it impossible to single people out, such as the hour at which a website is accessed and the gender of the visitor.[541] It is uncertain how companies would assess their own practices in this context. It is also unclear how far courts are prepared to go in extending the concept of personal data. Besides, for the individual it is difficult (if not impossible) to gauge what data and knowledge are behind the decision for which a small amount of her personal data are used. Data protection applies to this limited amount of personal data, but the consequences of volunteering may be more dire than expected, particularly as the decision is not based on this limited amount of data, but on the 'big' data of others.

It is also possible that big data affects individuals in the application phase without the use of personal data. Taking the medical research example, when an insurer decides to no longer reimburse a drug on the basis of knowledge (e.g., on costs versus benefits) gathered through big data, this affects individuals without it being directly linked to their personal data. Similarly, the offer of products or services in particular villages or parts of cities may be changed on the basis of big data, without personal data of the inhabitants being required for the analysis. In this scenario, the application phase is fully outside the scope of data protection law.

In sum, whether the Regulation applies to big data depends on whether personal data are processed, and whether and in which phase of big data personal data are processed depends on the particular big data project. However, general conclusions can be drawn as to the likelihood of each of the four categories of data being processed in each big data phase. All types of data can be processed in the acquisition phase. Identifiable data are often collected, but non-identifiable data are collected as well. In the analysis phase, identifiable data may be processed, but it is often unnecessary, and there are strong incentives to de-identify the data. Data that have been acquired as (directly or indirectly) identifiable in the acquisition phase will often have been de-identified. Consequently, the analysis phase is not necessarily covered by data protection law, even though it is in essence the origin of many of big data's negative effects. Alternatively, the combination of different datasets in the analysis phase can create new personal data. In the

---

IP addresses are not always personal data per se, *see Scarlet/SABAM* (n 441); *Breyer* (n 516). If, in a given case, one would be able to argue that an IP address and cookie do not constitute personal data, the regulation would not be applicable to this situation in which the knowledge of big data is applied to individuals.

540. Article 29 Working Party, 'Opinion 4/2007 on the Concept of Personal Data' (n 508) 15–16.

541. Cf. Schreurs and others (n 538) 254.

application phase, identifiable data may be processed to apply the model or knowledge derived from the previous two phases to an individual. In this case, the Regulation applies, but only to the limited amount of data that is used to target the individual. In the application phase the material scope does not include the model itself. It is also possible that no identifiable data are processed at all, leaving the application phase completely outside the material scope of data protection law. Table 4.1 shows the resulting eight hypothetical processing scenarios. This overview shows that the applicability of EU data protection law can differ according to each processing phase. In practice, many different scenarios occur, and combinations within phases are also possible. Data protection law applies to a phase if identifiable (i.e., directly or indirectly identifiable) data are processed, and does not apply when non-identifiable (i.e., de-identified or non-personal) data are processed.

Table 4.1 Processing Scenarios

	Acquisition	*Analysis*	*Application*
1	non-identifiable	non-identifiable	non-identifiable
2	non-identifiable	non-identifiable	identifiable
3	non-identifiable	identifiable	non-identifiable
4	non-identifiable	identifiable	identifiable
5	identifiable	non-identifiable	non-identifiable
6	identifiable	non-identifiable	identifiable
7	identifiable	identifiable	non-identifiable
8	identifiable	identifiable	identifiable

To give examples, most of which refer back to earlier illustrations: an example of the first scenario is meteorological big data projects, in which no personal data are processed. The situation in which aggregate data on shopping behaviour is bought and analysed, leading to models that are applied using people's loyalty cards (connected to identifiers), falls under scenario 2. In the biobanking example, personal data can be collected and subsequently de-identified, after which general decisions on treatment of specific diseases can be taken, which classifies as scenario 5. The credit scoring example from the financial services industry matches with scenarios 6 and 8.[542] If for any reason the data are not de-identified before entering analysis, it is scenario 7. Scenarios 3 and 4 are improbable, since creating identifiable information from non-personal data in the analysis phase

542. *See* subsection 2.3.1 of Chapter 2.

generally requires additional identifiable data (to be acquired in the acquisition phase).[543] Given the incentives and goals of big data, scenarios 5 and 6 are most likely to occur in the context of big data as described and delineated in Chapter 2. These different scenarios show once more that we need to assess what happens in big data in order to determine how data protection law applies to it and what its protective potential is, instead of declaring data protection applicable to big data as a whole. Table 4.2 summarises which types of data are processed in each of the phases of the big data process based on the four different types of data.

Table 4.2 Types of Data in Each Phase of the Big Data Process

Type of Data	*Phase*		
	Acquisition	*Analysis*	*Application*
Directly Identifiable Data	Yes	Yes, but incentive to de-identify	Yes, but limited
Indirectly Identifiable Data	Yes	Yes, but incentive to de-identify New data may be created	Yes, but limited
De-identified Data	Yes	Yes	Yes
Non-personal Data	Yes	Yes	Yes

4.3.3 Concluding Remarks

Data protection law only applies when personal data are processed; it does not apply to the processing of non-identifiable data. This dichotomy between identifiable and non-identifiable data is necessary in contemporary data protection law. A line needs to be drawn between data that are within the scope of data protection and data that are not regulated by it; otherwise, all (digital) information would be governed by data protection legislation. This would not be realistic, workable, or possible in practice. Nor would it match the balance that data protection law should achieve between protecting the rights and freedoms of the individual, while also enabling the free flow of data. Moreover, it would not even be desirable from the perspective of the protection of individuals, as it would water down the protection that the law

543. It is unlikely but theoretically possible, given the GDPR's definitions. From datasets that count as non-identifiable (de-identified or non-personal) datasets under the GDPR, personal data can be derived; legal non-personal data does not equal technical anonymous data. *See* for example Narayanan and Shmatikov (n 525).

offers.[544] Nonetheless, the distinction between identifiable and non-identifiable data is difficult to apply in practice, and it results in the only partial applicability of data protection to big data.

In the acquisition phase, all types of personal data (*directly identifiable, indirectly identifiable, de-identified,* and *non-personal*) can be processed. If directly identifiable data are collected, it is likely that these will be stripped of identifiers as soon as possible, turning the data into indirectly identifiable data, or 'anonymised', made into de-identified data. This is likely, because it diminishes the risks and consequences of security breaches, and as de-identified data are not regulated by data protection law, it alleviates the burden of compliance. For the protection of individual rights and freedoms through data protection law, this means that there is protective potential in the acquisition phase, since data in this phase are often within data protection law's material scope. The substantive norms of data protection law apply, as long as identifiable data are processed, and de-identifying identifiable data requires a legitimate processing ground.[545] Although the individual has no rights with respect to non-identifiable data in the acquisition phase, once these data are combined with identifiable data, they become identifiable data and thus enter the scope of data protection law.

The protective potential in the analysis phase seems rather fragmented. It is often unnecessary to process identifiable data during analysis, because big data is predominantly focused on general knowledge, categorisation, models, and predictions, instead of on information about specific individuals. Moreover, here de-identification also decreases risks and removes the burden of compliance, so there are strong incentives to de-identify before analysis. Identification may even be necessary, given the data protection by design and default obligations of the controller.[546] Given the likelihood that non-identifiable data are processed, the analysis phase shall often be beyond the material scope of data protection law, and because the substantive norms do not apply, data protection law has no protective role to play.

In the application phase two scenarios are possible. In the first scenario, an individual is affected by general big data decisions for which no personal data are processed. In such cases, the application phase is outside the scope of data protection. In the second scenario, an application phase decision is aimed at a specific individual. In this scenario, personal data are often processed, but the *amount* of personal data processed is usually rather limited. Predictive models or profiles, for example, do not necessarily require much personal data to be applied as input and are not personal data themselves. Consequently, because of the different ways in which big data can be applied to individuals, the applicability of data protection law in the

544. Cf. Zwenne (n 520).
545. *See* subsection 4.4.2.1.
546. *See* subsection 4.4.3.2.

application phase is very much dependent on the particular circumstances of the case.

Even when the application phase is within the scope of data protection law because personal data are used to apply big data's results to individuals, only the application phase itself is within the material scope of data protection law. After all, each phase and instance of processing needs to be judged on its own merits; the fact that personal data are processed in the application phase does not mean that personal data of the same individual are included in the data processing in the preceding acquisition and analysis phases. The substantive norms of data protection law therefore only apply to the application phase; personal data processing in the acquisition and analysis phases is not automatically drawn into the scope of protection when the application phase of big data is regulated by data protection law. In other words, there is a gap between the 'big' data that are processed in the acquisition and analysis phase on the one hand, and the limited amount of data used in the application phase on the other hand.

In sum, in all three phases personal data can be processed, but the material scope of data protection law, hinging on identifiability, is an insurmountable obstacle in the way of full protection of individual rights and freedoms through EU data protection law. The protective potential of data protection law's substantive norms of the following sections should primarily be sought in (or through) the acquisition phase and, to a lesser extent, the application phase, since these phases are expected to be covered by data protection law, substantially and partially respectively.

4.4 SUBSTANTIVE DATA PROTECTION NORMS

This section evaluates the application of the substantive data protection norms to the big data process, and the protection they offer against big data's negative impact on individual rights and freedoms. EU data protection contains many substantive data protection norms that can facilitate the protection of individual rights and freedoms in big data. Although opinions differ on whether EU data protection law is essentially risk regulation or whether it is inherently based on the concept of informational self-determination, the GDPR contains rules that reflect both ideas.[547] As they complement each other in big data, this section focuses on the potential of both types of rules. The substantive norms of the GDPR that are relevant for the protection of individual rights and freedoms in the context of big data can be grouped according to what they aim to achieve: making processing transparent and providing the individual with information, giving the

547. Cf. Raphaël Gellert, 'Data Protection: A Risk Regulation? Between the Risk Management of Everything and the Precautionary Alternative' (2015) 5 International Data Privacy Law 3, 5–7 and Koops (n 494) 21, and the sources cited therein.

individual control over her personal data, and regulating certain risks associated with personal data processing. The transparency rules are also a precondition for control: if an individual does not know that her personal data are being processed, who is doing this, and what the processing consists of, it is impossible for her to accomplish effective control over her personal data. Informational self-determination is essentially at the heart of the rules on transparency and control.[548] The rules of the third group on the other hand restrict the use of personal data, and contain obligations with respect to data protection impact assessments (DPIAs) and privacy by design/default, and consequently reflect a more risk-based approach. Grouping the evaluation of data protection's provisions into transparency, control, and risk mitigation allows us to draw conclusions on what approach seems to fit which big data issues best and whether an approach may never work, which serves as input for suggestions on improvements in Chapter 6.

Each of the following subsections broadly contains an explanation of the (new) rules and how they contribute to the protection of individual rights and freedoms, an analysis of how the rules apply in big data, and an evaluation of the extent to which the rules realise their potential in big data practice. The subsections pay specific attention to GDPR innovations, because these innovations were designed to respond to challenges of globalisation and new technological developments, with amongst others big data in mind, so much is expected of them in this context.[549] The innovations that are selected for discussion in this chapter represent the potential of the Regulation for the protection of individual rights and freedoms in the context of big data. They are the updated rules on automated decision-making including profiling, the right to erasure ('right to be forgotten'), and the right to data portability. Subsection 4.4.3.2 summarises the content of the subsections on transparency, control, and risk, by giving an overview of its potential and limitations.

4.4.1 Transparency

The intrinsic value of transparency and information obligations for individual rights and freedoms lies in limiting information asymmetries and showing the individual what happens with her personal data. This is particularly important for people's data protection right in the sense of

548. Cf. Antoinette Rouvroy and Yves Poullet, 'The Right to Individual Self-Determination and the Value of Self-Development: Reassessing the Importance of Privacy for Democracy' in Serge Gutwirth and others (eds), *Reinventing Data Protection?* (Springer 2009).

549. 'A Comprehensive Approach on Personal Data Protection in the European Union' (2010) Communication from the Commission to the European Parliament, the Council, the Economic and Social Committee and the Committee of the Regions COM(2010) 609 final 2–5, 18–19.

informational self-determination, to preserve people's personal autonomy, and to create awareness about discrimination. Transparency is also of instrumental value for individual rights and freedoms, as information is necessary to effectuate the control rights that are discussed in subsection 4.4.2. Through providing individuals with information, people can, for example, regulate the use of their data for health research purposes through consent, or object to automated decisions or evaluative measures in credit scoring. Such claims or objections are impossible without a measure of transparency.

4.4.1.1 Information to Be Provided at the Time of Acquisition of Personal Data

As part of the principle of fair and transparent processing (Article 5 (1) (a) GDPR), controllers have to inform individuals about the processing of personal data. Articles 13 and 14 of the Regulation stipulate what information has to be provided to individuals when the data are collected from them, or acquired through other means, respectively. Article 15 GDPR gives the data subject the right to access personal data that controllers hold about her, subject to amongst others reasonability conditions and respect for the rights and freedoms of others.

The information that has to be provided to the individual can be divided into: (1) *contact details,* (2) *information on the processing,* and (3) *restatements of rights of the data subject*. The contact details of the controller and the data protection officer ensure that the data subject knows who is processing her personal data and to whom to address her requests and claims. Regarding the processing, the data subject needs to be informed about the purpose and ground of the processing (Articles 5 (b) and 6 (1) GDPR), possible third party recipients, retention periods or criteria, and if the personal data are not collected from the data subject, also about the categories of personal data that are processed and the source of the data. The rights that need to be declared are the individual's rights of access, rectification, erasure, withdrawal of consent, and the possibility of lodging a complaint with a supervisory authority (Articles 7 (3), 15–17, 77 GDPR).[550]

Regarding the provision of information, Article 12 (1) GDPR states that the information should be provided 'in a concise, transparent, intelligible and easily accessible form, using clear and plain language'. Recital 58 of the Regulation shows that this provision was made with complex data processing in mind, such as big data:

---

550. This is a summary of the content of Articles 13 and 14 GDPR, with the exception of the obligations of Articles 13 (2) (f) and 14 (2) (g) to inform about automated individual decision-making, including profiling. These merit special attention due to their content and the fact that they specifically apply in the acquisition phase, hence they are discussed separately in the ensuing subsection.

This is of particular relevance in situations where the proliferation of actors and the technological complexity of practice make it difficult for the data subject to know and understand whether, by whom and for what purpose personal data relating to him or her are being collected, such as in the case of online advertising.

To summarise, at the time of acquisition of data the individual has to be provided with comprehensive and comprehensible information about the identity of the controller, the purposes of the processing and retention of personal data, and the rights that she has. If the data are acquired from the data subject herself, there is no possible exception to the controller's obligation to inform (Article 13 GDPR). However, in a big data context, these obligations do not function optimally. In addition, when the data are obtained not from the individual herself but through other means, for example through combining existing data sets or buying them from a data broker, Article 14 GDPR applies, which does contain exceptions. Both issues are explained below.

There are four justifications for not providing the data subject with information under Article 14 (5) of the Regulation, of which the second is the most important in the context of big data. No information needs to be provided if 'the provision of such information proves impossible or would involve a disproportionate effort'. If this exception applies, the individual does not have to be informed, but Article 14 (5) GDPR stipulates that the controller must take measures to safeguard the rights and interests of data subjects. This includes making the information accessible to the general public, for example, through publishing a publicly available privacy policy on the controller's website. An appeal to this exception is conceivable in big data, given the burden that the provision of information would constitute, in view of the amount of personal data that is not acquired from the data subject herself and newly created personal data, for example, in the online personalisation case. The individual can still demand the same kind of information on the basis of the access right of Article 15 (h) GDPR in such cases. However, this is somewhat paradoxical and probably useless, as in this scenario the individual has not received any information about the data processing. In other words, we can always request information from any company, but if we are not aware that it holds our personal data in the first place, the guarding and empowering function of transparency is a bit lost.

If the information obligations apply, there is a further difficulty with their functioning in big data. Often in a digital environment, but particularly in the acquisition phase of big data, it is doubtful whether controllers are able to properly inform data subjects about the purposes of the processing. This is closely connected to the principle of purpose limitation that is discussed in subsection 4.4.3.1. The potential applications of the results of the analysis in the application phase are often (partially) unknown at the moment of collection. As explained in Chapter 2, applications of big data are usually not entirely clear beforehand: much enthusiasm about big data can be summarised by the idea that big data can answer questions that have not yet been asked. And the value of big data lies not so much in the data itself, but in the outcomes of the analysis: the information, models, and insights obtained through big data.[551] These are often unknown in the acquisition phase, as organisations frequently do not yet know how valuable the data are going to be and what they will be used for.[552] Of course, general purposes of analysis and application may be known, such as marketing purposes or product enhancement. However, these purposes usually do not meet the requirements of specificity, and consequently, if not specified in greater detail, the transparency obligations are not met.[553]

As we shall see in subsections 4.4.1.2 and 4.4.2.1, information and transparency are inextricably linked to automated individual decision-making, including profiling, and consent. Difficulties surrounding properly informing individuals about data processing are a big stumbling block for achieving protection of individual rights and freedoms through consent, where even more obligations with respect to informing data subjects apply. But before turning to that point, the following subsection first reviews information obligations that relate specifically to the application phase of big data.

4.4.1.2 Logic Behind Automated Decision-Making

This subsection looks at the specific information duties with respect to automated decision-making. The provisions containing these duties are directed at big data-like types of personal data processing and aim at making the process of generating automated individual decisions, and the resulting consequences, more transparent for the individuals concerned.

Articles 13 (2) (f) and 14 (2) (g) GDPR on the information duties of the controller pay specific attention to *automated decision-making and profiling*. Neither the Directive nor the Regulation gives a definition of automated individual decisions, and originally the drafters of the Regulation did not intend to include a definition of profiling either.[554] However, following the

551. Bart Custers and Helena Uršič, 'Big Data and Data Reuse: A Taxonomy of Data Reuse for Balancing Big Data Benefits and Personal Data Protection' (2016) 6 International Data Privacy Law 4, 4.
552. Cate and Mayer-Schönberger (n 82) 68.
553. Articles 13 (1) (c), 5 (1) (b) and Article 29 Working Party, 'Opinion 03/2013 on Purpose Limitation' (n 111) 16.
554. Article 4 Proposal for a Regulation of the European Parliament and of the Council on the protection of individuals with regard to the processing of personal data and on the free movement of such data (General Data Protection Regulation), *COM(2012) 11 final*, 2012.

advice of the Working Party, a definition of profiling was added to Article 4 of the GDPR:[555]

> 'Profiling' means any form of automated processing of personal data consisting of the use of personal data to evaluate certain personal aspects relating to a natural person, in particular to analyse or predict aspects concerning that natural person's performance at work, economic situation, health, personal preferences, interests, reliability, behaviour, location or movements.[556]

Hence, automated individual decisions based on an *evaluation of personal aspects* of a natural person through personal data processing, constitute *automated individual decisions* in the sense of Article 22 GDPR. For the rules to be applicable, however, personal data must be processed (Article 2 (1) jo. 4 (1) GDPR and subsection 4.4.2). This means that the transparency obligations only exist if personal data are used for the evaluation. When a model is applied to an individual based on limited personal data of that individual, such as in the credit scoring example, the obligations apply. However, when no personal data are used for a decision, such as in the medical research example when certain drugs are not reimbursed anymore, or in the behavioural targeting example when people are targeted on the basis of group profiles and no personal data are processed to make decisions, the rules on automated decision-making, including profiling, are not triggered.[557] The scope of Article 22 GDPR is limited due to a number of factors, expounded on in subsection 4.4.2.2.

In this context, the information duties ensure that individuals are aware of the fact that they are profiled or subjected to other kinds of automated decision-making in the big data process. With respect to the *processing* part of profiling, i.e., when personal data are collected for the purpose of making an automated decision about that specific person, the general obligations to inform of Articles 13–15 GDPR apply. In the case of automated decisions and profiling, controllers also have to inform the data subject that automated individual decisions are being taken and/or that they are being profiled, as well as provided with 'meaningful information about the logic involved, as well as the significance and the envisaged consequences of such processing' (Articles 13 (2) (f) and 14 (2) (g) GDPR). As Article 15 of the Regulation gives the data subject a right of access that also pertains to information about profiling (Article 15 (1) (h) GDPR), automated decision-making, and the logic behind it, so the individual can also request this information herself at any time during the processing.

---

555. Article 29 Working Party, 'Advice Paper on Essential Elements of a Definition and a Provision on Profiling within the EU General Data Protection Regulation' (2013).
556. This definition is equally important for other rights on automated individual decision making, *see* subsection 4.4.2.2.
557. Schreurs and others (n 538) 254–256.

Explaining that profiling or other types of automated decision-making takes place does not seem to be difficult in the context of big data: information can be provided when decisions are being made. More complicated is the obligation to explain what the consequences and significance are for the data subject, and provide her with 'meaningful information about the logic involved'. Although the purpose of the evaluation of people or the decision can be known and clear, the reference to 'consequences' instead of the common GDPR expression 'purposes' indicates that merely stating the purpose of the decision is not enough. It seems insufficient for the controller to merely state her objective: she has to put herself in the position of the data subject, asking herself what future effects of the profiling or decision-making are relevant for the individual. The consequences of data processing can be far-reaching for individual rights and freedoms, not least because of the possible cumulative and long-term effects emanating from the application phase. It is unclear what the scope of this obligation is in big data, i.e., how far the obligation of explaining the consequences stretches, given what is necessary to inform and protect the individual vis-à-vis what can be reasonably expected of the controller.

The third part of the information obligation, the duty to provide information about the *logic* behind the decision, is the most interesting for big data. Algorithmic transparency has become a major topic on the agenda of NGOs, policy-makers, and academics in fields such as law, sociology, and computer science.[558] The EDPS summarises it as follows: 'as a society, we must be able to look into the "black box" of big data analytics in order to ensure that any particular analytics application can be safely deployed and will benefit us all'.[559] However, the potential of the GDPR's transparency obligation regarding the logic of decision-making and profiling depends on its scope.

Unfortunately, the exact scope of the obligation to give meaningful information about the logic involved is not clarified in the Regulation. Bygrave deems that the explanation of the logic behind a decision should at least contain information about 'the data categories which are applied, together with information about the role these categories play in the decision(s) concerned'.[560] There have been calls for specifically including the personal data on which the decision-making is based, as well as their source, in the transparency obligation, but this has not been transposed into

558. *See* amongst others Frank Pasquale and Danielle Keats Citron, 'The Scored Society: Due Process for Automated Predictions' (2014) 89 Washington Law Review; Pasquale (n 170), <https://epic.org/algorithmic-transparency> accessed 28 December 2016. Ben Wagner, 'Draft Report on the Human Rights Dimensions of Algorithms' (Council of Europe 2016) MSI-NET(2016)06.

559. European Data Protection Supervisor, 'Meeting the Challenges of Big Data: A Call for Transparency, User Control, Data Protection by Design and Accountability' (n 111) 10.

560. Lee Bygrave, 'Minding the Machine: Article 15 of the EC Data Protection Directive and Automated Profiling' (2001) 17 Computer Law & Security Report 17, 20.

the final Regulation.[561] Such an obligation would be a heavy burden on the controller that could also interfere with other people's rights and freedoms, as it is *their* data on which the knowledge and models used for the automated decision are based. Given these difficulties and the fact that it is not included in the Regulation, it seems unlikely that the obligation stretches as far as to include information about data of others and their sources. Considering the rationale behind transparency, both in general and in particular vis-à-vis objecting to automated decision-making,[562] it is more reasonable to expect that the explanation should clarify how decisions are taken, on which classification, criteria, methods, or model they are based, being both meaningful and 'concise, easily accessible and easy to understand', in clear and plain language.[563]

Still, such an obligation is not easy to apply properly in the application phase of big data.[564] How the big data process works and why it produces certain outcomes is difficult to comprehend, often even for the controller herself.[565] What exactly happens in the analysis phase and how this translates to the application phase is very difficult to explain and comprehend, because of the complexity and the possible use of machine learning algorithms. Because big data builds on correlations and not on causal relationships,[566] it is often impossible to give a definitive answer to the question of on what information the decision is based or why a decision has been taken. There may even be no such thing as *logic* behind big data decision-making. And if it is already difficult for controllers to understand the big data process, it is nearly impossible for the average data subject to understand what happens when she becomes part of big data and what the consequences will be. This leads to what Barocas and Nissenbaum call the 'transparency paradox': it is impossible to give the data subject complete information while at the same time informing her in an understandable way, because big data is simply too complex.[567]

Regarding the exception to the transparency obligation where the data are not acquired from the data subject herself: Article 14 of the Regulation also applies to automated individual decision-making, including profiling. This means that amongst others information does not have to be provided if this would be a disproportionate effort for the controller, or if it would make the realisation of the processing purposes impossible or very difficult. An

561. European Data Protection Supervisor, 'Meeting the Challenges of Big Data: A Call for Transparency, User Control, Data Protection by Design and Accountability' (n 111) 10.
562. *See* Article 22 GDPR and subsection 4.4.1.2.
563. Recital 58 GDPR.
564. Mireille Hildebrandt, 'The Dawn of a Critical Transparency Right for the Profiling Era', *Digital Enlightenment Yearbook 2012* (IOS Press 2012) 53–54
565. Cf. Jenna Burrell, 'How the Machine "Thinks": Understanding Opacity in Machine Learning Algorithms' (2016) Big Data & Society 1, 10.
566. Mayer-Schönberger and Cukier (n 83) 50–72.
567. Barocas and Nissenbaum (n 536) 2.

appeal by a big data controller to this exception is possible in big data, but in most cases of profiling and automated decision-making providing the profiled individual with information will not be disproportionate. Profiling or automated decision-making generally has a specific purpose, such as the offer or refusal of credit in the financial services illustration. In such cases, if the controller can evaluate the data subject and offer her something, the link will be strong enough to also enable the controller to reach out with information. In other cases, the exceptions can apply, the more because the controller does not have to actively seek identification of individuals to comply with the Regulation (Article 11 GDPR).

4.4.2 Control

EU data protection law puts much emphasis on individual control over personal data as a means of achieving the protection of data subjects. Combined with transparency, control rights empower the individual, giving her the tools to effectuate her own protection. This section homes in on the control rights that hold protective potential for individuals in big data.

The basic assumption of these rights is informational self-determination, individual control over one's personal data. Processing of personal data requires a legitimate processing ground, e.g., consent, and if personal data are processed the data subject has multiple possibilities to object to the (further) processing. From the perspective of the autonomy of the individual, a free and informed choice of the individual justifies the processing of personal data, and as such the idea of individual control seems clear and indisputable. However, in big data there are a number of issues with the mechanisms of control that limit their protective potential for individual rights and freedoms. The following subsections discuss consent and rights in relation to automated individual decision-making as the prime provisions to control the processing of personal data in the acquisition and application phases of big data. The focus then shifts to rights that are deemed innovations of the GDPR, being the right to erasure/right to be forgotten, and data portability, as part of control, to see whether the GDPR improves data protection law's capability to deal with big data issues in comparison to Directive 95/46/EC.

4.4.2.1 Legitimate Basis for Processing: Consent

Personal data may only be processed when there is a legitimate legal basis for processing (Article 5 (1) (a) GDPR).[568] This protects privacy and data

568. This principle is also laid down in Article 7 OECD Privacy Guidelines (n 23); Article 5 Convention 108 (n 23); Article 8 (2) Charter, and Article 6 Directive 95/46/EC.

protection through limiting the situations in which personal data may be processed and giving individuals the possibility to consent to processing, combined with the information duties as described above. But it also has potential for the protection of other individual rights and freedoms, notably personal autonomy, because individuals can decide for themselves when and how they want to have their personal data processed. However, as we shall see, its practical implementation is problematic in big data practice. After mapping out the principle and explaining the six possible grounds for personal data processing, this section zooms in on consent.

The regulation contains a closed list of grounds that make processing legitimate, as a specification of this general lawfulness principle. Processing is allowed when one of the following six grounds applies (Article 6 (1) GDPR):

(a) the data subject has given consent to the processing of his or her personal data for one or more specific purposes;
(b) processing is necessary for the performance of a contract to which the data subject is party or in order to take steps at the request of the data subject prior to entering into a contract;
(c) processing is necessary for compliance with a legal obligation to which the controller is subject;
(d) processing is necessary in order to protect the vital interests of the data subject or of another natural person;
(e) processing is necessary for the performance of a task carried out in the public interest or in the exercise of official authority vested in the controller;
(f) processing is necessary for the purposes of the legitimate interests pursued by the controller or by a third party, except where such interests are overridden by the interests or fundamental rights and freedoms of the data subject which require protection of personal data, in particular where the data subject is a child.

Processing personal data on grounds that are not enumerated is prohibited; however, some grounds are flexible.[569] This applies to all processing of personal data within the scope of the Regulation, with the exception of special categories of data for which the law contains specific requirements that are stricter, *see* Articles 9 and 10 and subsection 4.4.3.1. There is no hierarchy in the list and none of the grounds is generally preferred over others. However, in certain situations one of the grounds can be more suitable and therefore preferred, or the only one on which processing can be based given the circumstances. For example, authorities should not

569. *ASNEF* (n 455) [30–32].

ask the data subject for consent if they would process the data on the public-interest ground if consent is refused, as this would be misleading.[570]

In big data, the two most-used grounds are the legitimate interests ground (also called the 'balancing provision') of Article 6 (1) (f) GDPR and consent of Article 6 (1) (a) GDPR. The other four processing grounds are generally not applicable, for a number of reasons. Processing necessary for a contract (sub b) can occur somewhere in the big data process, but the contract ground only applies to data necessary for the entering into or performance of a contract. Therefore data cannot subsequently be used for other purposes, like big data analytics, when the initial acquisition was based on the contract ground. The same holds for compliance with a legal obligation (sub c): personal data that are processed to comply with a legal obligation cannot subsequently be used for big data purposes on the same legal ground. The vital interests ground (sub d) can only be used to protect an interest that is essential for someone's life, like processing personal data by emergency services in the case of an accident.[571] Processing on the basis of a public interest task (sub e) should have a basis in (national or EU) law[572] or in the exercise of official authority by the controller.[573] Use of this ground by public authorities for big data purposes is not ruled out, but in addition to this specific legal basis, processing must also be *necessary* for the specific public interest task or exercise of authority. Largely because of the necessity criterion it may be more appropriate for authorities wishing to get involved in big data to rely on another ground, like consent. Because of this, and because big data controllers are more often than not non-governmental entities, the public interest task is not discussed in more detail in this section. What is left are the legitimate interests ground and consent.

The legitimate interests ground is also referred to as the 'balancing provision', as it is about finding a balance between the legitimate interests of the controller (or a third party) and the rights and interests of the data subject. If the rights and interests of the data subject do not prevail over the legitimate interest that the controller or a third party pursues, personal data may be processed on the basis of Article 6 (1) (f) GDPR. Recital 47 indicates that the 'reasonable expectations' that the data subject has on the basis of her relationship with the controller should be taken into account in the balancing. A successful appeal to Article 6 (1) (f) GDPR therefore requires that the processing of the data matches the reasonable expectations that the data subject has of the controller and what the controller does with the data. The Working Party explains this as it being about the scope, time, and purpose of

570. *See* for example Article 29 Working Party, 'Opinion 15/2011 on the Definition of Consent' (2011) WP 187 13, 15–16.
571. Recitals 46 and 112 General Data Protection Regulation.
572. This legal basis must meet the criteria from the case law of the Court of Justice of the European Union and the European Court of Human Rights, Recital 41 General Data Protection Regulation.
573. Recitals 45 and 50 General Data Protection Regulation.

collection, and whether the data subject could have reasonably foreseen the processing.[574] The context and impact of the processing are thus of decisive importance. Therefore, whether the balancing provision can be applied is very much dependent on the particular circumstances of the case. Nevertheless, the fundamental rights to privacy and data protection are always a factor in the balancing.[575] They cannot be heedlessly surpassed and should weigh heavily against, for example, the commercial interests of controllers.

Recital 47 of the Regulation gives general descriptions of factors, but these are not specific and practical enough to be of much use. The Working Party has tried to fill this gap, which already existed under the Directive, by publishing an extensive opinion on the balancing provision in which different contexts and examples are explored.[576] In this opinion the Working Party explains that combining large amounts of data that were originally collected for other purposes in different contexts, as well as trading in data without safeguards and related profiling activities, cannot be based on the balancing provision.[577] If processing is based on the balancing provision, the data subject has the right to object to the processing, also when the data are processed for statistical purposes (Article 21 (1) and (6) GDPR). If there are no compelling grounds that override the interests, rights, and freedoms of the individual, the controller must comply with the request and cease to process the personal data.

According to the Working Party, as soon as it is a matter of targeting, price discrimination, and attempting to influence an individual, the processing cannot be based on the balancing provision.[578] The Working Party judges the application phase of big data as incompatible with the balancing provision. Many authors seem to implicitly agree, as they focus on consent instead of on the balancing provision in their discussions of big data, while at the same time explaining how problematic this is for big data processing.[579] It is most certainly problematic for big data entities, because, as we shall see, valid consent is difficult to achieve in big data. It could be argued that, depending on the context, small and non-invasive processing in big data can be based on the balancing provision, particularly if only used for the application and analysis phases. This would give big data entities more

574. Recital 47 General Data Protection Regulation.
575. Articles 7 and 8 of the Charter.
576. Cf. Recital 30 Directive 95/46/EC; Article 29 Working Party, 'Opinion 6/2014 on the Notion of Legitimate Interests of the Data Controller under Article 7 of Directive 95/46/EC' (2014) WP 217.
577. *Ibid* 26.
578. *Ibid* 31.
579. Cate and Mayer-Schönberger (n 82) 67; Bart Custers, 'Click Here to Consent Forever: Expiry Dates for Informed Consent' (2016) Big data & Society 1, 1; Yann Padova and Viktor Mayer-Schönberger, 'Regime Change? Enabling Big Data Through Europe's New Data Protection Regulation' 17 The Columbia Science and Technology Review 315, 321–323.

liberty and be an alternative for problematic consent situations (*see* below). From the perspective of individual rights, however, processing on the legitimate interests ground instead of on consent would mean less control, and consequently much less potential protection, because people's data can be processed without their permission.[580]

Not only in theory, but also in big data practice, consent is often the ground on which controllers base their processing.[581] Consent has become the primary mode of lawful processing online.[582] It is easier to provide evidence of a data subject's consent than to have certainty beforehand that, when all interests and rights at stake are balanced against each other, the controller has a legitimate interest that surpasses the interests of the individual and makes the processing of the data subject's personal data necessary. Consent is the only legal ground for processing without a necessity criterion; contrary to the other processing grounds, with consent, personal data can be processed even if processing is not necessary for the controller or a third party. However, this does not mean that it is automatically easier to obtain consent than to base personal data processing on one of the other five legal grounds.

Article 4 (8) of the Regulation gives criteria for consent, by stating that it means 'any freely given, specific, informed and unambiguous indication of [the data subject's] wishes, either by a statement or by clear affirmative action […]'. There are four main criteria in this definition: (1) *freely given*, (2) *specific*, (3) *informed*, and (4) *unambiguous indication of wishes, by statement or clear affirmative action*. When any one of these criteria is not met, consent is invalid. The Directive's definition of consent is similar, but it does not explicitly demand that the indication of wishes is unambiguous and made by statement or affirmative action.[583] Yet an even bigger change made by the Regulation is the specification of conditions for consent in Article 7 GDPR. Article 7 GDPR states amongst others that controllers should be able to prove that they have obtained consent, that it 'shall be as easy to withdraw consent as to give it', and that the request for consent should be intelligible and easily accessible. Consent is presumed not to be freely given if the 'performance of a contract, including the provision of a service', is unnecessarily made dependent on it, according to Recital 43 of the GDPR.

The problems with consent in big data can be divided into two categories. In the first place acquiring or giving consent can be difficult or

580. Cf. Frederico Ferretti, 'Data Protection and the Legitimate Interest of Data Controllers: Much Ado About Nothing or the Winter of Rights?' (2014) 51 Common Market Law Review 843.
581. Cf. Custers (n 579) 1.
582. Cate and Mayer-Schönberger (n 82) 67.
583. Kosta concludes that Directive 95/46/EC required affirmative action, *see* Kosta (n 491) 167. To a large extent, the extra requirements of the Regulation could be seen as codifications of prevailing interpretations of consent.

impossible because of the *nature* of big data. This problem is discussed below on the basis of the criteria that consent needs to be *specific* and *informed*. Second, it is possible that, even if legitimate consent has been realised, consent is insufficient to protect the individual against the negative consequences of big data.

The first issue is that valid consent needs to be 'informed' (Article 4 (11) and Recitals 32 and 42 of the Regulation). Informed consent is a well-known problem that does not only occur in the context of big data.[584] However, it is aggravated due to the *nature* of big data.[585] It implies that the data subject understands the facts and consequences of the processing and consent; information must be provided about all relevant aspects of the processing.[586] It also refers to the information obligations that the controller has under Articles 13 and 14 GDPR which, as explained earlier, amongst others concern information on what kind of personal data are processed for which purposes, who will acquire the data and what the rights of the data subject are, and the logic behind the decision-making. And the information has to be presented 'in an intelligible and easily accessible form, using clear and plain language' (Article 7 (2) and Recital 42 of the Regulation). As explained in subsections 4.4.1.1 and 4.4.1.2, given the difficulties with these obligations, not least the transparency paradox,[587] informed consent is a utopia in big data.

The second difficulty with consent is the specificity requirement, which is linked to the informed requirement. Consent is only valid when it is given in relation to one or more specific purposes (Article 6 (1) (a) GDPR). 'Purposes' of Article 6 (1) (a) of the Regulation has to be interpreted in accordance with the principle of purpose limitation and further processing of Article 5 (b) GDPR. This principle states that personal data may only be collected for 'specified, explicit and legitimate purposes', and that further processing must not be incompatible with the original purpose. According to the Working Party, the specificity requirement demands that, in that addition to the purposes, the scope and consequences of the data processing must be declared; consent should only apply within this specific context.[588] Therefore the request for consent cannot be vague. For the data subject, it needs to be clear what data are processed and why, and which processing activities are

584. There has been an ongoing discussion on (informed) consent in medical research and with respect to cookies, for example.
585. Cate and Mayer-Schönberger (n 82); Barocas and Nissenbaum (n 536); Alessandro Mantelero, 'The Future of Consumer Data Protection in the E.U. Re-Thinking the "Notice and Consent" Paradigm in the New Era of Predictive Analytics' (2014) 30 Computer Law & Security Review 643.
586. Article 29 Working Party, 'Opinion 15/2011 on the Definition of Consent' (n 570) 19.
587. The impossibility of providing the individual with information that is at the same time complete and understandable, because of the complexity of big data. *See* Barocas and Nissenbaum (n 536) 2 and subsection 4.3.2.1.
588. Article 29 Working Party, 'Opinion 15/2011 on the Definition of Consent' (n 570) 17.

within and beyond the scope of a given purpose. It needs to be clear for what purposes the data shall be processed *before* the consent is sought and the data collected. When the consent that is sought and given is too broad, it is invalid (Article 6 (1) (a) GDPR).[589]

The Working Party is of the opinion that processing of personal data for statistical purposes in big data can be covered by the notion of further processing.[590] This means that if personal data are acquired for a non-big data purpose in the acquisition phase, the ground on which the initial collection is based suffices for the analysis phase. The current legal bases for this assumption are Recital 50 and Articles 5 (1) (b) and 89 (1) GDPR, with the disclaimer that statistical purposes imply de-identification of personal data, and for the de-identification a legitimate processing ground is required. Yet for any kind of evaluation of, or decision-making about, individuals, separate consent is required.[591] In other words, consent given for big data analysis does not imply that consent is given for the application of knowledge or models, e.g., targeting or profiling, as this would clash with the reasonable expectations of the data subject and be incompatible with the original purpose. In sum, consent given for acquisition could stretch to the analysis phase if the data are de-identified (for which consent or another legitimate ground is required), but if the data are not de-identified, it is necessary to ask consent for analysis, specifying amongst others the purposes. Application requires specific consent.

Specifying the purposes of analysis can be difficult in big data. The idea of big data is, after all, to collect and combine datasets, often repurposing the data, in order to find new correlations and knowledge that can subsequently be used in ways that are not necessarily conceived of at the beginning of the process.[592] At the moment of collection the specific purpose of the processing is often unknown or unclear, and vague purposes like 'big data analysis' do not meet the criteria of purpose limitation.[593] The notion of 'further processing' only offers a partial solution, since this type of processing cannot be too far removed from the original purpose, as would be the case with, for example, the commercial analysis of personal data acquired for human resources purposes. In many cases it will be impossible to legitimately base big data processing on consent, because the consent would become too broad to be acceptable.[594] The consequence of these issues with both the balancing provision and consent, is that in practice they will be applied anyway, since they are usually the only two grounds of Article 6 (1) GDPR that are not completely ruled out beforehand (*see* above). This creates a discrepancy

589. For special categories of personal data, like data that reveal race or genetic data, or consent by children, special rules apply. *See* Articles 8 and 9 Regulation.
590. Article 29 Working Party, 'Opinion 03/2013 on Purpose Limitation' (n 111) 28.
591. *Ibid* 47.
592. Cf. Chapter 2 and Custers and Uršič (n 551) 4–5.
593. Mantelero (n 585) 652. *See also* subsection 4.3.3.1.
594. Padova and Mayer-Schönberger (n 579) 325–326.

between black-letter law and the application of legal provisions in practice, resulting in a decrease of protection for individuals.

The last big problem of consent in big data is the illusion of consent as an instrument to protect and achieve individual control in a digital environment. On the Internet people are confronted with requests for consent and privacy policies on a daily basis, yet this information is not regularly read.[595] In the context of big data, Kuner and others remark that the largest database in the world could probably be made up of obligatory yet unread privacy notices.[596] There are numerous reasons why these privacy policies are not read and why, despite much research, a solution to this issue has yet to be found.[597] Reading all privacy notices one is confronted with online would take incredible amounts of time, particularly as data collection is so widespread and common nowadays.[598] Reading them all would be an unfeasible burden on the individual; in 2008, researchers estimated that reading them would take more than a week of non-stop reading a year, or more than half an hour every day.[599] The texts are often long, unreadable, and complicated; comprehensive yet complicated and vague texts can be a formality used by controllers to dodge responsibility.[600] Moreover, on the Internet individuals often face a monopolist and a denial of services if one does not agree with the conditions regarding personal data sharing. This constrains free choice or even makes it impossible.[601] And even if people are offered and have absorbed all the information, they still make (irrational) choices in practice that do not match with their stated preferences and concerns.[602] Confronted with information overload both in terms of the information in a privacy policy and the number of consent requests online, people are inclined to simply accept without thinking.[603] Reasons are amongst others being tempted by benefits, such as being allowed to visit a website, using a service, receiving discounts, or using free apps, not being able to foresee the long-term consequences, or resignation to the idea that

595. Solove, 'Privacy Self-Management and the Consent Dilemma' (n 493) 1884.
596. Kuner and others (n 82) 48.
597. Cf. Zuiderveen Borgesius, *Improving Privacy Protection in the Area of Behavioural Targeting* (n 538), Chapter 7.
598. Solove, 'Privacy Self-Management and the Consent Dilemma' (n 493) 1888–1889.
599. Aleecia M McDonald and Lorrie Faith Cranor, 'The Cost of Reading Privacy Policies' (2008) 4 I/S: A Journal of Law and Policy for the Information Society 543.
600. Ravi Inder Singh, Manasa Sumeeth and James Miller, 'A User-Centric Evaluation of the Readability of Privacy Policies in Popular Web Sites' (2011) 13 Information Systems Frontiers 501; Cate and Mayer-Schönberger (n 82) 68.
601. Lee Bygrave and Dag Wiese Schartum, 'Consent, Proportionality and Collective Power' in Serge Gutwirth and others (eds), *Reinventing Data Protection?* (Springer 2009) 160.
602. Alessandro Acquisti and Jens Grossklags, 'Privacy and Rationality in Individual Decision Making' (2005) 3 IEEE Security & Privacy 26, 30–32.
603. Bart Schermer, Bart Custers and Simone van der Hof, 'The Crisis of Consent: How Stronger Legal Protection May Lead to Weaker Consent in Data Protection' (2014) 16 Ethics and Information Technology 171, 176–179; Custers (n 579) 3.

privacy and data protection on the Internet are a lost cause.[604] As Solove summarises: '(1) people do not read privacy policies; (2) if people read them, they do not understand them; (3) if people read and understand them, they often lack enough background knowledge to make an informed choice; and (4) if people read them, understand them, and can make an informed choice, their choice might be skewed by various decision making difficulties'.[605] In a digital big data environment, consent lacks effectiveness to be truly protective of individuals.

4.4.2.2 Automated Individual Decision-Making, Including Profiling

Automated individual decision-making has been discussed above with respect to the information duties regarding the logic behind decisions. However, the GDPR contains more rules on automated individual decisions. They seem to hold considerable potential for mitigating the negative effects of the application of big data on individual rights and freedoms, but many of the rules' criteria do not fully match with contemporary big data practices. The protective potential and limitations of the rules are elucidated below.

Protection in the context of automated decision-making was described as a 'core data protection principle, […] indispensable for defining the future agenda of data protection law and policy' as early as 2001.[606] The Regulation maintains the automated decision-making provision of Article 15 of the Directive but builds on it by adding profiling-specific rules to the automated decision-making provision, as well as to the information obligations described above and the right to object described below. Much is expected of these profiling provisions in the context of big data, because the rules potentially limit processing in the application phase of big data, where the risk of big data negatively affecting individuals is most prominent. The potential of the automated decision-making and profiling rules for the protection of individual rights and freedoms lies primarily in the protection against discrimination and loss of autonomy that it can offer. Through the rights, individuals can potentially prevent themselves being profiled and becoming part of discriminatory or manipulative decisions.

The rules on automated individual decision-making and profiling are found in section 4 of Chapter 2 on the principles of data protection. This

604. Tene and Polonetsky, 'Big Data for All: Privacy and User Control in the Age of Analytics' (n 84) 67; Antoinette Rouvroy, 'Of Data and Men: Fundamental Rights and Freedoms in a World of Big Data' (Bureau of the Consultative Committee of the Convention for the Protection of Individuals with Regard to Automatic Processing of Personal Data [ETS 108] 2016) T-PD-BUR(2015)09REV 23.
605. Solove, 'Privacy Self-Management and the Consent Dilemma' (n 493) 1888.
606. Bygrave, 'Minding the Machine: Article 15 of the EC Data Protection Directive and Automated Profiling' (n 560) 22.

section is titled 'Right to object and automated individual decision-making' and contains two articles: Article 21 GDPR on the right to object and Article 22 GDPR on automated individual decision-making, including profiling. At first glance, the articles seem similar. Both provide the individual with a right to refuse to be profiled. Upon closer examination the rights are distinct, and focus on different aspects of automated decision-making, including profiling.

Article 21 (1) GDPR provides individuals with the right to object to the processing of personal data, including profiling:

> The data subject shall have the right to object, on grounds relating to his or her particular situation, at any time to processing of personal data concerning him or her which is based on point (e) or (f) of Article 6(1), including profiling based on those provisions. The controller shall no longer process the personal data unless the controller demonstrates compelling legitimate grounds for the processing which override the interests, rights and freedoms of the data subject or for the establishment, exercise or defence of legal claims.

Article 21 GDPR is based on the right to object of Article 14 of the Directive and focuses on the *processing* part of profiling. It only applies when the processing is based on either the public interest ground or the balancing provision of Article 6 GDPR.[607] This seems limited, but it is explicable; as for consent there is the possibility to withdraw consent (Article 7 (3) GDPR), and for compliance with a legal obligation or the vital interests of the data subjects or others (Article 6 (1) (d) GDPR), it seems to be a deliberate choice of the legislator: vital interests and legal obligations override the preferences of the individual.

Article 22 (1) of the Regulation gives the individual the right not to be subject to an automated decision:

> The data subject shall have the right not to be subject to a decision based solely on automated processing, including profiling, which produces legal effects concerning him or her or similarly significantly affects him or her.

The right consequently does not apply to all automated individual decisions: the decision should create legal effects for the individual, or 'similarly significantly affect' her. In comparison to Article 21, Article 22 concentrates on the *decision* instead of on the processing.[608] Article 22 GDPR is based on Article 15 of the Directive, which regulates automated

607. Profiling is mentioned in Article 21 GDPR and in the heading of section 4 of Chapter 2 of the Regulation, but the right to object concerns personal data processing in general, *including* but not limited to profiling.
608. Bygrave, 'Minding the Machine: Article 15 of the EC Data Protection Directive and Automated Profiling' (n 560) 17.

individual decision-making in a similar way, and on the CoE's recommendation on profiling.[609] Article 22 also prohibits automated individual decisions based on the special categories of personal data of Article 9 GDPR such as race, health, or religion, except when the data subject's explicit consent is allowed and given (Article 22 (4) jo. 9 (2) (a) GDPR), or when it is necessary for reasons of substantial public interest and safeguards are in place (Article 22 (4) jo. 9 (2) (g) GDPR).

Profiling is a subset of automated individual decisions; the right bestowed upon an individual by Article 22 (1) GDPR also exists when automated individual decisions that do not qualify as profiling are concerned. Together Articles 21 and 22 GDPR give the data subject the possibility to oppose both the *processing* of personal data for profiling purposes and automated individual *decisions,* that may include profiling. But each provision also contains exceptions that limit the data subject's rights. In the case of an objection to (further) processing based on Article 21 (1) GDPR, the controller does not have to comply with the request if he proves that there are 'compelling legitimate grounds [...] which override the interests, rights and freedoms' of the individual, or if the personal data are processed for the 'establishment, exercise or defence of legal claims'. The right not to be subject to a fully automated decision does not apply if the decision is based on the explicit consent of the data subject or on a contract between the controller and data subject (Article 22 (2) (a) and (c) GDPR). In these cases, safeguards must be in place, which includes giving the data subject the possibility of obtaining human intervention from the controller and contesting the decision (Article 22 (3) GDPR). Additionally, if there are sufficient safeguards in place, Member States may implement other exceptions to the right not to be subjected to automated decisions in national law (Article 22 (2) (b) GDPR).

Summarising on the basis of the previous subsection and the transparency rules analysed in subsection 4.4.1.2, there are five main rules on profiling and automated decision-making: (1) the controller's *obligation to provide information*, (2) the data subject's *right of access to information*, (3) the data subject's right to *object to personal data processing*, (4) the data subject's right to *oppose automated individual decisions*, including profiling, and (5) the *prohibition* on automated decision-making based on *special categories of personal data*. The rules cover the whole big data process, but they do not apply under all circumstances. Most importantly, for the rules to apply there needs to be processing of personal data (Article 2 (1) jo. 4 (1) and subsection 4.2). If personal data are used to make the decision to target or profile the individual, Article 22 GDPR is applicable. But if the input for

609. Recommendation CM/Rec(2010)13 of the Committee of Ministers to member states on the protection of individuals with regard to automatic processing of personal data in the context of profiling 2010; Explanatory Memorandum to the General Data Protection Regulation 2012 9.

application of the decision does not constitute personal data, e.g., when people are targeted as groups, on the basis of group profiles that do not require personal data as input, or when general automated decisions that are not targeted at a specific individual are taken, the rules do not apply.[610]

In the application phase, data subjects have rights to actively resist automated decisions and profiling, through objecting against processing and by being able to refuse to be subjected to automated individual decision-making, which includes profiling. However, big data controllers can refuse the request of the data subject, if they have 'compelling legitimate grounds' (Article 21 (1) GDPR). If, for example, taking the specific data out of normal processing operations would be too big a burden whereas the risks for the data subject might at the same time be reduced, for example, because the data are pseudonymised, it seems reasonable to judge the refusal legitimate. Yet because of the absence of a definition of 'compelling legitimate grounds' in Article 21 (1) GDPR, it is impossible to say with certainty where the boundaries of legitimate refusal lie in practice.

The general possibilities to object and contest decisions, but in particular the prohibition of profiling and decision-making on the basis of special categories of data, counter discrimination in the application phase. The fact that Article 22 (4) GDPR is formulated as a prohibition for the controller instead of as a right that the data subject can invoke adds further weight to the protection. Individuals can also demand human intervention in the decision-making process, express their views, and challenge the decisions. This right to be heard and judged by humans instead of machines also supports personal autonomy.

The first issue is the scope of the right not to be subjected to automated decisions, including evaluative measures based on personal aspects. Of course, these decisions need to be based on personal data and targeted at the individual, so the rules do not cover the full application phase.[611] General decisions taken on the basis of knowledge that the analysis phase yields are outside the scope of Article 22 GDPR. And as the decisions need to have legal effect or 'similarly significantly affect' people, many big data applications are not covered by the rules. An effect which is similar to legal effects is a high threshold, also because the recitals refer to evaluations at work or credit applications.

The second issue is that the right to resist an automated decision of Article 22 GDPR is subject to three criteria, some of which clearly limit the scope of the right in the application phase of big data. The first criterion is that there needs to be a decision, which includes evaluative measures based on personal aspects of the data subject. Second, this decision should be based solely on automated processing. This means that when human decision

610. Schreurs and others (n 538) 254–255.

611. The Regulation only applies when personal data are processed, *see* Article 2. As this topic is extensively explained in section 4.2, it is not discussed in further detail here.

makers enter the big data decision-making or evaluation process, Article 22 GDPR does not apply and the individual cannot invoke the right not be subjected to the profiling or other decision. In the credit scoring case, for example, if credit is rejected based on big data analysis and predictions that lead to a score, and the individual is notified about the rejection face to face or through a phone call by an employee of the credit company, Article 22 GDPR does not apply. Decisions made by machines but communicated by people are beyond the scope of the automated individual decision-making rules. Third, the decision or evaluation must produce legal effects or 'similarly significantly affect' the individual. The notion of 'similarly significantly' is not expounded on in the Regulation. Recital 71 of the Regulation gives two examples of decisions that meet all the criteria enumerated above: the automated refusal of an online credit application and fully automated e-recruiting. In the context of profiling (as a subspecies of automated decision-making), the Recital mentions the analysis or prediction of personal aspects such as work performance, economic situation, health, preferences, reliability, behaviour, and location. But to this it adds the legal effects or *significantly affect* criterion, which implies that profiling based on the aforementioned personal aspects will not necessarily give the data subject the right not to be subjected to that type of profiling. The Working Party has argued that its successor, the EDPB, should be able to give guidance on this matter,[612] and Recital 72 of the Regulation also alludes to this. But until such guidance is offered, whether a specific decision or evaluative measure in big data 'significantly affects' an individual in the sense of Article 22 GDPR remains difficult to determine and must be judged on a case-by-case basis. Therefore, not all applications of big data that affect individuals lead to a right not to be subjected to that automated decision.

Automated decision-making or profiling may not be based on special categories of data, a measure which is intended to protect individuals against discriminatory treatment (Article 22 (4) GDPR). However, one particular characteristic of the big data process, discussed in section 2.5.2 and warned against by authors such as Barocas and Selbst, is that in big data, decisions or profiling can be based on non-special categories of data that serve as proxies for special categories of personal data.[613] In other words, even if special categories of personal data are not in the data set, other variables can correlate with personal data on, for example, race, health, or religion, and the profiling thus results in (intentional or unintentional) indirect discrimination.[614] Correlations can be obscure and hidden, and often it will not be the intention of the controller to discriminate. Although one might argue that this type of profiling is prohibited under Article 22 (4), it is also possible to

612. Article 29 Working Party, 'Advice Paper on Essential Elements of a Definition and a Provision on Profiling within the EU General Data Protection Regulation' (n 555) 4.
613. Calders and Žliobaitė (n 201) 49, 52–53; Barocas and Selbst (n 3).
614. Schermer (n 88) 49.

maintain that, since no special categories of data are processed and the profiling is based on different variables, this does not fall under Article 22 GDPR's prohibition. Moreover, even if it would fall under the prohibition, it would be difficult for controllers to detect the discrimination due to the particular characteristics of big data as described above, let alone reasonable to expect the individual to discover it.

But the biggest question related to the limitations of the profiling rules is similar to the issues regarding withholding consent described in the previous subsection: what happens if someone invokes her right to object or not to be subjected to an automated decision? Will that result in a refusal of services? A refusal of services is not prohibited by data protection law, and will generally be legitimate. External factors that were brought up before, like network effects, the difficulty with overseeing the consequences and valuing privacy and data protection, and the temptation of getting discounts or free services, have a strong influence on whether people will object to certain practices.[615]

All in all, the rules on automated decision-making and profiling facilitate the protection of individual rights and freedoms, notably privacy, data protection, non-discrimination, and personal autonomy, in the application phase of big data. As such, they could be(come) a core part of data protection in the context of big data as well.[616] However, when a decision does not target an individual, does not significantly affect her, or when the process is not fully automated, the application phase is outside the scope of Article 22 GDPR.[617] The provisions have their limitations in terms of applicability, and their potential depends on how the open norms will be filled in and how the rights will be effectuated in practice.

4.4.2.3 Right to Erasure

Here, the protective potential of the right to erasure in the context of big data is analysed (Article 17 GDPR). Article 17 GDPR is titled 'Right to erasure ("right to be forgotten")' and gained notoriety through the landmark right to be forgotten case, *Google Spain*.[618] In this case the CJEU decided, on the basis of the right of access and the right to object (Articles 12 (b) and 14 (a) Directive), read in conjunction with Articles 7 and 8 of the Charter, that individuals have the right to be delisted from search engine results and thus a (limited) right to be forgotten. At that time, the Regulation had not yet been

615. Hildebrandt, 'The Dawn of a Critical Transparency Right for the Profiling Era' (n 564) 51–52.
616. *See* the introduction under 4.2.
617. This criterion is not explicitly referred to as such in Article 22 itself, but the heading of the article contains the word 'individual' and the wording of both Article 22 and Recital 71 indicate individuals.
618. *Google Spain* (n 50).

adopted, but the case certainly raised and framed the discussion on Article 17 of the GDPR. Through this right to be forgotten element, Article 17 GDPR has an important function for the protection of privacy against an Internet that never forgets and gives others eternal access to information once it has been put online, although it may also have a chilling effect on freedom of expression.[619] However, Article 17 GDPR, based on the right to erasure of Article 12 (b) of the Directive, also has a second function.[620] It backs up other data protection rights, by giving data subjects rights to terminate the processing of personal data by having their personal data erased. In big data, the hiding from public view element is not of great concern, but the possibility to get data removed from the big data process shows potential for the protection of individual rights and freedoms, notably for the right to data protection and personal autonomy. This subsection explains what the right to erasure is and how it works in the big data process, concluding with an evaluation of its potential for the protection of individual rights in the context of big data.

Erasure in Article 17 of the Regulation is not only formulated as a right that can be claimed by the data subject but also as an obligation for the controller (Article 17 (1) GDPR). The obligation to erase the data exists if one of the grounds for erasure under sub (a)–(f) applies, which can be summarised as an obligation to erase when processing is unlawful under the Regulation.[621] Article 17 (3) GDPR lists the exceptions to the right to erasure, which are freedom of expression, establishing and exercising legal claims, and legitimate processing such as compliance with a legal obligation or a public interest task (Article 6 GDPR), reasons of public health in accordance with Article 9 GDPR, and archiving purposes in the sense of Article 89 (1) GDPR.

Apart from having to erase the data, the controller also has the duty to take 'reasonable steps, including technical measures' to inform other controllers that the data subject has demanded the erasure of personal data, if the (primary) controller has made these data public (Article 17 (2) GDPR). 'Public' is not defined in the Regulation, but read in conjunction with Article 19 GDPR, it likely refers to making the personal data available to any recipient not being the controller or processor itself. Although this rule may seem broad and disproportionately burdensome on the controller, the rationale behind it is probably that the first controller should have the responsibility when making personal data publicly available, as it has the

619. *See* in general on the 'right to be forgotten' Jef Ausloos, 'The "Right to Be Forgotten" – Worth Remembering?' (2012) 28 Computer Law & Security Review 143. On chilling effects: Stefan Kulk and Frederik Zuiderveen Borgesius, 'Google Spain v. González: Did the Court Forget About Freedom of Expression?' (2014) 5 European Journal of Risk Regulation 389; Giovanni Sartor, 'The Right to Be Forgotten: Balancing Interests in the Flux of Time' (2016) 24 International Journal of Law and Information Technology 72.
620. Explanatory Memorandum to the General Data Protection Regulation (n 609).
621. Sartor (n 491) 65–66.

power to prevent others from becoming controllers through repeating the publication of the personal data. An example is news websites that can prevent their web pages from becoming indexed by search engines' web crawlers through using the robots exclusion standard (robot.txt). But when the controller has not made the data public, she also has obligations to inform third parties: according to Article 19 GDPR, she must let every third party that has received the personal data from her know about the request for erasure, unless this would be disproportionate or impossible. She must also inform the data subject about these recipients if the data subject so desires.

The applicability of the right to erasure spans the whole big data process. In the application phase, where processing is often based on consent, the data subject can withdraw her consent (Article 7 (3) GDPR) after the controller has the obligation to remove the data (Article 17 (1) (b) GDPR), or demand erasure because she deems processing unlawful because of, for example, the lack of a legitimate ground (Article 17 (1) (d) GDPR).[622] Similar requests can be made in the analysis phase and application phase, with the addition of the possibility of the right to object to the processing of personal data as the basis for erasure (Article 17 (1) (c) jo. 21 (1) GDPR). Except for the processing for statistical purposes exception of Articles 17 (2) (d) and 89 (1) GDPR, it is not expected that the exceptions of Article 17 (2) GDPR shall apply in the context of big data. When personal data are de-identified and therefore count as anonymous and non-identifiable for the Regulation, of course no right to let these data be erased exists.[623]

The additional rules of Article 19 of the Regulation, requiring the controller to notify the recipients of the personal data to be erased and the data subject to be informed about these recipients, are an interesting addition in the case of big data. It means that the data subject can request erasure with the big data entity that processes the data, but also with other entities that are controllers of her personal data, controller currently being quite a broad definition.[624] For example, in the case that the personal data in the big data process are not acquired from the individual herself, the individual could request erasure from the party who collected the data from her, this party then being under the obligation to inform the big data entity about the erasure request. Article 19 GDPR creates a chain of notices and information duties when data have been transferred to parties other than the controller, and the individual can file her request with any controller in this chain. This applies throughout the whole big data process.

In effect, the right to erasure supports other data protection rights of the individual. It adds weight to the withdrawal of consent and the right to object and automated processing rules, by letting the data subject claim for erasure of personal data in addition to the termination of the unlawful processing.

622. *See* subsection 4.4.2.1.
623. *See* section 4.2.
624. *See* for example *Google Spain* (n 50) [28].

But it is not so much an innovation as a detailed continuation of the right to erasure of Article 12 (b) Directive,[625] with limited added value. After all, the bases on which the individual can claim erasure can be summarised as processing that is unlawful on the basis of other rights and principles of data protection.[626] Independent from the right to erasure, the data subject can also contest the processing on the basis of these other rights and principles, or through the withdrawal of consent or making use of the automated decision and profiling rules.

The notification obligation of Article 19 GDPR shows potential, because it takes the particularities of the current digital ecosystem into account: data are rarely collected by one controller, under whom they remain for the rest of their lifespan. However, the provision is limited in two ways. First, the controller does not have the obligation to notify the recipients of the data, when it would be impossible for her or 'involves disproportionate effort'. As with many of the open terms of the Regulation, the concept of 'disproportionate effort' is not elucidated anywhere. 'Disproportionate' clearly implies that impracticability is not a reason to refuse erasure; the assessment will likely be high. Nevertheless, what is proportionate and disproportionate remains vague. Second, the controller only has the obligation to *inform* both the recipient and the data subject. Therefore, after meeting this obligation, the responsibility to effectuate full erasure, i.e., erasure not only by the controller contacted by the data subject, but by all parties who have received the personal data and now process it, shifts back to the data subject. In spite of the transfer of data having been an action by the initial controller, probably with economic benefits, the data subject has to go to the effort of making sure these recipients also respect her right to erasure. Although full responsibility on the initial controller with respect to recipients would probably be a heavy burden on the controller,[627] from the perspective of the rights and interests of the individual, notably data protection and personal autonomy, the provisions could have been made stronger and more protective.[628]

In sum, the possibility to get big data entities to erase personal data that they have is important for the protection of individual rights and freedoms. However, in the context of big data where amongst others the value of Article 17 GDPR in the public right to be forgotten context is irrelevant, the right to erasure is a restatement and complementary safety net to the other rights of the data subject, rather than an innovation of special value.[629]

625. Koops (n 493) 258.
626. Sartor (n 491) 71.
627. Which would nevertheless be alleviated by the previously mentioned disproportionate efforts doctrine.
628. *See also* Alessandro Mantelero, 'The EU Proposal for a General Data Protection Regulation and the Roots of the "Right to Be Forgotten"' (2013) 29 Computer Law & Security Review 229, 234–235.
629. *See* the introduction to this subsection under heading 4.3.

4.4.2.4 Data Portability

This subsection assesses the GDPR's new right to data portability (Article 20 GDPR) in the context of big data. It finds that data portability is primarily directed at consumer-facing Web 2.0 services, such as social networks, but that it may have (indirect) beneficial effects in the context of big data.

Data portability can be seen as an evolution of the Directive's right of access (Article 12 Directive).[630] It gives data subjects the right to 'receive the personal data concerning him or her, which he or she has provided to a controller, in a structured, commonly used and machine-readable format', and the right 'to transmit those data to another controller without hindrance from the controller to which the personal data have been provided' (Article 20 (1) GDPR). As such, it has both a competition dimension and a consumer protection dimension; it was most likely created with social networking sites in mind.[631] Data portability is slightly different from the other rights discussed in this section, because data portability's function for the protection of individual rights and freedoms in big data lies just as much in the control it gives to individual users as in its potential to alter the current digital landscape, where big corporations are able to behave as monopolists.

The right to data portability as per Article 20 GDPR essentially consists of two parts: (1) the right to *receive* personal data from a controller, which corresponds to the earlier access right, and (2) the right to *transmit* those data unhindered to another controller.[632] This combined right only exists when the personal data have been provided to the controller by the data subject herself (Article 20 (1) GDPR) on the basis of either consent or a contract (Article 20 (1) (a) GDPR). Accordingly, data portability is primarily designed for consumers creating profiles and interacting with corporations online; other contexts in which other bases for processing apply, such as personal data that governments have about citizens, are excluded from data portability's scope (Article 20 (3) GDPR). For many big data projects it holds no relevance, such as the medical research and credit scoring illustrations, although it could find application in some, such as the online personalisation example.

According to Article 20 (1) GDPR, the personal data have to be provided in a 'structured, commonly used and machine-readable format', which is, like many of the Regulation's concepts, quite an open term.[633] This phrasing aims to find a middle way between being too strict by ordaining open or specific proprietary formats, and data portability becoming a paper tiger because of an absence of format criteria. Interoperability is encouraged,

---

630. Anita Bapat, 'The New Right to Data Portability' (2013) 13 Privacy and Data Protection 3, 3; Explanatory Memorandum to the General Data Protection Regulation (n 609).
631. Inge Graef, Jeroen Verschalken and Peggy Valcke, 'Putting the Right to Data Portability into a Competition Law Perspective' (2013) Law: The Journal of the Higher School of Economics 53, 62–63.
632. Zanfir (n 491) 157.
633. *Ibid.*

but controllers are not forced to create systems that are compatible with those of their (potential) competitors.[634] If technically feasible, the personal data should be directly transferred by the initial controller to the new controller, without the data subject having to receive or send/upload the data (Article 20 (2) GDPR). Under (4), explicit mention is made of the need to respect the rights and freedoms of other individuals in complying with the data portability request.

The right to data portability is not really a right that is used by individuals in the big data process to change how big data works for them. Data portability can be used to change to a different controller, but this does not automatically force the initial controller to remove the data and stop processing them (Article 20 (3) GDPR). The data subject could combine his data portability demand with an erasure request on the basis of Article 17 GDPR,[635] but the aim of data portability is not the erasure, but the *transfer* of the personal data: keeping the data and allowing them to be used by a different controller. As such, the right operates primarily outside of the big data process, because big data is the 'back-processing' by the controller for his own purposes, whereas data portability is the simultaneous 'front-processing' that the data subject has supplied, sees, and needs for making use of services online.

The truly innovative aspect of the right to data portability, which may have an effect on big data, is the right to *transmit* personal data to other controllers. By giving people the right to transfer their personal data unhindered by the controller they first provided it to, switching services and controllers will be made easier for data subjects. As such, it empowers individuals and supports their personal autonomy in addition to protecting their right to data protection. Notwithstanding its adaptation in data protection law and its connection to people's digital identity,[636] data portability is also about consumer empowerment, free choice, and a fear of lock-in and monopolies.[637]

The right to transmit may also have other, indirect positive effects. Because it is easier for individuals to switch services, the hope is that they will more readily do so, particularly when confronted with undesired practices, like manipulation and discrimination. As such, it is facilitative for many individual rights and freedoms, provided that it achieves its aims of changing the digital ecosystem. The latter aspect is the biggest limitation of the right to data portability: it is highly questionable whether it will achieve its aims, particularly as this depends on the knowledge and actions of data

634. Recital 68 and Article 20 (3) General Data Protection Regulation.
635. *See* subsection 4.4.2.3.
636. Zanfir (n 491) 151.
637. Peter Swire and Yianni Logos, 'Why the Right to Data Portability Likely Reduces Consumer Welfare: Antitrust and Privacy Critique' (2013) 72 Maryland Law Review 335, 349; Bapat (n 630) 4; Graef, Verschalken and Valcke (n 631) 57–60.

subjects, on which digital skills and network effects are probably very influential.[638] Moreover, even if the right will be used by individuals, the effects in practice could also be detrimental to data subjects' consumer interests.[639] As the scope of the right is still unclear, and there is no certainty about the effects of data portability in the future, it is impossible to conclude anything definite. The idea of data portability shows potential for the protection of individual rights and freedoms in theory, but its relevance depends on how it will be employed in practice, and the expectations are not very high.

4.4.3 Risk Mitigation

In addition to organising transparency and control for data subjects, data protection law also mitigates risks associated with personal data processing. The extent to which contemporary EU data protection law can be considered to be risk-regulation is open to question, but it is clear that to prevent certain risks of data processing turning into actual harm, there are provisions that do not focus on transparency and individual control.[640] Instead, the regulator has chosen to either limit the processing that is allowed under the law or imposed obligations on the controller with respect to mapping and preventing the risks associated with personal data processing in her organisation. For big data, the limitations on processing with the most potential for protecting individuals concern the processing of special categories of data (Article 9 GDPR), purpose limitation (Article 5 (1) (b) GDPR), and data minimisation (Article 5 (1) (c) GDPR). The obligations on the controller that could be valuable for the protection of individual rights and freedoms are those on DPIAs (Article 35 GDPR) and data protection by design and default (Article 25 GDPR). As they are linked to, or overlap with, other provisions elucidated above, their application in the context of big data is only briefly discussed below.

4.4.3.1 Special Categories of Data, Purpose Limitation, and Data Minimisation

Recital 51 of the GDPR states that 'Personal that are, by their nature, particularly sensitive in relation to fundamental rights and freedoms merit specific protection as the context of their processing could create significant risks to the fundamental rights and freedoms'. Article 9 (1) GDPR prohibits the processing of the enumerated special categories of data, also referred to as 'sensitive data', which are data on race or ethnic origin, political opinions, religious or philosophical beliefs, trade union membership, genetic data, data

638. Bapat (n 630) 4.

639. Swire and Logos (n 637) 349–365.

640. Lynskey, *The Foundations of EU Data Protection Law* (n 174) 81–83.

concerning health or sex life, and biometric data when used for identification purposes.[641] The prohibition can be lifted by one of the exceptions of Article 9 (2) GDPR, which include explicit consent, but even this exception can be prohibited by the Member States. It seems that the risks associated with these special categories of data, primarily related to discrimination on one of the sensitive attributes, justify overriding the informational self-determination of the individual, protecting her against herself.[642] In addition, given the risks, there are other obligations with respect to special categories of data, such as Article 22 (4) GDPR's prohibition against basing automated individual decision-making on these categories of data, and the requirement to conduct a DPIA when they are processed (*see* Article 35 and the later paragraphs in this subsection).

The prohibition against profiling people on the basis of sensitive data has been discussed in subsection 4.4.2.2 regarding the application phase. But the processing of special categories of data can also be problematic in the acquisition and analysis phase, for which Article 9 GDPR with its general prohibition and explicit consent exception are relevant. Amongst others, Article 9 protects people's private life through preventing the collection and further processing of sensitive data in the acquisition phase. As can be seen in Figure 2.2 in the conclusion of Chapter 2, although discrimination is not an issue in the acquisition phase, discrimination in the application phase originates from the analysis phase. The prohibition on collecting sensitive data and processing them in the analysis phase could prevent biases and outright discrimination from entering the analysis phase, ultimately preventing discrimination as a result of the application of big data. However, as explained in subsection 2.5.2.3 of Chapter 2 and subsection 4.4.2.2 above, discrimination in big data often happens indirectly, on the basis of variables that correlate with sensitive attributes but do not themselves constitute sensitive personal data in the sense of Article 9 GDPR. As such, the complete set of rules on special categories of data are of relevance and value in the specific scenario of direct discrimination, but they do not offer a solution to discrimination in big data in general.

Just like Article 9 GDPR on special categories of data, the purpose limitation principle of Article 5 (1) (b) GDPR restricts the use of personal data. Purpose limitation has been discussed extensively in this chapter already, such as in subsections 4.4.1.1, 4.4.1.2, and 4.4.2.1, because other provisions like the transparency obligations and consent refer to it and depend on its interpretation. Summarising what has been concluded in these previous subsections on purposes and big data: as the specific purposes may

641. In addition, Article 10 GDPR contains a general ban on the processing of personal data related to criminal offences.

642. Nikolaus Forgó, 'My Health Data – Your Research: Some Preliminary Thoughts on Different Values in the General Data Protection Regulation' (2015) 5 International Data Privacy Law 54, 57.

be unclear at the moment of acquisition of the personal data, as repurposing is a common practice, and because the concept of 'purpose' cannot be overly broad, there are irreconcilable problems with the proper application of purpose limitation and big data per se.[643] Theoretically, purpose limitation has protective potential as a restriction on processing, particularly in combination with the control rights of subsection 4.4.2. However, given the uncertainties with respect to its scope and the anticipated incompatibility with big data's aims, the actual protective potential seems limited.

The data minimisation principle of Article 5 (1) (c) GDPR relates to the purpose limitation principle, because it holds that personal data should be 'adequate, relevant and limited to what is necessary in relation to the purposes for which they are processed'. This is somewhat ambiguous, as the limitation to what is necessary is in the first place dependent on how broadly the purpose of processing is construed (*see* above) and in the second place depends on the definition of 'necessary', which is a quintessentially context-dependent concept. But setting aside the ambiguity of the definition, the mere *idea* of data minimisation already clashes with big data. On the theoretical level, the principle seems difficult to comply with, because of the friction between minimisation and big data's characteristic of gathering as much data as possible for multiple different, and possibly yet unknown, purposes. The actual assessment of what is excessive, however, depends on how broad purposes can be according to the interpretation of DPAs and the CJEU. Although protective of individuals, a very strict interpretation of data minimisation seems improbable, since data collection and processing is considered the foundation of the digital economy, including big data.[644] As Tene and Polonetsky note, 'data minimization is simply no longer the market norm'.[645] While we of course have to be careful in adapting law to practice, and we should not change the law simply because companies do not comply with it, it seems unlikely that a strict interpretation of data minimisation is adhered to in practice. Its restrictive effect on personal data collection and further processing could nevertheless aid a little in the protection of individual rights and freedoms. Much is dependent on how the concept of 'limited to what is necessary' and purpose limitation are interpreted and, for all three provisions in this subsection, how they are enforced.[646]

---

643. Article 29 Working Party, 'Opinion 03/2013 on Purpose Limitation' (n 111); Cate and Mayer-Schönberger (n 82) 68; Mantelero (n 585) 652, Custers and Uršič (n 551) 4–5; Padova and Mayer-Schönberger (n 579) 325–326; Corien Prins and Lokke Moerel, 'On the Death of the Purpose Limitation Principle' (International Association of Privacy Professionals 2015) Working Paper.
644. 'Towards a Thriving Data-Driven Economy' (2014) Communication from the Commission to the European Parliament, the Council, the Economic and Social Committee and the Committee of the Regions COM(2014) 442 final.
645. Tene and Polonetsky, 'Big Data for All: Privacy and User Control in the Age of Analytics' (n 84) 260.
646. *See* subsection 4.5.

4.4.3.2 Data Protection by Design/Default and DPIAs

The obligation to implement data protection by design or default and to conduct DPIA require organisations to map the processing in their organisation and implement measures to protect the personal data.[647] Consequently, it forces those engaging in big data to map the risks associated with the processing, and take measures to protect individuals' personal data accordingly. Despite issues with the explanation, implementation, and enforcement of these provisions, the obligation on controllers to assess the processing before engaging in it can be beneficial for the protection of individuals in big data.

Data protection by design is derived from the concept of 'privacy by design', which, in the words of Cavoukian, 'prescribes that we build privacy directly into the design and operation, not only of technology, but also of operational systems, work processes, management structures, physical spaces and networked infrastructure'.[648] In the GDPR, this idea of proactively protecting individuals' data protection rights through consciously implementing them in the architecture of processing systems and using privacy enhancing technologies is implemented in Article 25 (1) GDPR, which reads as follows:

> Taking into account the state of the art, the cost of implementation and the nature, scope, context and purposes of processing as well as the risks of varying likelihood and severity for rights and freedoms of natural persons posed by the processing, the controller shall, both at the time of the determination of the means for processing and at the time of the processing itself, implement appropriate technical and organisational measures, such as pseudonymisation, which are designed to implement data-protection principles, such as data minimisation, in an effective manner and to integrate the necessary safeguards into the processing in order to meet the requirements of this Regulation and protect the rights of data subjects.

The second paragraph of Article 25 GDPR refers to 'privacy by default', demanding that the same technical and organisational measures are used to ensure that the purpose limitation and data minimisation principles are complied with, and that access to the data is properly restricted and secured.

Implementing privacy or data protection by design principles is possible in big data; there are many techniques and technologies available to this

647. The discussion in this subsection follows the order maintained in the GDPR, but ideally the assessment precedes the implementation of data protection by design/default measures.
648. Ann Cavoukian, 'Privacy by Design: The Definitive Workshop' (2010) 3 Identity in Information Society 247, 248.

end.[649] Aiming at a balance between preventing privacy and data protection harm while preserving data quality in the acquisition and analysis phases, its implementation could prevent privacy and data protection harm, primarily in the acquisition and analysis phases.[650] As it is in effect an obligation to comply with data protection law through technical and organisational measures, it supports and reinforces the protective potential of data protection law's substantive norms as described earlier in this section. For example, it aids Article 9 GDPR's function of protecting against discrimination in online personalisation, because it demands that the limitation on processing special categories of data is implemented in the systems that are used to target individuals. The added benefit is that data protection principles, and through them the protection of individual rights and freedoms as elucidated above, get an ex ante effect because they are built into the systems. The controller has to take data principles into account in the design and build them into the system, which may relieve some of the pressure of ex post enforcement by individuals or DPAs.

But, as with many of the GDPR's provisions, it all depends on how the obligation is explained, implemented, and enforced in practice. And with Article 25 GDPR that is a complicated matter. One of the main challenges is the definition of 'appropriate technical and organisational measures', which is obviously vague. This vagueness arguably may make it a weak and unenforceable obligation. Regarding the protection of data against illegitimate access and abuse, security measures must already be in place, due to Article 32 GDPR on security measures, mandatory breach notification under Articles 33 and 34 GDPR, (national) liability, and reputation damage that may result from data breaches.[651] Yet for many other provisions of the GDPR, this is not the case. At the same time, some vagueness is necessary to make the obligation technology-neutral and time-proof, and prevent it from being strict to a point of stifling innovation.[652]

Second, it has been argued and shown that depending on how literally Article 25 GDPR's expression 'meet the requirements of the Regulation and protect the rights of data subjects' is taken, it is very difficult to comply with Article 25 GDPR in practice. Tools and methods to enhance data protection and privacy are available, but a complete transcription of data protection principles into technical and organisational measures is impossible, for many reasons.[653] For instance, many of the GDPR's provisions contain abstract

649. D'Acquisto and others (n 492).
650. Cf. Anna Monreale and others, 'Privacy-by-Design in Big Data and Social Mining' (2014) EPJ Data Science 1.
651. Eric Tjong Tjin Tai, 'Aansprakelijkheid bij datalekken' (2016) 150 WPNR: Weekblad voor Privaatrecht, Notariaat en Registratie 459.
652. Bert-Jaap Koops and Ronald Leenes, 'Privacy Regulation Cannot Be Hardcoded. A Critical Comment on the "Privacy by Design" Provision in Data-Protection Law' (2014) 28 International Review of Law, Computers & Technology 159, 161–162.
653. *Ibid* 164–167.

expressions or open norms that require human interpretation or an extensive assessment. Another example is that complying with one principle can conflict with complying with others. An example is the obligation to collect additional personal data such as birthdate to differentiate between people who can consent and who cannot due to their age, which clashes with data minimisation.[654] Of course, the first sentences of Article 25 GDPR make the compliance obligation less strict, by stating that amongst others the cost of implementation, nature, scope context, purposes, and (degrees of) risks have to be taken into account. But in doing so it also waters down the obligation and makes it difficult to judge when it is met.

In conclusion, as a concept, privacy and data protection by design can be of great value for the protection of privacy and data protection in the acquisition and analysis phase, an effect that could trickle down to the protection of other fundamental rights and freedoms such as non-discrimination and freedom of expression, possibly even in the application phase. Yet by its nature it is not a full-blown data protection right that can easily be enforced in practice, and it is thus dependent on the willingness of big data entities to implement it.

Since the big data process involves new technologies that pose a high risk to individual rights and freedoms and may involve profiling, the Regulation also demands that controllers carry out a DPIA (Article 35 (1) GDPR). This assessment must consist of at least the following points (Article 35 (7) GDPR):

(a) a systematic description of the envisaged processing operations and the purposes of the processing, including, where applicable, the legitimate interest pursued by the controller;
(b) an assessment of the necessity and proportionality of the processing operations in relation to the purposes;
(c) an assessment of the risks to the rights and freedoms of data subjects referred to in paragraph 1; and
(d) the measures envisaged to address the risks, including safeguards, security measures and mechanisms to ensure the protection of personal data and to demonstrate compliance with this Regulation taking into account the rights and legitimate interests of data subjects and other persons concerned.

The DPIA essentially demands that controllers map how the personal data processing works in their organisation, requiring them to review how data protection law applies in their specific case. This is where the omnibus approach of EU data protection law reflects a consciousness of sectoral

654. Ugo Pagallo, 'On the Principle of Privacy by Design and Its Limits: Technology, Ethics and the Rule of Law' in Serge Gutwirth and others (eds), *European Data Protection: In Good Health?* (Springer 2012) 343; Koops and Leenes (n 652) 165–166.

differences and the need to adapt one's behaviour to the particularities of the specific processing context. For the protection of individual rights and freedoms, it is particularly important that controllers are explicitly forced to review the risks to rights and freedoms beforehand, and have to document how they plan to prevent these risks from turning into harm. As such, it has much potential in a way akin to the data protection by design requirement. However, it also suffers from the same weaknesses with respect to enforcement. For obvious reasons, Article 35 does not contain straightforward standards. And although it is clear that controllers should have proof of the impact assessment vis-à-vis DPAs, it is largely up to them how to conduct a DPIA. In practice, instead of focusing on individuals and complying with data protection law, DPIAs could become assessments of legal risks and liability. All in all, however, the fact that controllers have to devote attention to individual rights and freedoms and EU data protection law, could only be seen as beneficial for the protection of individual rights and freedoms in the context of big data.

The findings of this section on substantive data protection norms are summarised in subsection 4.6, which matches them with the level of protection that the normative concepts of the right to privacy and data protection require, as determined in Chapter 3. The following section first discusses the EU enforcement landscape, as an indispensable part of the conclusion on the protective potential of EU data protection law.

4.5 ENFORCEMENT OF DATA PROTECTION LAW

Ultimately, in practice the protective value of EU data protection law for individual rights and freedoms hinges on compliance. And whether big data entities comply with the law depends to a great extent on the sanctions for non-compliance and how the rules are enforced.

Under EU data protection law, if the data subject's rights are infringed, she may seek redress through filing a complaint with a DPA (Article 77 GDPR). Alternatively, she may seek judicial redress and be entitled to compensation for damages (Articles 78–79 and 82 GDPR). However, generally individuals do not tend to enforce their rights.[655] This may be because they do not know about their rights or the infringement, because the infringement is made up of multiple small interferences, because they do not suffer tangible or economic harm, because enforcing rights is a burden that

655. Viktor Mayer-Schönberger, 'Beyond Privacy, Beyond Rights – Toward a "Systems Theory" of Information Governance' (2010) 98 California Law Review 1853, 1874–1877; European Union Agency for Fundamental Rights, 'Access to Data Protection Remedies in EU Member States' (2013) 7.

takes time and could entail high costs, or maybe they simply do not care.[656] Whatever the case, Max Schrems is the exception rather than the rule; we cannot expect individuals to vouch for the protection of individual rights and freedoms in general, and this is also not expected of them, as there are other ways in which data protection law is enforced. NGOs now have the possibility to lodge complaints on behalf of data subjects (Article 80 GDPR), and the GDPR is enforced by DPAs.

EU data protection law has long suffered from a general enforcement deficit, with DPAs having limited powers, and lacking the competence to impose fines on large data processing corporations that could procure a (lasting) deterrent effect.[657] Moreover, there have been concerns over the impartiality of DPAs in multiple countries, their ties to national governments casting doubt on independent oversight over data processing by the authorities, and the possible removal of personal data from the jurisdiction and oversight of DPAs.[658] Fortunately for the protection of individuals, much has changed in recent years. Under the GDPR, fines may be imposed to a maximum of EUR 20,000,000 or 4% of the annual worldwide turnover of a company.[659] It is still not as much as, for example, the 10% of annual total turnover that can be imposed under competition law, yet it is a clear message that is expected to have a deterrent effect on even the largest of companies.[660] The level of the fine is dependent on the data protection rule that is infringed, and the contextual factors that relate to the nature of the infringement and the actions taken by the controller or processor (Article 83 (2) GDPR). Regarding the provisions discussed in this chapter: infringing the transparency or control rules, or those related to special categories of data, purpose limitation, and data minimisation, can lead to a fine up to EUR 20,000,000 or 4% of the annual worldwide turnover of an undertaking (Article 83 (5) (a) and (b) GDPR). If the controller does not meet his obligations on DPIAs and

---

656. Cf. Neil Robinson and others, 'Review of the European Data Protection Directive' (RAND Corporation 2009) 35–36.
657. European Union Agency for Fundamental Rights, 'Data Protection in the European Union: The Role of National Data Protection Authorities – Strengthening the Fundamental Rights Architecture in the EU II' (Publications Office of the European Union 2010) 6, 42–43.
658. *Commission v Germany* (n 459); *Commission v Austria* (n 459); *Commission v Hungary* (n 29); *Schrems* (n 32).
659. Under the Directive imposition of sanctions was largely left to the discretion of the Member States, which did not lead to fines that were commonly perceived as high. Article 24 Directive 95/46/EC and European Union Agency for Fundamental Rights, *Handbook on European Data Protection Law* (Publications Office of the European Union 2013) 132–133.
660. Article 23 (2) and (4) Council Regulation (EC) No 1/2003 of 16 December 2002 on the implementation of the rules on competition laid down in Articles 81 and 82 of the Treaty 2003 (OJ L01/01); Christopher Kuner, 'The European Commission's Proposed Data Protection Regulation: A Copernican Revolution in European Data Protection Law' (2012) Bloomberg BNA Privacy and Security Law Report 1, 12.

privacy by design/default, it can cost him up to EUR 10,000,000 or 2% (Article 83 (4) (b) GDPR).

Higher fines and more powers for DPAs are likely to positively influence compliance with data protection law. Moreover, the increased attention in the media for privacy, the protection of personal data, and the behaviour of companies and governments in this area have put privacy and data protection higher on the agenda of controllers and processors.[661] Reputation is an important asset in the commercial sphere, and losing it can have serious economic consequences.[662] Still, enforcement of EU data protection law through DPAs suffers from a number of serious deficiencies that have been met with strong criticism, and are not completely resolved under the GDPR.[663] The issues identified in the past continue to be relevant; increased fines and cooperation mechanisms will not conclusively solve issues related to enforcement and rights awareness.[664] In particular, the problems of understaffing and lack of financial resources at DPAs will not disappear. Most likely, given the pervasiveness of data processing, these problems have only worsened with the dawn of big data over the past few years. DPAs have to prioritise the allocation of their resources, and can only focus on a tiny proportion of those who process personal data.

4.6 LACUNAE IN PROTECTION VERSUS NORMATIVELY REQUIRED LEVEL OF PROTECTION

This section summarises the overall protection offered by the GDPR in each phase, and homes in on lacunae in the protection of individual rights and

661. Grant and Crowther (n 493) 304–305.
662. *See* for example Verizon's response when it learned about a massive data breach at Yahoo after it had placed a USD 4.8 billion takeover bid. Sam Thielman, 'Yahoo Hack: 1bn Accounts Compromised by Biggest Data Breach in History' *The Guardian* (15 December 2016); James Fontanella-Khan and Hannah Kuchler, 'Verizon Takeover in Doubt after Yahoo Reveals Second Cyber Hack' *Financial Times* (15 December 2016); *See also* Kevin M. Gatzlaff and Kathleen A McCullough, 'The Effect of Data Breaches on Shareholder Wealth' (2010) 13 Risk Management and Insurance Review 61.
663. Cf. Kenneth Bamberger and Deirdre Mulligan, 'Privacy in Europe: Initial Data on Governance Choices and Corporate Practices' 81 The George Washington Law Review 1529, 1549–1550.
664. Douwe Korff, 'Existing Case Law on Compliance with Data Protection Laws and Principles in the Member States of the European Union' 62–64; European Union Agency for Fundamental Rights, 'Data Protection in the European Union: The Role of National Data Protection Authorities – Strengthening the Fundamental Rights Architecture in the EU II' (n 657) 6, 42–43, 50; European Commission (DG Justice, Freedom and Security), 'Comparative Study on Different Approaches to New Privacy Challenges in Particular in the Light of Technological Developments' (2010) DK/100120 43–44; Kristina Irion and Giacomo Luchetta, 'Online Personal Data Processing and EU Data Protection Reform' (Centre for European Policy Studies 2013) 28–29.

freedoms in big data left by the GDPR. It matches these lacunae with the normative concepts of privacy and data protection derived from Chapter 3. The aim of this analysis is to reach a conclusion on the GDPR's potential and limitations for protecting against big data's negative impact, and the extent to which the GDPR *should* protect individual rights and freedoms. To this end, the previous sections on the protective potential and limitations of EU data protection law are summarised. The results are then matched with the negative effects in each phase as described in Chapter 2 (*see* Figure 2.2). On the basis of this analysis, a typology of gaps can be created that gives insight into the underlying problems. These lacunae also indicate whether the normative fundamental rights level demands a different implementation on the secondary EU data protection law level, or whether the issue is beyond the scope of data protection law and requires a different solution.

Some of data protection law's rules do not target one phase in particular. The right to data portability is, as explained, not expected to be of great use in practice, but the obligations on DPIAs and data protection by design and default, hold much protective potential. They force controllers to review their own organisation and processing of personal data and determine how data protection principles apply in their specific situation. Depending on the implementation, principles on security, data minimisation, purpose limitation, and the collection of special categories of data amongst others, would be embedded in the system to a certain degree. This may increase compliance and could prevent interferences with people's privacy and data protection rights and, to a limited degree, discrimination and inequality resulting from big data. Yet, as with all substantive data protection norms, their effect depends to a large extent on how the rules are enforced in practice. *See* Figure 2.2 in Chapter 2.

Three different causes can lie at the root of the lacunae in protection, and the lacunae can thus be divided into the following three types:

(1) *Insufficient protection through the EU privacy and data protection framework:* the EU privacy and data protection framework applies to a big data phase and addresses concerns for individual rights and freedoms in that phase, but the regulation does not or cannot afford protection of individuals regardless of whether their personal data are used.

(2) *Non-regulation, with data processing at its core:* (part of) a big data phase is not regulated by the EU privacy and data protection framework, and therefore the framework as such is of no protective value in this phase. The processing of (non-identifiable) data is at the core of the problem.

(3) *Non-regulation, data processing of negligible significance*: (part of) a big data phase is not regulated by the EU privacy and data protection framework, and therefore the framework as such is of no protective value in this phase. Data processing, whether it be

identifiable or non-identifiable data, is not at the core of the problem; the negative impact is not inextricably linked to the processing of data.

Summarising, the question is whether the negative impact of big data that exists in spite of the EU privacy and data protection law framework is not mitigated by it because its rules do not offer sufficient protection even though they apply (*lacuna 1*), or because the framework is not applicable at all (*lacunae 2 and 3*). In the latter case, the second distinction centres around the question of whether data processing is at the heart of the problem, or whether the negative issue is in essence something else. The following subsections discuss the potential and limitations of data protection law vis-à-vis the negative impact of big data and the lacunae and resulting conclusions on EU data protection law's task in this context for each of the three big data phases.

4.6.1 Acquisition Phase

As concluded in Chapter 2, in the acquisition phase it is the accumulation of personal data, the combination of datasets, and the opacity and complexity of the big data process that negatively affect personal autonomy, privacy and data protection, and freedom of expression. The transparency norms target the opacity and complexity of the big data process. Through the obligations of Articles 13–15 GDPR, people should receive information about the processing, which consists of information about the purposes of the processing, retention times, and possibly the types of data that are processed. However, if the data are acquired from sources other than the individual herself, this obligation can be circumvented through Article 14 GDPR's exception that is likely to apply in the big data process. Moreover, it is questionable to what extent controllers are able to explain the purposes of the processing, and in the acquisition stage there is no obligation to explain the consequences or the logic behind the big data process. These aspects weaken the information duties' ability to overcome problems with autonomous choices and data protection in the acquisition phase.

The negative effects emanating from the accumulation of data in the acquisition phase are mitigated primarily through the control rights. If the controller is able to base the processing on the balancing provision, the principle of lawful processing does not provide individuals with the means to control and restrict the processing of their personal data. Nevertheless, in practice consent is generally the designated processing ground. Consent is complemented by other control rights: the rights to withdraw consent, to object to the processing of personal data, and to erasure. These rights all strengthen the notion of control, provided that the controller does not successfully reject the request on the basis of an exception. And the general prohibition on the processing of special categories of data without explicit consent from the data subject is a strong additional safeguard against the harm that may arise from processing sensitive personal data in the acquisition phase, such as discrimination and privacy violations. In theory, control rights such as consent enable the individual to limit the interferences with her data protection and privacy rights, and can prevent the chilling effects that data collection can have on freedom of expression. However, in practice there are many issues with control rights. Taking consent as an example: in the first place it is difficult for controllers to acquire proper consent due to the requirements that it must be specific and informed. If these requirements are interpreted strictly and according to the Working Party's explanations, it is nearly impossible to acquire valid consent due to big data's specific characteristics, such as its complexity and the uncertainties surrounding future data processing. A wide interpretation would be more workable in practice, but would also considerably weaken the value of consent for the protection of the rights and freedoms of individuals. The second problem is that it has been demonstrated that consent in a digital environment is often illusory, and does not adequately protect individuals. The reasons are manifold: individuals are amongst others overwhelmed by the amount of (complex) information they have to read, they cannot foresee the consequences of consenting to data processing in the long run, or they are tempted by the benefits of consenting, as consent to personal data processing is often the only way to obtain certain services or benefits, such as using social networks. The individual is plagued and tempted from all sides on the Internet, without having a clear perception of the consequences of data processing and big data, or of the importance of privacy and data protection for her as an individual and for society at large.

In conclusion, there is a type 1 lacuna (*insufficient protection*) in the acquisition phase. Data protection law generally applies, because personal data are usually processed during acquisition.[665] To a certain extent, the combination of data protection law's transparency and control rights protects privacy and data protection, and fosters personal autonomy in the acquisition phase. It also has an enabling function for the protection of freedom of expression and non-discrimination, because surveillance and discrimination can be mitigated through exerting individual control over the processing of personal data. But unfortunately, these protection mechanisms are not able to cope with new technological realities and big data. The prime issues are the difficulties with comprehensively explaining big data and its (future) consequences to the average individual, the gargantuan task of online privacy management, the 'privacy paradox', the potential for manipulation, and the lack of oversight compared to the ubiquitousness of data collection.

---

665. *See* Figure 2.2 and Table 4.1 and subsection 4.3.2 in general on the different processing scenarios and the likelihood of personal data being processed for each big data phase.

The acquisition phase is within the scope of the normative concepts of the rights to privacy and data protection, as personal data are processed. However, as the normative concepts primarily demand that individuals have a certain measure of control over their personal data, and that they are protected against abuse and non-authorised surveillance, it seems that the secondary legislative level meets the normative concepts' demands. In the acquisition phase, it is not a case of lacking data protection legislation; it is a matter of established principles that match with the fundamental rights level, yet that do not offer as much protection as they used to due to socio-technological changes. It may be possible to strengthen the transparency and control rights, but in this context it must be mentioned that the GDPR already contains many strict conditions for consent and transparency, that have been made more explicit in comparison to the Data Protection Directive.[666] Moreover, it has been suggested that in a digital environment we should not put too much trust in control as a preferred mechanism of protection, which particularly applies to big data.[667] Due to the forces at play in the digital environment, it is not effective, nor will it become so when accompanied by stricter requirements.[668] Chapter 5 discusses possible alternative solutions to deal with big data issues regarding the acquisition phase as touched upon in this subsection.

4.6.2 Analysis Phase

The analysis phase is a general lacuna in the regulation of big data. As most personal data will have been de-identified before they enter analysis, and these data are therefore outside the scope of data protection law, the means to exert influence over the analysis through the GDPR are virtually non-existent. Consequently, there is a type 2 lacuna (*non-regulation, core = data processing*), as the GDPR likely does not apply, but the issues stem from the processing of usually non-identifiable data.

The analysis phase is the *source* of many of the negative effects that big data can have in the acquisition phase, as here the models or knowledge that are used in the application phase are generated. The biggest problem for individual rights and freedoms seems to be that the people whose data are used for the analysis and the people to whom the outcomes of the analysis are applied, are unable to exert influence over the analysis. Neither the acquisition phase group of people who provided their personal data for

666. Cedric Burton and others, 'The Final European Union General Data Protection Regulation' (2016) Bloomberg BNA Privacy and Security Law Report 1, 5.
667. Solove, 'Privacy Self-Management and the Consent Dilemma' (n 493) 1903; Koops (n 493) 251–253; Bart van der Sloot, 'Do Data Protection Rules Protect the Individual and Should They?' (2014) 4 International Data Privacy Law 307, 323.
668. Cf. subsection 4.4.2.

de-identification and analysis, nor the application phase group of people who bear the consequences (positive or negative) of the outcomes of the analysis, are able to exert legal control or demand transparency on the basis of data protection law. For the acquisition phase, group de-identification after acquisition and subsequent analysis of the de-identified data may result in 'hidden collaboration'; through their (de-identified) data decisions are made that they might not have agreed with if they had known about them. For the acquisition phase group the lack of control over the model that is applied to them is problematic: they might have control over the input or the generation of knowledge or models in the analysis phase. In this sense, personal autonomy is at stake for both groups. Non-discrimination can also be said to be at stake, because discrimination in the application phase generally results from discriminatory models created in the analysis phase.

The only exception would be if people are identifiable through the data, in which case they could use their right to withdraw consent or object to the processing, and their right to erasure, to try to remove themselves from the analysis. In such cases, the prohibition on processing special categories of data without explicit consent may mitigate against direct discrimination entering the analysis phase. Nevertheless, it is only relevant for this type of discrimination: the prohibition does not prevent the various kinds of indirect and hidden discrimination from entering into the knowledge, models, and predictions. Moreover, as explained, the chances of identifiable data being de-identified before analysis are considerable.[669]

Comparing the (issues in) the analysis phase with the normative concepts of privacy and data protection, the fundamental rights to privacy and data protection do not seem to demand a different implementation at the secondary level regarding the analysis phase, as personal data are not likely to trigger the applicability of the normative concepts to the analysis phase. With respect to the *outcomes* of analysis this may be different, particularly with respect to the normative concept of privacy. But the outcomes are part of the application phase, discussed in the next subsection.

4.6.3 Application Phase

The negative impact of big data in the *application phase* is the most difficult to describe clearly, as the applications of big data, and therefore also its consequences, are extremely diverse. People's private life can be at stake due to decisions made on the basis of the knowledge yielded by big data, or they can be discriminated against in various manners, or their reception of information can be affected. Moreover, people can be manipulated, persuaded and coerced in various small ways. All of these consequences can be significant and immediate, but also small and cumulative, and have a cascade

669. *See* subsection 4.3.2 and Tables 4.1 and 4.2.

of long-term effects on the rights to personal autonomy, non-discrimination, privacy and data protection, and personal autonomy. Often, the harm will be a consequence of the processing of a limited amount of personal data of a person, after which a decision is made about this individual, on the basis of the model resulting from the analysis phase. Because of the variety of applications of big data the application phase does not show a clear image of the gaps in protection. Because of the diversity in negative impact and gaps, there are also a multitude of possible solutions. Yet essentially, all different cases of application can be categorised in three different scenarios.

In the first scenario, personal data of an individual are used to make decisions about that individual. An example is online personalisation such as behavioural targeting based on identifiers. In this case data protection law applies, because personal data are processed. When a decision is based on (limited) personal data, the general rules on transparency, control, and risk also apply, albeit with the limitations described above. This means, *inter alia*, that sensitive data cannot be used as input for a decision, preventing direct discrimination. Moreover, consent for personal data processing can in theory be withheld, thus blocking automated decisions based on personal data. As explained above, both mechanisms suffer from serious flaws, and will not fully prevent inequality or diminishing personal autonomy, but they are helpful in establishing individual control over big data applications.

Ultimately, the possibility to oppose automated individual decision-making or enquire into the logic behind the decision is the most important mechanism of data protection law in the application phase. These automated decision-making rules show great promise for addressing the negative impact of big data on *all* individual rights and freedoms, i.e., negative effects on personal autonomy, privacy and data protection, non-discrimination, and freedom of expression. They have the potential to mitigate the negative impact of the application phase for all different individual rights and freedoms by creating transparency and giving individuals the right not to be subjected to such decisions. Yet they also suffer from a number of problems. First of all, as explained in detail in Chapter 4.3.2.2, the criteria of the profiling rules are too narrowly circumscribed to be applicable to the majority of big data applications. This is primarily so because they set a high bar through the criterion of 'legal or similarly significant effects'. This means that the special transparency and control rules only apply to high-impact decisions. But low-impact decisions can also be manipulative and a threat to personal autonomy and freedom of expression, particularly as the future becomes increasingly personalised in many small but cumulative ways. These situations, illustrated in Chapter 2 through the online personalisation example, are beyond the scope of the automated decision-making rules. In addition, high-impact decisions that are based on the automated processing of personal data, but non- or semi-automated when they are applied to individuals are also excluded, because Article 22 GDPR does not apply when there is human intervention in the process of taking the decision. This means that if human controllers use the knowledge that big data yields to make decisions about people, people cannot challenge the decision on the basis of data protection law. For example, fully automated credit scoring is within Article 22 GDPR's scope, but when the decision to reject a credit application is communicated by an individual, the provision does not apply. And third, providing information might not even achieve the goal of empowering the individual, as the explanation of big data and its consequences may be so complex that it obfuscates the meaning for the average individual. Consequently, in this scenario there is a lacuna of the second type (*insufficient protection*) in the application phase. The rules of the GDPR apply, but due to the particularities of big data they do not always apply, and in general they do not offer an adequate level of protection of individual rights and freedoms.

When looking at the normative concepts of the rights to privacy and data protection, it is questionable whether these limitations of secondary EU data protection law are problematic. This type of application of big data is within the scope of the normative concepts, but secondary data protection law seems to meet the concepts' demands. As long as personal data are protected, and data protection principles such as having a legitimate ground for processing are abided by, the GDPR matches the Courts' interpretation of privacy and data protection. The fundamental rights level does not require a higher standard of protection against the negative effects of automated decision-making, for example, in the guise of eliminating the high-impact criterion. It does not require data protection law to solve all negative effects on other individual rights and freedoms either. As explained above, there is an important enabling effect emanating from data protection law for these other freedoms, such as non-discrimination. However, this is a by-effect; it is not an aim in itself, required from data protection law at the constitutional level. Under the normative concepts of the EU fundamental rights to privacy and data protection, it is not the responsibility of data protection law to solve these issues; solutions should be sought elsewhere. Chapter 5 gives suggestions on where to find such solutions.

In the second scenario, decisions are based on individual characteristics but no personal data are processed, such as in the example of group profiling.[670] As the GDPR does not apply and it is about the application of the outcome of big data and the effect thereof, this qualifies as a type 3 lacuna (*non-regulated, core ≠ data processing)* in protection. Here, it becomes even clearer that frequently it is not so much the collection of (personal) data or the processing that is at the heart of the issue, but its effects. These can be imminent and high-impact, but also small and cumulative, as in the online personalisation example.[671] Without personal data, the normative concepts

670. *See* 4.3.2 and 4.6 and Schreurs and others (n 538).

671. Online personalisation can be based on personal data, which places it in the first (targeted) application phase scenario, or on general characteristics or group attributes that do not constitute personal data, which would place it in the second scenario. There

do not demand different implementation; the lack of protection of individual rights and freedoms in these cases cannot be perceived as an imputable shortcoming of EU data protection law.

The third possibility is the scenario in which *general* decisions are made that affect individual rights and freedoms. In such situations, the application of big data is not aimed at individuals, but affects their individual rights and freedoms nonetheless. As no personal data are processed, these situations are beyond the scope of data protection law. Therefore, this is a gap that fits in type 3 (*non-regulation, core ≠ data processing*), as there is no link between the (personal) data of the individual and the general decision being made. However, the use of the notion of 'gap' in the context of this scenario of general decisions can be misleading. The impact here is of a general nature, and not aimed at specific individuals. A decision can depend on the analysis of data that may have been personal at a certain point in time, but here it is purely the *effects* of a decision based on big data that are at stake. With respect to the normative concepts of the right to privacy and to data protection: these general decisions may trigger the right to privacy of their own accord, but they are far removed from data protection law and the big data process. For severe cases, for example, when the health of people living in a certain area is at stake due to pollution or toxic waste after the government has allowed for the building of a chemical plant in a specific location on the basis of big data analysis, an appeal to the fundamental rights to privacy may be possible purely because of the consequences of the decision. Yet the normative concepts do not require a different implementation in data protection law to cover such cases. This gap in protection of individual rights and freedoms should not be closed through data protection law. Rather, it is requisite that we acknowledge that big data stands at the core of decisions that can pose a threat to individual rights and freedoms, but are unrelated to privacy and data protection. It needs attention from other areas of law to mitigate these problems; big data and its potential negative effects cannot be regarded solely through a data protection law lens.

4.7 CONCLUSION

This chapter has explored the potential and limitations of EU data protection law, regarded by many as the prime instrument to regulate big data, to protect individual rights and freedoms. In an attempt to determine to what extent contemporary data protection law is up to the challenge, the material scope of the GDPR, the substantive norms that focus on transparency, control, and risk, and the enforcement of these norms have been reviewed. All things considered, it has become apparent that the GDPR contains many rights,

is discussion on where the exact border lies in such cases given the ambiguity of the definition of personal data, as explained in, amongst others, section 4.2 of Chapter 4.

obligations, and principles that are of great importance in the context outlined above and in Chapter 2. At the same time, it seems that a few specific characteristics of the GDPR's provisions, and some aspects of data protection in general, interfere with a satisfactory level of protection. Here, the conclusions about the different data protection elements are summarised to answer the core question of what the potential and limitations of the data protection law approach to big data are, after which an explanation follows of the implications of this result for the broader enquiry into the protection of individual rights, and the possible need for alternative solutions to big data issues.

The biggest hurdle for protection of individual rights and freedoms lies in data protection law's material scope of application. Data protection law only applies to personal data, therefore non-personal and de-identified data are not within its scope. The rationale is that when data do not relate to identifiable individuals, there is rarely a privacy risk in the processing for the data subject. However, in big data there are also risks for individual rights and freedoms other than data protection, such as personal autonomy, freedom of expression, and non-discrimination.

The general issue here is that, because of its limited scope of application, much of the potential of data protection law for the protection of individual rights and freedoms is lost, simply because the rules do not apply. The acquisition phase is covered when personal data are processed, but much non-personal data that will eventually affect individuals can enter big data, such as in the example of environmental pollution.[672] The analysis phase is usually not (fully) covered by data protection at all, even though this is where the knowledge, models, and predictions are created that will affect people's individual rights and freedoms. This means that transparency and control through data protection are absent in the analysis phase, in spite of this phase being the *source* of the negative effects of big data's application in practice. It is even possible that the application phase is beyond the scope of data protection, for example, in cases of group profiling, and when general decisions that do not target specific individuals are taken on the basis of big data. No personal data are used to apply the findings of big data in these cases, so data protection law does not govern the application, but the decisions affect individual rights and freedoms nonetheless.

Moreover, because of the *disconnectedness of the phases*, de-identified processing in the analysis phase can still cause issues for the rights to privacy and data protection of people other than the data subject of the acquisition and analysis phase, when the outcomes of analysis are applied in the application phase.[673] Personal data can be collected for a relatively limited

672. *See* subsection 4.3.2.

673. The disconnectedness of the phases refers to the difference between the data that are collected from a group of people in the acquisition phase and used in the analysis phase on the one hand, and the group of people to whom the outcomes of the analysis are

and innocent aim, after which the acquired data can be de-identified. The data then end up in the analysis phase, about which the data subject was not informed, and did not need to be informed according to the law. The whole process was outside the scope of data protection law, but the data subject unknowingly and without any control becomes part of a big data project. This 'hidden collaboration' is permitted by law, but it may be possible that the data subject would not have consented to the acquisition of her data had she known about the analysis and application phase, for example, because the purpose and application of a specific big data process are morally unacceptable to her, or because it negatively affects others, for example, through discriminatory effects, and she wants to prevent that.

In the same way as the acquisition phase is disconnected from the analysis and application phases, the application phase is disconnected from the acquisition and analysis phases. The millions of data that are collected and analysed to *create* the knowledge, models, or predictions, are in principle unrelated to the data that are used to *apply* the knowledge, models, or predictions. Of course, it is possible that the data of the application phase later also end up in a new acquisition phase. But the point is that *application* of big data rests on a limited amount of personal data, whereas behind it there are a wealth of data from other people or sources. When a person applies for a loan, for example, and gives consent for the processing of data about her most recent holiday destination, favourite computer game, and her pet, on the basis of millions of data a correlation could be found in the analysis phase between her answers and a high risk of not paying the interest. For the individual, it is impossible to gauge the risks of providing this seemingly limited amount of innocuous data. Even though she has control over the data she provides in the application phase, the decision is based on information that she has not provided herself, but that instead has been acquired from legion other sources collected in the acquisition phase and processed in the analysis phase. Being cautious with providing personal data is therefore of limited relevance in the age of big data, because one does not have control about what others produce and consent to. And it also works the other way around: big data makes it possible to distil rules from the data of a small group of people, which can then be applied to everyone. On the basis of familiar characteristics, predictions and decisions can be made about people, without having to ask these new people for much information. The (presupposed) minority that consent to the use of their personal data influences the possibility of control over big data of people that belong to the

---

applied in the application phase, on the other hand. These groups can overlap; people whose data are used for analysis can be the people to whom the outcomes of analysis are applied later on as well. However, the (personal) data in the acquisition and analysis phase are disconnected from the application phase: in the application phase it is the resulting model or prediction that is applied, possibly with the aid of limited personal data collected from the second group of people.

non-consenting majority. Paradoxically, in big data the informational self-determination of one person may lead to the limitation of the informational self-determination of others.

If data protection law applies, its prime mechanism to tackle big data issues is a combination of transparency and individual control over personal data processing. Yet in the case of consent to collection and further processing, this runs aground because in practice it is nearly impossible to comply with the legal requirements, which leads to non-compliance and can therefore even lead to erosion of data protection law. It also does not achieve its goal because research shows that consent is highly problematic in a digital environment, in which individuals are tempted by free offers, dazed by privacy policies, and unaware of consequences, practices, and values online. This is a general problem, not caused by big data as such, but it emphasises the problems with trying to protect rights and freedoms through individual control. A third practical problem is big data's limited value due to the disconnectedness issue described above, which is inherent in big data. After consent has been given, data can be de-identified and then used for any purpose, as a result of which the individual then becomes part of a big data project without having any influence over the analysis or the outcome and application.

This leaves us with the rules that address particular risks, and focus on defaults and obligations on controllers, starting with the GDPR's innovations. The innovations show a move away from standard data protection principles, to rules that target particular issues of our times (the right to be forgotten) and combinations with other legal fields such as competition law (data portability). They represent the increasing importance and changing societal function of personal data, which finds its way into data protection law. Data portability shows potential, because it may enhance the freedom of choice of individuals and shows potential for curtailing the power of 'data monopolists', when individuals make use of their acquired extra autonomy by responding to undesired practices such as manipulative or discriminative conduct by big data entities through switching platforms or services. However, its practical effect is uncertain, and other innovative elements such as the right to be forgotten do not address the real problems of big data for individual rights and freedoms.

In the end, the most promising rules seem to be those on automated decision-making. Now that 'including profiling' has been added to these rules' definition in the GDPR, they appear designed for the application phase of big data. Unfortunately, they fail to live up to their potential. Besides being easy to circumvent through adding a human element somewhere in the process, their scope is limited to *fully automated high-impact decisions*. Inconspicuous decisions and manipulations often go unnoticed and do not always seem a problem when each personalisation is assessed individually instead of as part of a larger whole. Yet, as Chapter 2 has shown, personalisation and persuasion have become the norm, and an environment consisting of small but cumulative manipulations can be just as detrimental as high-impact fully automated decisions. The rules are ineffective against this problem; the bar is set too high in terms of decision types.

This is where the right to object, with a broader reach than the automated decision rules, comes in, as it is not subject to such specific criteria as 'legal or similarly significant effects'. Combined with the right to erasure and the possibility to withdraw consent, data subjects can have themselves removed from the big data process. As such, these are part of control but different from prior consent in the acquisition phase because of their ex post effect: the possibility to reconsider one's decision or resist further processing. Opting out from (parts of) the big data process is a direct way of countering big data's possible negative effects. However, the issues with consent demonstrate that many issues with this general individual control-based approach remain. And as with all the aforementioned rights and obligations, the rules are only as strong as the extent to which they are enforced through DPAs and courts, and affected by other compliance-enhancing factors, such how much (reputational) damage organisations suffer when they do not comply.

To summarise, there are four problems that make data protection law unfit as a sole solution to big data issues. First of all, its limited scope of application causes significant gaps in protection, because parts of the big data process are not regulated by data protection law. Second, the specificity of the criteria of many of its rules and innovations, such as automated individual decision-making, makes their scope too narrow to truly mitigate all big data harm. Third, EU data protection law relies heavily on individual control over personal data as a protection mechanism, which is misplaced in a digital environment in general, and in big data in particular. Fourth, even if the rules were to be adapted to big data, more defaults were introduced, and the enforcement and oversight were to be flawless, big data still causes issues for individual rights and freedoms that are not addressed by data protection law. The normative concepts of the rights to privacy and data protection require the protection of individuals and their data, but they do not demand the protection of other individuals, save for personal autonomy to a limited extent. Under the normative concepts the enabling effect of privacy and data protection law is a by-effect, but not an aim in itself. So not only is data protection law not capable of mitigating all negative effects of big data; it is also not its *task* to do so.

These conclusions do not mean that data protection is completely ineffective in big data. On the contrary: this chapter has also shown that individual rights and freedoms are protected through data protection, not only the right to privacy or data protection itself, but also personal autonomy, freedom of expression, and non-discrimination. Most examples of innovation show both potential and limitations at the same time. For example, there is certainly potential for the protection of individual rights and freedoms, notably data protection and personal autonomy, in the Regulation through all the rights that individuals can exercise with respect to their own data. Positive effects also extend to non-discrimination and freedom of expression. Due to big data's particularities, data protection law cannot mitigate all negative effects on individual rights and freedoms, but it does smooth the rough edges by addressing the most obvious direct consequences. Depending on the use of the rights and compliance with the obligations, it can take away a share of the negative impact on privacy, data protection, and freedom of expression in the acquisition phase while respecting (but not preserving) individuals' personal autonomy.

However, as postulated in the introduction to this chapter: blind trust in data protection as the sole solution to big data's negative impact on individual rights and freedoms is unwise. Due to big data's characteristics, data protection law is insufficient as a sole solution. Moreover, big data affects many individual rights and freedoms, against which secondary EU data protection legislation cannot and should not protect. It is necessary to accept that not every big data issue can be traced back to the rights to privacy and data protection, and to look for alternative solutions to complement the EU framework on privacy and data protection. A first step in this direction is taken in the ensuing chapter.

Chapter 5
Potential Solutions and a Combined Approach

5.1 INTRODUCTION

This chapter is about the way forward, following the conclusion that the EU privacy and data protection law framework is insufficient to fully protect individual rights and freedoms in the age of big data, in spite of its high level of protection. The takeaway from the previous chapters is that personal data function as a proxy for intervention, and as such their regulation can overcome many issues, but that we must also acknowledge that not all problems of big data are privacy and data protection problems, and not all problems are located in the processing of personal data per se. This means, that in many cases, data protection law is not the right means to protect individual rights and freedoms against the negative impact of big data. For the protection of individual rights and freedoms, it is necessary to explore different legal avenues for dealing with the issues that big data creates.

The previous chapter identified three different types of gap in protection of individual rights and freedoms in big data (*lacuna 1: insufficient protection through the EU privacy and data protection framework; lacuna 2: non-regulation, with data processing as its core; lacuna 3: non-regulation, data processing of negligible significance)*. After matching these gaps with the normative concepts of the fundamental rights to privacy and data protection, it concluded that secondary data protection law is not required to mitigate negative effects of big data in all phases for all individual rights and freedoms. On the basis of the case law of the ECtHR and the CJEU, the constitutional level does not even seem to demand a level of protection that goes beyond what is currently offered by the GDPR.[674] Whereas a solution to the first type of lacuna may consist of changing (substantive) data protection law, for the second and third lacunae this would not be a fitting solution, as here the other individual rights and freedoms do not extend through privacy and data protection law. As these situations are beyond the scope of privacy and data protection law, they necessitate a different approach. Therefore, we must conclude that protection of individual rights and freedoms against big data's negative impact cannot be effectuated through the EU framework on privacy and data protection law alone; it calls for an integral approach that combines different legal solutions.

This chapter aspires to explain the necessity of a combined approach. It describes domains that could be part of a combined approach, because they address gaps in the protection of individual rights and freedoms in the context of big data. It does not give concrete solutions that should be implemented in practice. The chapter therefore consists of two parts. First, it gives an overview of possible legal alternatives, to see which alternative approaches merit further discussion and research. Second, it argues that a combined approach is necessary, in which different legal approaches are combined that each solves different aspects of the complex problem of big data's negative impact on individual rights and freedoms. The overview of the possible legal solutions to the issues found consists of a review of possible alternatives, intended to show the direction in which our attention and efforts should go when looking for solutions. Through tracking the academic discourse on big data and related issues and solutions over the past few years, a range of solutions has been identified. These solutions are subdividable into three categories: (1) *changes* in the EU privacy and data protection framework, (2) applying legal instruments from *other areas of law* to big data, and (3) *tailored solutions,* i.e., legislation designed to address specific parts and problems of big data. This chapter does not aspire to give a conclusive in-depth analysis of each possibility under these headings, or determine whether it should be implemented in practice. The goal is only to show the broad range of possibilities, and provide an appraisal of their potential from the perspective of protecting the individual rights and freedoms that are the focus of this book. As such, this overview functions as *inspiration* for further research, providing input for a further discussion on how existing tools can be employed in a big data context, what legislative measures may be successful and which ones can be disregarded.

674. We must keep in mind, however, that the case law of the Courts is rather casuistic and the context is generally different from the big data context as described in this work. *See* Chapter 3.

5.1.1 Literature Review

This chapter focuses on the possible alternative solutions for the gaps in the protection of individual rights and freedoms against the negative impact of big data. Point of departure are the lacunae in protection. This chapter therefore focuses on solutions that may be able to fill these gaps in protection against the negative impact of big data on individual rights and freedoms where data protection law does not, because data protection law either does not function optimally or does not apply to a particular negative effect. The solutions are derived from the discourse on big data of the past few years: its issues and possible solutions, including general aspects that are part of big data, such as profiling or online data collection.[675] In this respect it builds on the literature of previous chapters, and additional works that direct their attention towards solutions in particular.

The sources used can be further divided into subtopics according to the category of alternative interventions to which they relate. Most sections focus on general literature such as commentaries first, to map the areas of consumer law, competition law, and non-discrimination law, for example.[676] A large proportion of the sources consulted focus on newly proposed solutions, venturing beyond the big data context into the areas of proposed solutions and the evaluation of these solutions.[677] Some of the cited sources consist of literature on the interplay between privacy, data protection, and other areas of law.[678] Sources of a more policy-based or practical nature are also included where they provide additional insights into developments in these areas or show how alternative solutions are already employed in

675. For example Solove, 'Privacy Self-Management and the Consent Dilemma' (n 493); Schermer (n 88); Richards and King (n 85); Maurice Stucke and Allen Grunes, *Big Data and Competition Policy* (Oxford University Press 2016).

676. JGJ Rinkes, 'Europees consumentenrecht' in EH Hondius and others (eds), *Handboek consumentenrecht: een overzicht van de rechtspositie van de consument* (Uitgeverij Paris 2011); Willem van Boom, 'Unfair Commercial Practices' in Christian Twigg-Flesner (ed), *Research Handbook on EU Consumer and Contract Law* (Edward Elgar 2016); Alison Jones and Brenda Sufrin, *EU Competition Law: Text, Cases, and Materials* (Oxford University Press 2016); European Union Agency for Fundamental Rights, *Handbook on European Non-Discrimination Law* (n 40).

677. Nadezhda Purtova, *Property Rights in Personal Data: A European Perspective* (Kluwer Law International 2012); Lawrence Lessig, 'Privacy as Property' (2002) Social Research 247; Corien Prins, 'When Personal Data, Behavior and Virtual Identities Become a Commodity: Would a Property Rights Approach Matter?' (2006) SCRIPT-ed 270; Nicholas Diakopoulos, 'Algorithmic Accountability: Journalistic Investigation of Computational Power Structures' (2015) Digital Journalism 398; Nicholas Diakopoulos and Sorelle Friedler, 'How to Hold Algorithms Accountable' (2016) MIT Technology Review; Mike Ananny and Kate Crawford, 'Seeing Without Knowing: Limitations of the Transparency Ideal and Its Application to Algorithmic Accountability' (2016) New Media & Society 1.

678. Inge Graef, 'Market Definition and Market Power in Data: The Case of Online Platforms' (2015) 38 World Competition 473; Natali Helberger, Frederik Zuiderveen

(national) practice.[679] The integrated approach and conclusions suggested build on this literature and the previous chapters.

5.2 OVERVIEW OF POSSIBLE LEGAL ALTERNATIVES

This section presents the possible alternative legal alternatives to deal with big data's negative impact. These alternatives are the result of following the legal discourse on big data, its negative impact, and possible solutions over the past few years of this research. They are bundled according to type: solutions that consist of amending data protection law to make it more effective in big data (subsection 5.2.1), employing areas of law other than privacy and data protection law to deal with big data's negative effects on individual rights and freedoms (subsection 5.2.2), and the possibility of creating tailored regulatory measures to deal with (parts) of big data that cause particular issues (subsection 5.2.3). There are also differences between these alternative solutions with respect to the phases in which they can be of added value and which issue or negative effect on particular individual rights and freedoms they address. These aspects are elucidated in the following subsections that map out the general background of the solutions, explain how they could be of relevance in big data, discuss what conceivable drawbacks there are, and evaluate whether the alternatives merit further discussion and research.

5.2.1 Amending Data Protection Law

This section gives an overview of different avenues for amending data protection law to increase its protective potential in the context of big data. Data protection law can be amended in a myriad of ways, but here the focus lies on changes that target aspects that have been found to decrease its potential in big data as described in Chapter 4, to improve how the secondary legislative level meets the normative concepts. Therefore, the ensuing

Borgesius and Agustin Reyna, 'The Perfect Match? A Closer Look at the Relationship Between EU Consumer Law and Data Protection Law' (2017) 54 Common Market Law Review 1427.

679. European Data Protection Supervisor, 'Privacy and Competitiveness in the Age of Big Data: The Interplay Between Data Protection, Competition Law and Consumer Protection in the Digital Economy' (n 87); *Apple Sales International* [2013] Landsgericht Berlin 15 O 92/12; 'Bundeskartellamt Initiates Proceeding against Facebook on Suspicion of Having Abused Its Market Power by Infringing Data Protection Rules' (2 March 2016) <http://www.bundeskartellamt.de/SharedDocs/Meldung/EN/Pressemitteilungen/2016/02_03_2016_Facebook.html>; Autorité de la concurrence and Bundeskartellamt, 'Report "Competition Law and Data"' (2016).

subsections focus on changes in application criteria of provisions that show potential in big data, changes that circumvent or aim to solve issues with individual control, and improvements in enforcement.

The first possibility is to change substantive data protection norms, such as the automated decision-making rules, to increase their effectiveness in big data. Two other suggestions derived from the literature to amend data protection law are more innovative. The first is creating property rights in personal data. The second is the idea of broadening the scope of application of data protection law to encompass all (digital) data, personal or not. These three possibilities are discussed under their respective headings below.

5.2.1.1 Changes in Substantive Data Protection Law

Some of the GDPR's rules do not function well in big data. Notwithstanding its recent conception, a number of the GDPR's provisions were not created having in mind the complex processing of large and diverse datasets, de-identification, disconnected processing phases, network effects, and ubiquitous data processing and brokering. To a certain extent, these deficits are technical legislative shortcomings that could be adapted to these new technological realities through changing substantive data protection law.

The automated decision-making rules are a key example. Conceptually, they show great promise in the context of big data, as many negative effects in the application phase of big data may be mitigated through enabling people in understanding how they are subjected to automated individual decisions, and giving them the means to refute such decisions.[680] Yet much of this potential is not realised because of the criteria that make the provisions only applicable to fully automated high-profile decisions, which greatly limits their scope. Leaving aside any valid reasons for including these criteria when the provisions were drafted, they could of course be taken out of the profiling provisions, making the rules applicable to any kind of automated individual decision-making, regardless of human involvement or its insignificance. Individuals would get the opportunity to learn about and resist any automated decision, which strengthens their personal autonomy. However, the protective (enabling) effect of data protection law's profiling rules would still depend on control exercised by the individual herself. Control implies free choice, overseeing the consequences, and functional transparency. These are all to a degree lacking in the application phase of big data, particularly due to the ubiquitousness of big data decision-making that targets individuals.

Another approach that could be explored against the background of the difficulties with control rights is changing data protection law to include more defaults, and possibly even introducing more prohibitions. Acquisition

680. *See* subsections 4.4.1.2 and 4.4.2.2 of Chapter 4.

of personal data under certain circumstances may be prohibited or require explicit consent. Yet data protection law may not be the right place for such prohibitions. EU data protection law is an omnibus regime, applying across sectors, that legitimises data processing and confers rights upon individuals.[681] True prohibitions and provisions that address specific sectors are rare in the GDPR. Many of the problems with transparency and control referred to above seem to exist because of information asymmetries and power imbalances between the individual and the big data entity. As we shall *see* below, such prohibitions, defaults, and criteria on how to establish fairness in the exercise of control fit more in the realm of consumer protection. Power imbalances and abusive behaviour that can result from it may also be addressed by competition law. These ideas are discussed below, but first the ensuing part of this subsection addresses other alternative approaches within the realm of data protection law.

Enforcement of data protection law could also be improved. Two ways to increase the effectiveness of enforcement are stricter sanctions for violations of data protection law and creating possibilities for collective action.[682] The GDPR already improves the Directive in this respect; the maximum fines are increased (Article 83 GDPR), and the possibility of representation by non-profit bodies is introduced in Article 80 GDPR. Much is expected of these changes, but the effectiveness of these new competencies depends on how they are employed in practice, e.g., how DPAs will use their power to impose sanctions for violations of data protection law. Class action supports individuals seeking redress, as it creates collective power and facilitates the sharing of costs, risks, and other burdens involved in litigation, which is of particular relevance in the context of violations of data protection law, where cases are complex and individual harm is often difficult to assert.[683] General class action possibilities in data protection cases have been introduced in multiple Member States, such as Belgium and France, but there is no harmonised law or practice in the EU. The opportunities could be broadened further, particularly given that collective action shows much promise set against the backdrop of the specific enforcement issues discussed in Chapter 4.4.

5.2.1.2 Propertisation of Personal Data

An alternative idea, professed to give individuals more control, is the propertisation of personal data. This idea originates from the US, but it has

681. Lynskey, *The Foundations of EU Data Protection Law* (n 174) 15–38.
682. *Ibid* 261f.
683. European Union Agency for Fundamental Rights, 'Access to Data Protection Remedies in EU Member States' (n 655) 32.

received attention in the EU as well.[684] Proponents claim it would create an environment of negotiation instead of emphasising liability and compensation.[685] It would also match more closely with contemporary online personal data processing, where personal data represent a commercial value and are perceived as an asset.[686] In big data, it seems to be primarily relevant in the acquisition phase, where it may strengthen people's control rights. However, the protective value of property rights in personal data hinges on how this right would be shaped and what entitlements it would generate for individuals and other parties. Even if it were to take the form of a non-transferable, non-exclusively licensable property right, its added value for the current EU legal privacy and data protection framework would most likely be limited.[687] It is questionable whether such a right alone would be capable of changing individuals' bargaining power. Many environments, such as the finance and online personalisation illustrations, suffer from information asymmetries and power imbalances; it is unlikely that property rights rhetoric would improve this situation for individuals. Property rights rhetoric also hints at the commodification of personal data, which has been argued to be damaging for people's fundamental rights with respect to personal data.[688] Furthermore, it raises many new questions, for example on how personal data created by others than the individual herself should be governed, regarding its compatibility with the free flow of information and freedom of expression, and regarding enforceability. In terms of feasibility and effects it does not merit priority in further research and discussion on solutions to big data issues.

5.2.1.3 Broadening the Material Scope of Data Protection Law

Some of the limitations of data protection law's potential to protect individual rights and freedoms in the context of big data result from its

684. Cf. Nadezhda Purtova, 'Property Rights in Personal Data: Learning from the American Discourse' (2009) Computer Law & Security Review 507; Pamela Samuelson, 'Privacy as Intellectual Property' (2000) Stanford Law Review 1125; Paul Schwartz, 'Property, Privacy, and Personal Data' (2004) Harvard Law Review 2056; Purtova (n 677); Egbert Dommering, 'Recht op persoonsgegevens als zelfbeschikkingsrecht', *16 Miljoen BN'ers? Bescherming van persoonsgegevens in het digitale tijdperk* (Stichting NJCM-Boekerij 2010) 83–99.
685. Lessig (n 677); Purtova (n 677) 137–139.
686. This holds true for both data users, such as companies, as well as individuals, *see* Sarah Spiekermann, Jana Korunovska and Christine Bauer, 'Psychology of Ownership and Asset Defence: Why People Value Their Personal Information Beyond Privacy', *Proceedings of the International Conference on Information Systems* (AIS Association for Information Systems 2012); Sarah Spiekermann and others, 'The Challenges of Personal Data Markets and Privacy' (2015) 25 Electronic Markets 161, 161–162.
687. Prins (n 677) 270–303.
688. European Data Protection Supervisor, 'Opinion 4/2017 on the Proposal for a Directive on Certain Aspects Concerning Contracts for the Supply of Digital Content' (2017) 4/2017 7–10.

limited scope.[689] Data protection law only applies if personal (i.e., identifiable) data are processed, which may keep a big data phase outside its scope, notably and frequently the acquisition phase.[690] A solution may be to broaden data protection law's material scope of application. It can be broadened to include *all* data, thereby having data protection regulate all 'data' instead of sole data related to identifiable individuals.[691] With this approach all (digital) data would fall under the GDPR, regardless of whether they concern identifiable individuals or not, which means that de-identified and non-personal data would also be covered. The idea is that in the big data era the distinction between identifiable and non-identifiable data has become meaningless, and all data can become personal data and affect the individual. For this newly covered category of non-identifiable data there would be a *data protection light* regime that would focus on the duties of the controller, instead of on individual control exerted by the individual. These duties, such as securing the data and complying with principles of data minimisation, purpose limitation, and legitimate processing, would then apply to any kind of automated data processing.[692] This solution would draw the currently often-unregulated analysis phase, from where many of the negative effects originate, within the scope of protection. By demanding safeguards regarding data processing and focusing on duties with respect to the data, it would shift some responsibility from the (control rights of) individuals to the entities using big data. In this respect, it partially circumvents the individual control issues by putting the burden on the data user.

However, this possibility has many drawbacks. Regulating all data would likely create a complicated and burdensome system, both for big data processing and beyond, that involves a high risk of non-compliance and erosion of data protection law. Declaring all data to be covered by data protection law would not make the assessment of which duties and obligations apply any easier, as controllers would still have to analyse in which category the data that they process fit in order to decide what level of risk corresponds to their processing, what regime covers the data, and which obligations they would have to comply with. Moreover, in big data it targets analysis, but in society at large it would affect all automated or systemic data processing. People or entities that process data that are unrelated to individual rights and freedoms, such as a local store owner that digitises her inventory list, would become instantly and probably unconsciously subject to data protection rules under this system, and to procedures to demonstrate compliance. This would be a substantial burden for a massive number of new controllers, particularly in light of the fact that the current broad definition of

689. This is explained in detail in section 4.3 of Chapter 4.
690. *See* Tables 4.1 and 4.2 in subsection 4.3.2 of Chapter 4.
691. Bart van der Sloot, *Privacy as Virtue: Moving Beyond the Individual in the Age of Big Data* (Dissertation University of Amsterdam 2017) 189–193.
692. *Ibid* 191.

personal data is already perceived as burdensome by entities processing personal data. As such, it would also obstruct the free flow of information, which is one of the objectives of data protection law (Recital 3 GDPR). It would likely also decrease public support for data protection regulation. Additionally, even though its precise merit as a solution depends on which data protection rules would apply to this new category of data, in general a broader material scope of data protection law does not seem promising, as it leaves *inter alia* problems with the substantive rules of the GDPR and many negative effects resulting from the application of big data intact. As such, it seems far removed from being a feasible solution that reflects a careful balancing of interests to merit priority in further research.

5.2.2 Employing Other Fields of Law

Given the limitations of data protection as a complete solution against big data's negative impact, it is requisite that the potential of other areas of law is also explored. This becomes most obvious in the application phase scenarios identified in Chapter 4 where there are clear negative effects on individual rights and freedoms other than the rights to privacy and data protection. Data protection may or may not be applicable to such scenarios, but when for example people are discriminated against on the basis of big data, non-discrimination law can and should apply, in its own right and as a complement to data protection law. A combined approach, for example, complementing data protection law with consumer protection legislation, may also be viable where data protection law does not function optimally. In some cases, it may be that data protection law applies, but that personal data processing is not the only aspect of a problem. For example, when there are power imbalances between big data entities and individuals, such as in the case of monopolies or data-requesting services that people deem indispensable, it becomes interesting to see whether competition law could be useful in mitigating big data's negative effects. The three areas of law (consumer law, competition law, and non-discrimination legislation) that are generally deemed to be of interest and value in the context of big data are discussed successively below.

5.2.2.1 Consumer Law

Consumer law aims to protect the (economic) interests of individuals vis-à-vis businesses, from the perspective that there may be power imbalances and information asymmetries between businesses and consumers.[693] Consumer protection is a general objective of the EU (Article 12 TFEU), and

693. Rinkes (n 676) 31–34.

there is much (patchwork) harmonisation in the form of directives.[694] Existing EU instruments that can be of direct relevance for big data are the Consumer Rights Directive, the Unfair Commercial Practices Directive, and the Unfair Contract Terms Directive.[695] Consumers and data subjects are two different (legal) categories that can overlap. Consumer law and data protection are not mutually exclusive; both can apply at the same time, and in some aspects they may supplement each other in the context of big data. Recent developments such as the proposal for a Digital Content Directive, and opinions and actions from EU and national supervisory bodies (discussed below), already demonstrate convergence.[696]

Consumer law instruments may be of relevance in big data in the commercial sphere, as in big data people's data can be processed when purchasing, or in exchange for, goods or services. Examples are online services offered by social media platforms or search engine providers. This primarily occurs in online big data acquisition, where data is often acquired this way. Depending on the circumstances, data subjects can qualify as consumers, and the social media platform or search engine provider as the business in the business-to-consumer relationship. As such, consumer law instruments may apply, for example, in the context of online data processing such as that described in the online personalisation illustration in Chapter 2.

One of EU consumer law's main mechanisms is empowering consumers through *informing* them.[697] Many of these information obligations overlap with the information that individuals are already entitled to under data protection law, which is also broader when it comes to the information

694. *Ibid* 38.
695. Directive 2011/83/EU of the European Parliament and of the Council of 25 October 2011 on consumer rights, amending Council Directive 93/13/EEC and Directive 1999/44/EC of the European Parliament and of the Council and repealing Council Directive 85/577/EEC and Directive 97/7/EC of the European Parliament and of the Council ('Consumer Rights Directive') 2011 (OJ L 304/64); Directive 2005/29/EC of the European Parliament and of the Council of 11 May 2005 concerning unfair business-to-consumer commercial practices in the internal market and amending Council Directive 84/450/EEC, Directives 97/7/EC, 98/27/EC and 2002/65/EC of the European Parliament and of the Council and Regulation (EC) No 2006/2004 of the European Parliament and of the Council ('Unfair Commercial Practices Directive') 2005 (OJ L 149/22); Council Directive 93/13/EEC of 5 April 1993 on unfair terms in consumer contracts 1993 (OJ L 95/29).
696. European Data Protection Supervisor, 'Privacy and Competitiveness in the Age of Big Data: The Interplay between Data Protection, Competition Law and Consumer Protection in the Digital Economy' (n 87); Proposal for a Directive of the European Parliament and of the Council on certain aspects concerning contracts for the supply of digital content, COM/2015/0634 final 2015. Article 3 (1) of the proposal stipulates that the consumer protection rules of the proposal for a Digital Content Directive apply when a price is paid and when the counter performance is the provision of personal data. As such, the proposal seems to accept the possibility of 'paying with data' and aims to ensure consumer protection in such situations.
697. Rinkes (n 676) 32–34, 39–41.

to be provided regarding data processing.[698] Yet in terms of remedies there is added value. Under consumer law, non-compliance with information obligations may constitute unfair commercial practices and breach of contract, with the possibility of terminating the contract or claiming damages under national law.[699] These possibilities, which can be invoked by the individual herself, may strengthen the position of the individual vis-à-vis (powerful) businesses, particularly in the acquisition and analysis phase.

Another avenue would be unfair commercial practices regulation. In the US, the equivalent (unfair business practices) has proven its worth as the primary doctrine dealing with consumer privacy.[700] It has been argued that there are no obstacles to applying the EU-equivalent rules, i.e., the rules of the Unfair Commercial Practices Directive, in EU online privacy and data protection cases too.[701] The Unfair Commercial Practices Directive addresses unfair influencing of consumers through misleading and aggressive commercial practices and thereby strengthens free choice of consumers.[702] This instrument may be used to assess the fairness of persuasive practices, amongst others practices such as behavioural targeting as described in the third illustration in Chapter 3.[703] As such, unfair commercial practices regulation adds assessment criteria and prohibited practices that do not depend on personal data processing, which can be of value in the context of manipulation and loss of personal autonomy in the acquisition and application phases.

Some Member States already have experience in applying consumer law in cases concerning personal data acquisition and further processing. In Germany, the law implementing the Unfair Contract Terms Directive has been used to prohibit certain standard clauses in contracts that gave consumers no option other than to accept behavioural targeting and transfers

698. Helberger, Zuiderveen Borgesius and Reyna (n 678) 10–12.
699. Article 5 Consumer Rights Directive; Article 6 Unfair Commercial Practices Directive; *Ibid* 11–13.
700. Cf. Chris Jay Hoofnagle, *Federal Trade Commission Privacy Law and Policy* (Cambridge University Press 2016).
701. Emilie Kannekens and Nico van Eijk, 'Oneerlijke handelspraktijken: alternatief voor privacyhandhaving' (2016) Mediaforum 102. Although the scope of the applicability criterion 'transactional decision' is not fully clear and may be an issue in situations that do not involve monetary compensation, it seems sufficiently broad to be applicable in many online big data cases as described in this subsection, *see* European Commission, 'Commission Staff Working Document – Guidance on the Implementation/Application of Directive 2005/29/EC on Unfair Commercial Practices' (2016) SWD(2016) 163 final 36–39.
702. Boom (n 676) 388.
703. Cf. subsection 2.3.3 of Chapter 2; Natali Helberger, 'Profiling and Targeting Users in the Internet of Things – A New Challenge for Consumer Law' in Reiner Schulze and Dirk Staudenmayer (eds), *Digital Revolution: Challenges for Contract Law in Practice* (Nomos/Hart 2016); Helberger, Zuiderveen Borgesius and Reyna (n 678) 23–27.

of data to third parties.[704] Such clauses were prohibited amongst others because there would be an unreasonable disadvantage for consumers, constituting significant imbalances between the rights and obligations of the parties.[705] Similar proceedings have taken place in France and Norway regarding user agreements for services such as Google, Facebook, LinkedIn, Instagram, and Tinder.[706] These examples show how consumer law could add to data protection law, by taking aspects such as imbalances between parties and fairness into account.

In sum, consumer law focuses on consumer autonomy while taking imbalances between parties into account. Particularly in the online data processing environment these imbalances are a factor of major importance, as it is the enabler for many negative effects of big data, and a reason why data protection law does not function optimally. Although there are uncertainties regarding the application of (EU) consumer law in the context of data processing and online contexts, it is an area that deserves further research in the context of protection against the negative effects of big data.[707]

5.2.2.2 Competition Law

Competition law strives to maintain market competition through the regulation of anti-competitive behaviour. In the context of big data and competition law in the EU, merger control and the regulation of (abuse of) dominant positions may be relevant.[708] Merger regulation determines under what conditions companies can merge or acquire other companies. It allows for the possibility of preventing companies from becoming dominant in a certain market. This is ex ante control through public enforcement, to avoid companies acquiring a position that would enable them to engage in abusive behaviour.[709] Through the prevention of dominance, which can lead to limited choice for consumers or exploitative behaviour towards them, it can be relevant in the context of big data. By regulating companies, it may be of value with respect to big data in the commercial sphere. In the context of big data, competition law is primarily discussed with respect to online companies that are large in terms of user share or the amount of data they possess, such as Google.

Under regulation of dominant positions, when a company holds a dominant position in a given market it is prohibited from abusing that

704. *Apple Sales International* (n 679).
705. *Ibid* 8–11; Helberger, Zuiderveen Borgesius and Reyna (n 678) 21.
706. Helberger, Zuiderveen Borgesius and Reyna (n 678) 19–22.
707. *Ibid* 28–30.
708. Jones and Sufrin (n 676) 92–110. Other areas are cartels and state aid, but they are not likely to be relevant in the big data context.
709. Council Regulation (EC) No 139/2004 of 20 January 2004 on the control of concentrations between undertakings (the EC Merger Regulation) 2004 (OJ L 24/1).

position.[710] Abusive behaviour is generally divided into exploitative abuse and exclusionary abuse. Exploitation is directed at consumers, for example through unfair pricing. Exclusionary conduct consists of abusing a dominant position to exclude a competitor from the market.[711] Regulation of both forms can be of relevance in big data: exclusionary abuse in a similar (ex post) vein to merger control above, and exploitative abuse regarding unfair behaviour towards individuals, possibly even in the context of data protection principles, as explained below.

Over the years, a number of mergers have been reviewed by the Commission which have a big data dimension, notably the acquisitions of DoubleClick by Google, WhatsApp by Facebook, and LinkedIn by Microsoft.[712] However, the Commission authorised all three transactions, and big data considerations were generally not deemed an issue in the decisions.[713] There is attention for personal data in the context of competition as well, notably by the French *Autorité de la concurrence* and the German *Bundeskartellamt,* who take a different approach.[714] Together, they drafted a report assessing data-related anti-competitive conduct, how data can be a source of market power, and how big data can contribute to market power.[715] Afterwards, the *Bundeskartellambt* started an investigation into Facebook on account of abuse of market power by infringing data protection rules.[716]

To summarise, at the moment in general dominant positions and mergers are not assessed on the basis of the (personal) data that companies possess, but on aspects such as the functionality that companies' services offer.[717] But there are (national) developments that show an increased interest in the interplay between big data, competition law, and even data protection law, and explore new avenues for employing competition law in big data

710. Article 102 TFEU and Council Regulation (EC) No 1/2003 of 16 December 2002 on the implementation of the rules on competition laid down in Articles 81 and 82 of the Treaty (n 660).
711. Jones and Sufrin (n 676) 258–270.
712. *Google/ DoubleClick* [2008] Commission Decision COMP/M.4731; *Facebook/ Whatsapp* [2014] Commission Decision COMP/M.721; *Microsoft/Linkedin* [2016] Commission Decision COMP/M.8124.
713. However, they do play a role, *see* for example the 2017 Commission decision in which Facebook was fined EUR 110 million for providing incorrect or misleading information under the merger rules that related to the matching of Facebook identities with WhatsApp phone numbers. European Commission, 'Mergers: Commission Fines Facebook €110 Million for Providing Misleading Information about WhatsApp Take-over' (2017) Press Release.
714. Autorité de la concurrence and Bundeskartellamt (n 679).
715. *Ibid* 11–54; cf. 'The Commercial Use of Consumer Data – Report on the CMA's Call for Information' (Competition and Markets Authority (UK) 2015).
716. 'Bundeskartellamt Initiates Proceeding against Facebook on Suspicion of Having Abused Its Market Power by Infringing Data Protection Rules' (n 679).
717. Graef (n 678) 504.

contexts. Many objections can be made with respect to abuse of a dominant position in relation to privacy and data protection, and difficulties in assessing data markets and competition in general, but competition law can have general positive effects in the context of big data.[718] At least some of the problems in the acquisition and application phases are caused by information asymmetries and power imbalances between big data entities and individuals, which leads to *inter alia* significant limitations of the proper functioning of individual control rights. From another perspective, it has also been argued that big data must be taken into account in competition law because of the competitive advantages it creates, and the long-term effects that big data can have on competition and consumer welfare.[719] In the context of big data, competition law deserves (and will undoubtedly receive) further attention in discussions and research.

5.2.2.3 Non-discrimination Legislation

A third legal area that can be of value in protecting individuals against the negative effects of big data is non-discrimination legislation. Non-discrimination is protected as a fundamental right by amongst others Article 14 ECHR and Article 21 CFREU.[720] It prohibits direct and indirect discrimination, but the contexts in which and grounds on which discrimination is prohibited depend on the legislative framework.[721] In the EU, non-discrimination legislation has long been limited to the context of employment on the basis of sex, but since 2000 its scope has broadened considerably.[722] In the employment context, the grounds of race, ethnicity, sexual orientation, religion, age, and disability were added, and to the discrimination on the basis of race, ethnicity, and gender the contexts of education, welfare, social security, goods, and services.[723] EU non-discrimination legislation has continued to develop, but it remains patchwork legislation and does not (yet) cover everything that would be protected under

---

718. Robert McLeod, 'Novel but a Long Time Coming: The Bundeskartellamt Takes on Facebook' (2016) 7 Journal of European Competition Law & Practice 367. The use of competition law in the context of big data is sometimes met with reservations or resistance by those well-versed in competition law, particularly when it is suggested that competition law should be used as an instrument to advance privacy and data protection law goals, as this would not be coherent with competition law's objectives.
719. Cf. Stucke and Grunes (n 675).
720. *See* subsection 1.2.4.2.4 of Chapter 1.
721. European Union Agency for Fundamental Rights, *Handbook on European Non-Discrimination Law* (n 40) 57, 119.
722. *Ibid* 14, 67–75.
723. Council Directive 2000/43/EC of 29 June 2000 implementing the principle of equal treatment between persons irrespective of racial or ethnic origin 2009 (OJ L 180/22); Council Directive 2000/78/EC of 27 November 2000 establishing a general framework for equal treatment in employment and occupation 2000 (OJ L 303/16).

the fundamental rights.[724] However, the national laws of the Member States generally match the constitutional level of protection.[725]

In the context of big data, non-discrimination is likely of additional, if not indispensable, value. There is no need to exclude data protection law from such situations; both can apply at the same time in a given case, and both can mitigate non-discrimination.[726] Yet in such cases, discrimination law seems the most appropriate response, acknowledging again that often, particularly in the application phase of big data, it is not about an individualised person that is intertwined with her personal data but about the effect that big data may have on her life. The character of the undesired effect may already point in the direction of a specific legal regime: obviously, non-discrimination law pertains to manifestly discriminatory practices, and should generally be applied in such cases.

In practice, however, its application may be more complex. For example, as explained previously, discrimination in big data can be difficult to uncover.[727] Additionally, one of big data's main novelties is the degree of differentiation that can be achieved through it, for example in segmenting customers: differentiation does not (necessarily) equal discrimination. Big data gives rise to many borderline cases, bearing in mind the discussions on price discrimination for example, which is not prohibited.[728] It is difficult to generalise, as the scope of non-discrimination law with respect to big data is dependent on the context of a big data project and the (national) legislation pertaining to it. But in any case it deserves attention as an additional instrument to be taken into account in further discussion about solutions to big data issues.

5.2.3 Tailored Solutions

The last category of alternative legal approaches to big data's negative impact is the creation of new regulatory measures that specifically deal with (problematic) aspects of big data. This should not be seen as merely a last resort for when all else fails; it is a sui generis approach in which parts of the big data process and the problems it causes are deemed new and delineated from other issues, which can make them the subject of proposals for new

724. Cf. the EC's website listing and tracking legislative developments in the area of non-discrimination <http://ec.europa.eu/justice/discrimination/law/index_en.htm> accessed 15 May 2017.
725. Cf. Isabelle Chopin and Catharina Germaine, 'A Comparative Analysis of Non-Discrimination Law in Europe 2016' (Directorate General for Justice and Consumers 2016) European network of legal experts in gender equality and non-discrimination.
726. Cf. subsections 4.2 and 4.4.3.1 of Chapter 4.
727. *See* subsection 2.5.2.3 of Chapter 2.
728. Zarsky (n 213); Zuiderveen Borgesius, 'Online Price Discrimination and Data Protection Law' (n 214) 9.

regulation. Under the headings of algorithmic transparency and related terms, and big data ethics in general, this topic has received much attention over the past few years. A similar approach with a different angle is sector-specific regulation. When big data issues reveal themselves only or particularly in certain sectors or contexts, a sector-specific approach may be appropriate. These three possibilities are discussed in turn below.

5.2.3.1 Algorithmic Transparency

Algorithmic transparency centres around opening up algorithms to the public, usually through allowing access to the code.[729] From the active recent discussions, various flavours of this idea have emerged. There are different proposals or ideas in relation to, for example, the target audience of the information, which shows that algorithmic transparency can have different aims. Providing transparency to people who are targeted in the application phase aims to strengthen individual control and transparency, while it can also be about allowing experts such as internal auditors, journalists, researchers, or government institutions including supervisory authorities to scrutinise algorithms to evaluate them on fairness and lawfulness.[730] The trouble with algorithmic transparency directed at individuals who are subjected to big data decision-making is that it aims for increased knowledge and control; two factors that have been repeatedly identified as weaknesses in the current protective scheme. In addition to the general issues with control and transparency as enumerated on many occasions previously, there is only a very small group of people in society with the technical expertise in understanding these algorithms; it will not increase the average individual's capacity to make sensible choices.[731]

Access may however be valuable for certain groups. For journalists and researchers, it would make research into the fairness of algorithms easier and less time consuming and costly, and as such would create more space for watchdog oversight, knowledge, and clarifications on the basis of their research.[732] Legal oversight could be effectuated through algorithmic audits

729. Diakopoulos and Friedler (n 677).
730. Cf. Mayer-Schönberger and Cukier (n 83) 180–182; Cf. Ananny and Crawford (n 677) 5; Pasquale (n 170).
731. Diakopoulos (n 677) 411.
732. *See* for example ProPublica's 'Machine Bias' investigations, e.g., Julia Angwin, Terry Parris Jr. and Surya Mattu, 'Breaking the Black Box: What Facebook Knows About You' *ProPublica* (28 September 2016); Julia Angwin and others, 'Machine Bias: There's Software Used Across the Country to Predict Future Criminals. And It's Biased Against Blacks.' *ProPublica* (23 May 2016); Julia Angwin and Surya Mattu, 'Amazon Says It Puts Customers First. But Its Pricing Algorithm Doesn't' *ProPublica* (20 September 2016).

by supervisory authorities.[733] However, algorithms used in big data are highly complex and the feasibility of assessing their outcomes should not be overestimated. To begin with, it requires time and considerable technical expertise. Additionally, the outcomes and fairness of algorithms can generally not be gauged on the basis of the code alone. Particularly with self-learning systems and without knowledge about the input data, only having access to the code may not be meaningful.[734] With these caveats, algorithmic transparency remains an avenue that merits further research.

5.2.3.2 Big Data Ethics

Big data ethics has become something of a buzzword, like big data itself – discussed in special round-table discussions, big data and ethics councils, and in proposals ranging from introducing binding legal obligations on for example transparency and data security similar to those mentioned in the other alternatives discussed in this subsection, to self-regulation and incorporating ethical reviews and possibly ethical review boards in entities engaging in big data processing.[735] Positive aspects of these initiatives are that they are not limited to personal data processing and can focus more on procedures and outcomes. Additionally, more abstract notions such as fairness can be taken into account. This is an advantage, as frequently in big data the fairness of the process and treatment of people in general are at stake, instead of an individualised person who is intertwined with her personal data. Whether this shows promise depends on the context: in academia and medical research ethical review boards are common, but in many situations, such as in the online behavioural advertising sector, the positive effects are probably more limited. There will not be much support for costly and time-consuming reviews, and they are more likely to become

733. Which supervisory authorities this should be and what values their evaluation should be based upon, is still open to question. To be meaningful the assessment should go beyond what is unlawful in terms of possible personal data processing or direct discriminatory effects, and incorporate other aspects of fairness. Cf. danah boyd, 'Transparency ≠ Accountability' <https://points.datasociety.net/transparency-accountability-3c04e4804504> accessed 21 June 2017.

734. Ananny and Crawford (n 677) 5–13.

735. *See* amongst others Richards and King (n 85); Jacob Metcalf and Kate Crawford, 'Where Are Human Subjects in Big Data Research? The Emerging Ethics Divide' (2016) Big Data & Society; Effy Vayena and others, 'Elements of a New Ethical Framework for Big Data Research' (2016) Washington and Lee Law Review; European Data Protection Supervisor Decision establishing an external advisory group on the ethical dimensions of data protection ('the Ethics Advisory Group') 2015; Omer Tene and Jules Polonetsky, 'Beyond IRBs: Ethical Guidelines for Data Research', *Future of Privacy Forum – Big Data Ethics* (2015); Mandy Chessel, 'Ethics for Big Data and Analytics' (IBM 2014); the Council for Big Data, Ethics, and Society <http://bdes.datasociety.net/> accessed 20 March 2017, and workshops such as at the Future of Privacy Forum, <https://bigdata.fpf.org/> accessed 20 March 2017.

box-ticking exercises for compliance instead of meticulous analyses of the ethical and social implications of a given big data project. Additionally, parts of these processes can or may already be incorporated in DPIAs, or in similar assessments that are conducted for compliance purposes or because clients demand proof of specific ISO-certifications.[736] Still, particularly for specific sectors, it could be taken into account in further discussions.

5.2.3.3 Sector-Specific Regulation

The final alternative possibility of this section is the creation or using (sector-specific) regulation to tackle big data issues that emerge in specific sectors or contexts. As explained above, data protection law is omnibus regulation; it follows a general design and is not meant to pertain to particular sectors or technologies.[737] But from the illustrations of Chapter 3 on credit provision in the financial services industry, biobanks in medical research, and online personalisation, as well as from the multiple big data processing scenarios of Table 4.1 of Chapter 4, we can infer that some big data issues are particular for a given case. If an area is clearly demarcated and features specific contextual factors, sector-specific regulation may be developed or already be in place, such as in the financial sector and medical sector. Parts of the big data process and its implications may be regulated through such sector-specific regulation, or the rules may be supplemented with big-data specific directions.

In biobanking for example, contextual factors such as the type of samples and data, the safeguards and special infrastructure needed for storage and sharing, and the specific demands on consent and safeguards on usage given the (medical) research purposes, have made sector-specific regulation common.[738] Such regulation may counter big data issues, or specific rules in the big data context may be added. It may, for example, feature procedural safeguards and include the previously mentioned algorithmic auditing or ethical standards and reviews, or address risks of particular outcomes. This type of regulation, which can also consist of codes of professional ethics or sectoral self-regulation, should not be overlooked in the discussion on regulating big data.

---

736. For example, general standards regarding data security (the ISO 27000 series) or sector-specific standards that include data processing and management, such as ISO 20252 for market research.

737. Lynskey, *The Foundations of EU Data Protection Law* (n 174) 15–29.

738. Cf. Jennifer Harris and others, 'Toward a Roadmap in Global Biobanking for Health' (2012) 20 European Journal of Human Genetics 1105; Deborah Mascalzoni (ed), *Ethics, Law and Governance of Biobanking National, European and International Approaches* (Springer 2015).

5.3 A COMBINED APPROACH TO BIG DATA

This subsection starts with a recap of what has been concluded in previous chapters. It then sets out the idea of an integrated approach to big data: there are as many solutions to big data as there are problems, we must acknowledge that different problems merit different solutions, and that a combination of different solutions is necessary to protect individual rights and freedoms in big data.

The EU privacy and data protection framework is extremely important for protecting individual rights and freedoms against big data's negative impact. But perceiving everything about big data as a privacy and data protection problem is detrimental to the protection of individual rights and freedoms. The EU privacy and data protection framework cannot mitigate all negative impact, and does not have to, as part of the negative impact is beyond the scope of the rights to privacy and data protection. Perceiving everything about big data as a privacy and data protection problem ignores the other individual rights and freedoms and negative effects that are at stake. Also, such an approach may ultimately lead to an erosion of data protection law through overstretching its scope. We need to look at the big data process with an open mind instead of only through a privacy and data protection lens and evaluate every negative effect on its own merits.

The possible solutions to big data issues are as diverse as the problems, ranging from changing data protection law, or focusing on other areas of law such as consumer law or non-discrimination legislation, to creating regulatory measures and opting for sector-specific regulation. These solutions may supplement the protection offered by data protection law, or be in a better place to mitigate certain negative effects. After all, frequently it is not so much the collection of (personal) data or the processing that is at the heart of the issue, but the negative effects it may have on individuals. These can be imminent and high-impact, but also small and cumulative, as in the online personalisation illustration for example. In essence many of the problems are just as much (or more) problems of discrimination, power-imbalances, and weak positions of individuals as data protection issues, in spite of their source and use of personal data as a means to apply the outcomes of big data to individuals. If the outcome of big data is discriminatory, or if unfairness is caused by a power imbalance between the data subject and the big data entity, the rights to privacy and data protection are arguably not the essence of the issue, hence they probably are and should be addressed by other areas of law. For example, in cases of discrimination non-discrimination laws are obviously of additional (and likely necessary) value. Not only do (tools from) other areas of law show much potential in the targeted first scenario of the application phase; they also seem more appropriate.

No solution, not even new regulatory measures such as rules on algorithmic transparency, can function as a panacea through which the other negative effects can be mitigated. There is no one-size-fits-all solution to the problems that big data can cause. The focus should be on how different solutions can complement the EU privacy and data protection framework and each other. This also requires enforcement efforts: big data should be on the agenda of regulators and authorities, not just data protection authorities, but also consumer, competition, or other supervisory authorities. This seems to require cooperation and coordination amongst particularly different supervisory authorities. This is partially true and on some occasions happening already, considering amongst others the national and EU initiatives in the field of competition law as described under section 5.2.2.2 above. Where data protection law and other areas of law come close to each other, such as when competition law authorities decide to investigate abusive behaviour in the form of data protection principles, efforts may have to be coordinated to make sure they will not overlap.

But often such cooperation and coordination are unnecessary, as efforts do not have to overlap because the specific problems they address are distinct. Particularly with respect to the negative effects that big data can have on individual rights and freedoms in the application phase, it may not be needed. Many negative effects that flow from processes that we call big data actually consist of harm that exists in society irrespective of big data. For instance, differentiating on the basis of ethnicity when applying for a job is discrimination, irrespective of whether it is based on data analysis or human judgment. It is, and should be, addressed by non-discrimination legislation. For a large part a combined approach simply requires that the big data process and its negative effects are not reduced to privacy and data protection problems, but instead are evaluated on their own characteristics. Researchers, policymakers, and enforcement agencies should assess issues with an open mind; cases or problems should not be categorised as privacy and data protection problems as soon as personal data are at stake. For example, when a person has a weak position vis-à-vis a company that provides an important service, and the service is made conditional on collecting her personal data, she is not only a data subject but also a consumer.

In sum, the way forward is a combined approach to big data. As we have seen, there is no single big data problem; there are a multitude of different negative effects, unsatisfactorily protected by the EU privacy and data protection framework, due to a variety of gaps. Similarly, there is no holy grail of solutions. What happens in practice, the effects this has on individual rights and freedoms, and how the legal framework applies, is not homogenous throughout the whole three-phase big data process, nor in every practical application of big data. The answer lies in acknowledging that big data and its negative side effects are not a singular concept and accepting that the problems can only be solved through a combination of solutions.

5.4 CONCLUSION

This chapter presents an alternative approach to mitigate the negative impact of big data, following the conclusion that the privacy and data protection law approach does not, does not have to, and cannot offer adequate protection against big data's potential negative effects on individual rights and freedoms. Through compiling the possible solutions that could be relevant and have been proposed in discussions on big data and related topics, and assessing how they could be of value, conclusions have been drawn on their potential, and the need for an approach that combines multiple solutions.

These solutions have been summarised under three headings that describe their character: (1) *changes* to the current EU privacy and data protection law framework; (2) application of *other areas of law* in a new way in the context of big data, or a shift in the focus of (supervisory) authorities that are not DPAs to big data; and (3) completely *new* regulatory measures. Each solution has its merits and drawbacks, but some show more potential or disadvantages than others. As this chapter merely aims to explore the possibilities for further research, the list of alternatives is non-exhaustive and does not offer policy recommendations. Depending on the issues that big data may cause in the future, other solutions may be required. Nevertheless, despite these disclaimers and the concise analysis, some preliminary conclusions can be drawn regarding which (combination of) legal alternatives should be prioritised in discussions and research focused on searching for answers, and which may be dismissed in advance.

Amending data protection law may seem a viable option. However, for several reasons it should not be the focus of attention. First of all, the GDPR contains some major improvements from the perspective of the protection of the individual, for example in terms of enforcement possibilities. The landscape will change with these possibilities; suggesting drastic changes seems premature. Also, keeping in mind the efforts and discussion that it took to reach a compromise on the new data protection rules, the likelihood of suggested changes making it into law and changing something for the benefit of individuals in the foreseeable future seems small. And lastly, as explained in Chapter 4, it is not the *task* of data protection law to mitigate all negative consequences that big data can have on individual rights and freedoms. Although it sometimes can, its enabling function is a by-effect and not an aim in itself.

This is where the second category of possible legal alternatives (employing other fields of law) comes in. Under this heading, consumer law, competition law, and non-discrimination law have been discussed. All areas seem to have potential in the context of big data, and first developments are emerging, particularly in Member States. One reason why consumer law, competition law, and non-discrimination law show much potential, is that some of the gaps and problems discussed are intrinsically issues of (unfair) competition, a weak position of consumers, or outright discrimination. If such gaps and problems form the essence of a problem, the areas of law that focus on these problems specifically seem an obvious avenue for further research, particularly in how these problems manifest itself in big data contexts. In addition to addressing the issues that they are designed for in big data, these areas of law could offer supplementary protection to problems that do fit within the realm of data protection law. An example has been described above, where consumer law is used to address unfair contract terms pertaining to the processing of personal data and data protection law. However, in such cases there may be more drawbacks, such as conflicts and legal uncertainty. Caution is required, yet both possible applications of other areas of law merit further attention.

In the context of the above, new regulatory measures may not seem indispensable. Yet alternatives such as algorithmic transparency regulation and sector-specific regulation address specific issues and may be of value in particular contexts, and therefore deserve attention. There is, however, no need for 'sui generis big data regulation', because this incorrectly presupposes that big data and its issues are something completely new and unregulated. As shown above, many legal domains regulate or could regulate parts of big data, and data protection law already offers much protection in a large part of the big data process. The most important point is to acknowledge that there is no one-size-fits-all solution; what happens in and because of big data is diverse and demands a combined approach. And negative effects that appear in one phase can have their source in another. The effects of regulation of one phase could flow to other phases, mitigating other issues and possibly obviating the need for more regulatory intervention.

The main conclusion is that in big data, problems should be analysed open-mindedly, without a particular legal framework in mind. It is crucial that we acknowledge that big data stands at the base of decisions that can pose a threat to individual rights and freedoms, but that are only remotely related to privacy and data protection. It needs attention from other areas of law to mitigate these problems; big data and its potential negative effects cannot be regarded solely through a data protection law lens. Different problems require different solutions, and solving them requires a practical, balanced, and structured approach. Data protection law and authorities are not the only legitimate caretakers of individual rights and freedoms in the context of big data. Only through a combination of the EU privacy and data protection framework with other solutions and areas of law can adequate protection of individual rights and freedoms in the age of big data be ensured.

Chapter 6
Conclusion

6.1 INTRODUCTION

This chapter summarises and analyses the main findings of this research, on the basis of which the main conclusions are drawn, including the answer to the research question. Before the main findings are summarised in the following sections, this introduction first gives an outline of the research design.

This work is about the protection of individuals against the negative impact that big data may have on their private lives. Many positive and promising developments result from big data, but the massive collection and use of data also raise a host of issues. At the centre of this work is the position and protection of the individual whose personal data are used in big data, or who experiences the negative consequences of the application of big data. In the EU, the rights to privacy and data protection are the focal points in the discussion of this dark side of big data for individuals. They are perceived as being the primary rights at risk, as well as the solution to the problems that big data creates.

The importance of the rights to privacy and data protection is acknowledged in this book, but it is argued that this perspective is too narrow. The effects of big data on the lives of individuals transcend privacy and data protection. By conceptualising big data as a process that consists of the acquisition and analysis of (personal) data and the application of the outcomes thereof, it finds that the potential consequences may also be particularly severe for personal autonomy, freedom of expression, and non-discrimination (Chapters 1 and 2). The question that arises in this context is what the potential and limitations of the EU legal privacy and data protection framework are with respect to the protection of individual rights and freedoms against big data's potential negative impact, and to what extent they should mitigate the negative effects of big data on individual rights and freedoms in general. This latter aspect, the extent to which it can be seen as data protection law's *task* to mitigate this harm, is assessed on the basis of the normative concepts of the fundamental rights to privacy and data protection in the EU. These normative concepts are derived from an analysis of Article 8 ECHR and Articles 7 and 8 CFREU and their interpretation by the ECtHR and CJEU (Chapter 3).

An analysis of EU data protection law leads to a conclusion on data protection law's capacity to protect the rights to privacy and data protection itself, and its enabling effect through which it indirectly protects these other individual rights and freedoms (Chapter 4). Data protection law offers a high level of protection for both the rights to privacy and data protection, and (indirectly) to the other individual rights and freedoms as well. However, data protection law does not function optimally in the context of big data, and many of big data's negative consequences for individual rights and freedoms turn out to be beyond the scope of the rights to privacy and data protection. The protection offered by data protection law is insufficient to fully protect individual rights and freedoms against the negative consequences of big data.

This work therefore concludes that to protect individuals' rights and freedoms, it is necessary to look beyond the privacy and data protection paradigm. The only way to resolve the problems arising from big data is an integrated approach that consists of other legal solutions that complement each other and reflects the multi-faceted nature of the problem at hand (Chapter 5).

Sections 6.2– 6.4 below summarise the substantive parts of this research. This is followed by conclusions on big data, data protection law, and the protection of individual rights and freedoms in subsection 6.5. Subsection 6.6 ends with implications, solutions, and predictions that together form the envisioned way forward in light of the conclusions on the limitations of the privacy and data protection law approach to the protection of individuals in big data.

6.2 BIG DATA

Chapter 2 discusses the concept of big data and the resulting possible negative consequences for the rights and freedoms of the individual. The meaning of the term 'big data' depends on the context in which it is used. It is commonly assumed that the term was first used in 2011, linked to three factors that refer to data, being *volume, velocity,* and *variety.* These factors were introduced as characteristics of new possibilities for data management and analysis that were considered a result of technological developments that increased these possibilities and made them cheaper. However, over the years the term has been used in various new ways, ranging from a marketing term that refers to the mere analysis of a large amount of data and is used as a means to attract attention and generate income, to a generic reference to a socio-technological phenomenon with far-reaching consequences for the way in which we regard knowledge and societal developments.

6.2.1 Three-Phase Model of Big Data

Considering the diversity in interpretations, a further delineation of big data is required. After all, when the content of the term and its consequences are not clear, it is impossible to determine how it is regulated and how it should be regulated. Therefore a process-oriented logic is applied, which facilitates a normative and legal analysis of big data. The common denominator of the different interpretations that are in use is that in all cases big data can be seen as a process in which data are collected and analysed, with the aim of subsequently applying the results of this analysis. In practice, it is obviously a complex and iterative process, but in general these three phases of acquisition, analysis, and application can be distinguished in big data projects. This three-phase model makes it possible to conduct a normative and legal analysis of big data.

In Chapter 2 the different phases are elucidated and illustrated using three practical examples of big data: credit in the financial services industry, biobanks in medical research, and online personalisation. In brief, the phases consist of the following steps. In the acquisition phase, data are collected. They can be acquired from the individual herself, but they can also be bought from data brokers, or for example created through combining different datasets. Thereafter follows the analysis of the data. The analysis is automated using specialised software programs that are continuously being developed. From this analysis flows information in different forms, for example, as knowledge, models, or predictions. In the application phase, this information is used as a basis for decisions. These can be general decisions, for example, about building infrastructures or prescribing new (combinations of) drugs for specific diseases. But often it concerns decisions that are targeted at the individual, such as the rejection of a credit application or the adjustment of the prices of flights on a website.

For the normative and legal analysis, it is important to give thought to the fact that the people whose data are gathered and serve as input for analysis and the people to whom the results of analysis are applied are two different groups. Depending on the big data project at stake they can overlap, where data from the application phase lead to new input. But in general, the acquisition and analysis are separated from the application; a model is developed using the data of people from the first group and can subsequently be applied to an unlimited new group of people.

6.2.2 Negative Consequences for Individual Rights and Freedoms

After the explanation of the three-phase model follows an analysis of the possible negative consequences on individual rights and freedoms that can result from each phase. Notwithstanding the positive influence that big data can have on the lives of individuals and society as a whole, which is not denied in this work, given the research question most attention is paid to the negative aspects of big data. The conclusion is that every phase can negatively influence individual rights and freedoms in its own way, because different actions take place in each of the phases. In the acquisition phase, the risks primarily lie in the large-scale collection and combination of (personal) data. This has negative effects on the rights to privacy and data protection, but personal autonomy and freedom of expression are at stake as well. The knowledge that one's behaviour is monitored and that data on behaviour is tracked and saved for future use can influence people's behaviour, the choices they make, and the information that they gather and produce.

In the analysis phase the effects seem more limited, because often data will be processed in a form that makes it impossible to trace them back to identifiable individuals, as will be explained in more detail below. But the analysis phase is the source of many of the negative effects that crystallise in the application phase, such as discrimination. As a rule, neither the people whose data are the source of analysis nor the individuals that experience the negative consequences in the application phase can exert any influence over what happens in the analysis phase. Essentially, there can be said to be a negative effect on personal autonomy: there is not much influence over what is done with data, or which data and models underpin a decision.

In the application phase the full range of negative effects may materialise, that is, negative impact on the rights to personal autonomy, privacy and data protection, non-discrimination, and freedom of speech. Personal autonomy is under pressure, because of the possibilities to personalise, persuade, coe,rce, nudge, and manipulate that big data creates. It must be borne in mind that it is not about *high-impact* decisions only; small but cumulative instances of personalisation can also have a lasting influence on the individual's free choice, development, and identity. Given the increasing knowledge and possibilities, and the scale at which it takes place, particularly in the digital environment, it is important to also heed this cumulative personalisation, as well as the long-term consequences that it can have for individuals' future. With respect to privacy and data protection in the application phase, roughly the same problems occur as in the acquisition phase. In addition, the application of big data can result in self-standing interferences with the personal sphere, independent of the processing of personal data. Personalisation can also negatively affect the free gathering of information and ideas. And finally, the application of big data can lead to (direct or indirect) discrimination.

6.3 THE FUNDAMENTAL RIGHTS TO PRIVACY AND TO DATA PROTECTION

Central to Chapter 3 is the scope of the fundamental rights to privacy and to data protection in the EU, to determine their normative content with regard to big data. The chapter examines what the fundamental rights involve in the context of big data, and what they demand of the protection that secondary EU law offers. The chapter focuses on the stand-alone value of these rights, as well as on the protective function that they fulfil with respect to other individual rights and freedoms, which is referred to as the *enabling function* of the rights to privacy and to data protection in this book. It results in a normative conceptualisation of the rights to privacy and to data protection. An interference with these normative concepts should trigger legislative protection at the secondary legislation level, which is the subject in Chapter 4. In addition, for the protection of individual rights and freedoms other than privacy and data protection through the *enabling function*, the rights to privacy and/or to data protection need apply to a given effect of big data. Where this is not the case, these rights are not protected against the negative impact of big data through the privacy and data protection law framework, and it is not the task of the framework to do so. This affects what is required from data protection law with respect to protecting individual rights and freedoms other than the rights to privacy and to data protection, which is evaluated in Chapter 4.

6.3.1 Interpretation of Fundamental Rights in the Context of Big Data

Article 8 ECHR and Articles 7 and 8 CFREU are compared, being part of the most important fundamental rights instruments in the EU. Complaints about violations of the ECHR and CFREU can be brought before the ECtHR and the CJEU. The ECtHR has, in its long tradition of case law on Article 8 ECHR, to a large extent shaped the content of the right to (informational) privacy in the EU. The interpretation of the rights to privacy and to data protection by the CFREU is strongly influenced by the Strasbourg case law, mainly because the right to privacy in the Charter is a *corresponding right* in the sense of Article 52 (3) CFREU that has to offer minimum protection in accordance with Article 8 ECHR. The Charter adds a separate right to the protection of personal data to the EU fundamental rights level.

The interpretation of these fundamental rights in the light of big data is difficult for multiple reasons. The judgments of both Courts are casuistic and strongly embedded in the context of the cases at hand, which usually deal with interferences (through actions or neglecting to act) by states. Concrete cases on big data and explicit references to the enabling function are uncommon. However, through relinquishing the procedural context and instead looking at the normative content of the rights, in combination with the interpretative doctrines of the Courts such as the *living instrument* and *practical and effective* doctrines of the ECtHR, meaning can be given to the scope of the rights and to the level of protection that is required in secondary legislation.

6.3.2 Normative Conceptualisation of the Rights to Privacy and Data Protection

The successive analysis of Articles 8 ECHR and 7 and 8 CFREU in Chapter 3 leads to a relatively coherent image of the normative concepts of the rights to privacy and data protection with respect to big data as interpreted by the ECtHR and the CJEU. The right to privacy encompasses personal data processing in all phases, for which the interpretation is linked to Convention 108 and includes metadata and location data. However, personal data processing does not automatically lead to an interference; it depends on circumstances such as sensitivity of the data, reasonable expectation of privacy, and the scope of the processing. In any case there are minimum requirements that need to be met to protect the individual. These requirements include limitations on storage and retention times, and obligations to take measures to protect the personal data, amongst others to prevent unauthorised access and abuse. Independent of personal data processing, the right to privacy is at stake when there is an interference with the home or correspondence, or in the sphere of sexual activities, social life, personal relationships, or personal, moral, or physical identity. This can be the case when the application of big data results in a decision that interferes with these interests. Given the diversity in possible applications of big data, it is impossible to give a detailed comprehensive overview of such cases.

The scope of the normative concept of privacy with respect to personal data seems very broad, but the right to data protection is still of added value. It adds, amongst others, specific requirements related to the processing of personal data. Article 8 CFREU is more precisely formulated than Articles 8 ECHR and 7 CFREU; it contains detailed requirements that the processing of personal data is based on consent or another legitimate ground, rights on access to data and rectification, and the necessity of having independent oversight on compliance.

The enabling function of privacy and data protection is acknowledged in the literature, but there are not many explicit references to be found in the case law of either Court that discusses the rights to privacy and to data protection. Personal autonomy is regarded by the ECtHR as part of the right to privacy, and with that the facilitating function of privacy for personal autonomy is inherent in the normative concept of the right to privacy. However, because an interference with personal autonomy has never been explicitly established by the ECtHR, its exact scope is undetermined.

Regarding freedom of expression, the CJEU has made the connection in its case law and has thereby acknowledged the facilitating function, but this enabling function is not formulated as a duty of the right to privacy or data protection. The limited attention for the enabling function is likely due to the fundamental rights tradition in the EU: the rights to privacy and to data protection have stand-alone value, and other rights and freedoms are protected by their respective fundamental rights and freedoms, which are generally analysed separately when they are also part of a case. These conclusions on the normative scope of the rights to privacy and to data protection reappear in Chapter 4, where they are compared to the conclusions on the scope of EU data protection law, to assess its duty to protect individual rights and freedoms.

6.4 DATA PROTECTION LAW

Chapter 4 analyses to what extent current EU data protection law, in the guise of the GDPR, protects individual rights and freedoms, can protect them, and is required to protect them. To answer these questions, this chapter is divided into four parts, which discuss whether EU data protection law applies to big data, how its substantive norms function in this context, how it is enforced, and whether the normative concepts of the rights to privacy and to data protection demand a different implementation of secondary legislation.

6.4.1 Scope of Application

The first part of the chapter analyses when the regulatory framework applies within the big data process. Decisive for this question is the definition of 'personal data' and the associated concept of 'identifiability'. The material scope of EU data protection law depends on whether personal data are processed, and therefore on the criteria that make up the concept of 'personal data'. In the context of big data, the crucial criterion is 'identified or identifiable', which refers to whether data can be traced back to natural persons. On the basis of this criterion, four types of data can be distinguished: directly identifiable data, indirectly identifiable data, de-identified data, and non personal data. The first two types are within the scope of the GDPR and are here referred to as *identifiable data*. The other two types are not within the scope of the law and are referred to as *non-identifiable* data.

On the basis of this division, multiple processing scenarios are possible. When only non-identifiable data are processed in a given big data phase, the regulation does not apply, and accordingly there is no protective effect emanating from EU data protection law. Whether and in which phase identifiable data are processed depends on the specific big data project. There are projects in which personal data are processed in all three phases, which makes the regulation applicable without reservations. But there are also projects that do not collect and use personal data in the acquisition and analysis phases, but that can nevertheless have an impact on the individual in the application phase. An example is when a government allows for the building of a chemical plant in a specific location on the basis of big data analysis of non-identifiable data, and the health of people living in that area is at stake due to pollution or chemical waste. Generally, it will be the case that personal data processing often, but not necessarily, occurs in the acquisition phase and (to a limited extent) in the application phase, but not in the analysis phase. After all, there are strong incentives for entities engaging in big data to process data in a non-identifiable manner. In big data (analysis) there is generally no interest in specific individuals: general patterns are what matters. There is usually no necessity to keep data in an identifiable state. De-identification ensures that the GDPR is no longer applicable. If data protection rules are not applicable, principles such as purpose limitation, data minimisation, and the necessity of having a legitimate processing ground do not apply. This increases the possibilities for big data, while decreasing the risk with respect to, *inter alia*, compliance, which explains this strong incentive. The conclusion is that EU data protection law does not apply to (parts of) the big data process in some cases, and consequently big data partially avoids protection through the GDPR. This constitutes the first lacuna in the protection of individual rights and freedoms.

6.4.2 Substantive Norms and Enforcement

The second part of Chapter 4 analyses how the substantive norms of the GDPR function in the context of big data, if EU data protection law is applicable. This analysis focuses on rules that are of relevance in big data, given the actions in the different phases and the possible negative effects in every phase, with additional attention for the potential of innovations in data protection law resulting from the GDPR, like the right to data portability. The analysis of the potential and the limitations of substantive data protection law is divided into rules that should make data processing *transparent* for the individual, rules that aim to give the individual *control* over the processing, and rules that intend to map out or regulate specific *risks*.

The duties to inform individuals about the aims and the way in which data are processed, and the logic and consequences of automated individual decisions (including profiling), constitute the rules that shape transparency. These rules address the acquisition phase, and the application phase in particular when there is automated individual decision-making. Control rights that are of importance are the requirement for a legitimate ground for processing and the accompanying consent requirement, the right not to be subjected to automated individual decision-making, the right to erasure (right to be forgotten), and the right to data portability. Together the rules on transparency and control create the necessary preconditions for the individual's informational self-determination: enabling awareness about, and insight into, personal data processing and being able to influence it. This informational self-determination safeguards personal autonomy and the right to data protection, and can (indirectly) mitigate discrimination and have protective effects on the general rights to privacy and to freedom of expression. However, in the context of big data this protection does not reach its full potential. One of the reasons for this is that the scope of the rights is limited due to their criteria for application. For example, the automated decision-making rules are limited to *high-impact* decisions. Profiling and personalisation can alter people's choices and lives in small but cumulative ways, which is not addressed by these rules. Moreover, accurate predictions do not always require much personal data from the person to whom big data is applied. Although designed with big data in mind, these provisions are to a certain extent already outpaced by technological developments.

Additionally, in practice it is often difficult to meet the criteria that exist with respect to informing the individual and acquiring her consent, for example because future applications and consequences are unknown or insufficiently clear at the moment of personal data acquisition. But the most important reason is that individual rights and control do not function well in an environment of online data collection in a data-driven economy, and application of big data. Given the complexity and ubiquitousness of digital personal data processing, the management of online privacy and data protection has become an almost impossible task for the individual. Moreover, the supply of personal data frequently functions as a requirement and counter performance for the provision of (online) services, whereas the (negative) consequences of personal data processing are often of an abstract nature, or only substantiate in the long run or within the context of cumulative processing instances or decisions. For individuals, it may seem as if they are not directly affected by the processing of their personal data. These are additional reasons to assume that adequate protection of individual rights and freedoms in the context of big data cannot be achieved through transparency and control by the individual alone.

The rules of the GDPR that are directed at mapping or regulating specific risks primarily address the entities that process personal data or are responsible for the processing. As such, the rules largely avoid the drawbacks associated with the aforementioned rules of the informational self-determination sphere. Important in the context of big data are the rules that (conditionally) prohibit the processing of special categories of data, the principles of purpose limitation and data minimisation, the obligations regarding DPIAs, and the rules on implementing data protection by design and default. The limited prohibition on the processing of personal data that are perceived sensitive fulfils an important function in the protection of the rights to data protection and to privacy. It can also function as a means to mitigate discrimination, through limiting the processing of data related to grounds for discrimination such as ethnicity, sex, or religion. Yet it is of no avail in cases of indirect discrimination, which is a genuine danger in big data because certain (combinations) of data can serve as *proxies* for special categories of personal data. DPIAs and data protection by design and default demand, in brief, that big data entities map their processing activities and the associated risks and take (technical) measures to try to safeguard individuals' data protection rights. The obligation to assess risks and possible safeguards in order to protect the rights of individuals prior to the processing of their personal data in all likelihood has a positive influence on the protection of the individual. But there are doubts about the practical implementation and enforcement of such rules, and as such about the protective potential of these provisions. The same holds for the provisions on purpose limitation and data minimisation. In conclusion, these rules seem to impose important limits on the processing of personal data on the one hand, but appear irreconcilable with big data, which can ultimately lead to enforcement issues.

As regards enforcement of data protection law, its effectiveness has long been criticised. However, with the entry into force of the GDPR, things may change. The GDPR improves enforcement possibilities, amongst others through substantially higher fines. However, due to *inter alia* the ubiquitousness of personal data processing and the continuing friction between law and practice, enforcement of data protection law will remain a problem in big data to some degree.

6.4.3 Scope of Protection of Data Protection Law for Individual Rights and Freedoms

The last part of Chapter 4 explains the lacunae that exist in protection of individual rights and freedoms in big data when analysing the GDPR. It matches these lacunae with the normative concepts of privacy and data protection from Chapter 3, to draw conclusions on the potential and limitations of the data protection law approach to issues in big data, and assess to what extent data protection law *should* address these effects.

The lacunae in protection are divided into three types, according to the causes that lie at their foundation: whether data protection law is applicable, and if it is not, whether data processing is the core of the problem or not. In the first type of lacuna, the EU privacy and data protection law framework applies, but it offers insufficient protection. This cause is at the root of most of the acquisition phase problems. It can also be at stake in the application phase, for example, if people are targeted on the basis of personal data, but the automated decision-making rules do not apply because the decisions are not high-impact, or there is human intervention in the process. There are multiple reasons underlying this lacuna: as explained above, control and transparency do not function well in the context of the data-driven economy in general, and small but cumulative big data applications in particular. Second, the criteria that apply to the GDPR's rights, for example those on automated decision-making as explained above, do not yield broad protection in big data. The second type of lacuna exists when data protection does not apply, yet data processing is at the heart of the issue. This frequently occurs in the analysis phase, as most personal data will have been de-identified before they enter analysis, and these data are therefore outside the scope of data protection law, but the risks lie in the processing of the data. In such cases, the means to exert influence over the analysis through data protection law are virtually non-existent, and there is no task for data protection law as no personal data are processed. In the third type, the framework is not applicable, and data processing is *not* the essence of the problem. This situation occurs in the application phase where, in addition to targeted personal data-based decisions, non-targeted decisions are made. These decisions do not rely on personal data for application, but can affect individuals' lives nonetheless, as explained above.

On the basis of the summary of how data protection law functions in the context of big data and the taxonomy of lacunae in protection, conclusions can be drawn about the normative concepts of the rights to privacy and to data protection, and how EU data protection law corresponds with them. As elucidated above, in the insufficient protection lacuna, data protection law applies but is not entirely up to the challenge of big data. EU data protection law does, however, seem to meet the level of protection that is required under the normative concepts of the rights to privacy and data protection law. In effect, the fundamental rights level demands a measure of informational self-determination, i.e., through the rights bestowed upon the individual under Article 8 (2) CFREU, and obligations regarding safeguards to protect personal data to be taken by those processing the data. Data protection law contains such rights and provisions, even though there are issues with their scope of application and protection in the context of big data.

A significant number of the big data problems, particularly (part of) those occurring in the analysis and application phases, does not fall within the scope of the normative concepts of privacy and data protection. If this is the case, there is no place for an enabling effect. Accordingly, these are stand-alone problems. For type 2 and 3 lacunae, particularly if data processing is not the core of the issue, there is no clear link between a problem and the rights to privacy and to data protection. In such cases, the biggest problems seem to reside in information asymmetries and power imbalances that data-driven decision-making generates, and the effects of certain decisions that may harm individuals. This can even be the case if the data protection law applies. An example is problems in the acquisition phase, where asymmetrical relationships involving, for example, network effects can be regarded as an important cause. Therefore, it is key to acknowledge that not every problem of big data constitutes a privacy or data protection law problem. Data protection law should not be regarded as a panacea in the context of big data. The problems need to be assessed and addressed based on their individual characteristics. This observation strongly influences the preferred approach of big data as maintained in this work, which is explained below.

With respect to the normative concepts of the rights to privacy and data protection, it could be argued that under the living instrument and practical and effective doctrines and the increasing attentiveness of the CJEU regarding the protection of privacy and personal data, a broader interpretation of the rights to privacy and data protection would be appropriate, as the current interpretation of the concepts does not achieve a broad measure of protection in the light of technological advancements and the data-driven economy. This broader interpretation would then also influence what would be expected of the secondary legislative level. However, currently there do not seem to be concrete starting points that evince such an approach by (either one of) the Courts. In addition, many big data problems cannot be construed in 'traditional' privacy and data protection terms of protection of informational self-determination and the personal sphere; they consist of stand-alone negative impact on individual rights and freedoms. These points, and their implications for the protection of individual rights through the EU legal privacy and data protection framework, are elucidated in the concluding thoughts below.

6.5 CONCLUSIONS

Big data is often considered a phenomenon, but it should be regarded as a means: a tool that can be used to improve the lives of people on many fronts (i.e., financial, social, health), but that can also be used to harm them, occasionally both at the same time. The large scale processing of *personal* data is often considered the core of big data, and there is also a general consensus that further major characteristics include the variety of data and sources involved, and the speed with which the data can be processed. Partly for this reason, privacy and data protection law have been the point of departure for the legal discussion on big data. But big data is not only about the large scale of the data that are processed, or the velocity or variety, but also about 'big' in the sense of its *scope*. It is about the ubiquitousness and widely diverse types of use that are made of it, such as finding useful knowledge, data-driven decision-making, and categorising, predicting, and profiling of people on a large scale.

These negative effects are strongly felt in the application phase. What is done with the knowledge, how it is applied, and what the results are, represent the main problem of big data. This is not only comprised of high-impact decisions, such as direct discrimination through big data decisions, but also the small cumulative effects, such as ubiquitous online personalisation. Individuals' daily lives are increasingly based on optimised and personalised decisions. The deterioration of personal autonomy is not felt in full, because it involves only small decisions and effects. But they all add up and influence a person's life, identity, and chances in the long run. Individual awareness has a central role to play here, but further deliberation and research into the long-term effects of small but cumulative instances of big data and personalisation, and their effects on core values of liberal societies, is also necessary. Also problematic in this context are the labels of objectivity and neutrality that are often attached to big data. It is a misconception that when there are enough data, truth and objectivity automatically appear. When decision-makers rely too much on big data, biases and errors may result that are difficult for individuals to refute. With big data as a basis, transparency, accountability, and appeal against decisions become difficult to achieve. But these issues will generally be beyond the privacy and data protection law domain, particularly when general, non-targeted decisions are concerned. Taking an example from the biobank illustration: when certain drugs are not reimbursed anymore following big data analysis, on the basis of costs of effectiveness, this is informed decision-making on the basis of big data. However, even though this decision may be opposable for many different reasons, it is not the processing of personal data or the analysis that make it so. In sum, although the processing of data is the core, making privacy and data protection (law) the point of departure in both societal and legal discussions about big data, big data issues transcend the normative interests protected by privacy and data protection.

This work therefore observes a privacy, data protection, and big data problem that goes beyond the traditional understanding of fear for infringement of individuals' informational privacy as a result of big data. The focus on privacy and data protection law itself in the context of big data is part of the problem. Certainly, the core of big data is large scale (personal) data processing, and there is undeniably a risk of a deflation of privacy and data protection, particularly in the acquisition phase. However, these issues represent only a part of the big data problem. And because of the focus on data processing, we might lose sight of the fact that the risks or damage of big data are only partially about the loss of informational privacy. They are just as much about other consequences of data processing; the possible detrimental effects on personal autonomy, freedom of expression, and non-discrimination, and the information asymmetries, power imbalances, and unfairness that can arise from the data-driven economy and data-driven decision-making.

Part of this problem may be neutralised through the rights to privacy and data protection. The legal protection of privacy and personal data facilitates the protection of other individual rights and freedoms, particularly through data protection regulation. Negative effects such as discrimination or 'chilling effects' on freedom of expression can be mitigated through prohibitions and measures promoting individual control over personal data, primarily because they can nip the processing that lies at the foundation of the negative consequences in the bud. Personal data therefore function as a *proxy* for the protection of individual rights and freedoms. As such, the regulation of personal data indirectly protects other rights and freedoms. This *enabling function* of privacy and data protection is recognised in the literature. EU data protection regulation acknowledges it (i.e., Recital 4 and Article 1 (2) GDPR), and the Courts allude to it occasionally (*see* the summary in subsection 6.3 above). However, its potential should not be overestimated in the context of big data. From a legal doctrinal perspective, the protection of individual rights and freedoms is not an aim in itself against which the specific data protection rules should be tested. Protection always goes through an interference with the rights to privacy and personal data protection; the law cannot by-pass this to protect these other interests. An overly strong focus also under-appreciates the diverse nature of the problems that big data creates: as explained above, not all big data problems travel through the rights to privacy and to data protection. Additionally, the protective potential of the EU privacy and data protection law framework itself is limited in multiple ways.

In the first place, parts of big data collection and processing are beyond the scope of protection of the EU legal privacy and data protection law framework, because data protection law does not apply. This means that with respect to a large share of *big data assets*, no information or transparency obligations exist. Notwithstanding the fact that the control that the individual can exert over these data is limited, if not non-existent, in practice it leads to information asymmetries and an increase in opacity. Moreover, it demonstrates that the opportunities to scrutinise crucial factors in the decision-making process within big data entities are limited.

Additionally, even if it applies, the level of protection offered in the context of big data by the EU legal privacy and data protection law framework is limited, in spite of the many achievements of data protection law and the improvements under the GDPR. Data protection law, as omnibus (and compromise) legislation, does not always seem able to cope well with technological advancement and the data-driven economy. The automated decision-making provisions for instance seem to hold great promise, because big data decisions in the application phase are responsible for a range of different negative effects. However, the criteria determine that the profiling rules only apply to high-impact decisions, in cases where there had not been any human intervention in the process. But as one of big data's significant problems is the many minor but cumulative decisions that influence individuals' lives in small and inconspicuous ways, it is clear that the profiling rules are of little help against big data's cumulative negative impact. The same holds for rights that aim to give the individual control over her own data. Contemporary data protection law operates from an idea of individuals in isolation, of personal data silos, which does not match big data reality in which different types of data from different people and things all influence a single person's daily life, chances, and position in society. Finally, as elucidated above, some effects and decisions can simply not be attributed to the processing of (personal) data; they relate to how people or entities with decision-making power respond to certain knowledge. We can refer to these cases as consequences of big data, but such consequences do not necessarily concern the EU legal privacy and data protection framework.

In sum, data protection law has an important function as a solution to big data issues. It does not only provide for informational self-determination and measures protecting personal data as required by the fundamental rights to privacy and to data protection; it also has indirect protective value for the rights to personal autonomy, non-discrimination, and freedom of expression. However, it is not the aim of data protection law to be the panacea against all big data's negative effects. Neither can it fulfil this role, since the protected subject matter of privacy and data protection law is limited. Data protection law does not always apply to big data, and not all big data problems are privacy and data protection problems in essence. Therefore, this research advocates an approach in which data protection law is supplemented by other legal solutions, to provide an integrated solution to the negative impact that big data may have on individual rights and freedoms.

6.6 THE WAY FORWARD

The envisioned way forward, following the conclusion that to protect individuals' rights and freedoms it is necessary to look beyond the privacy and data protection paradigm, is an integrated approach in which multiple legal solutions are combined. This stems from the idea that it is necessary to assess the problems individually and see which legal solution fits best, because of the multi-faceted nature of the problem at hand.

To this end, several legal alternatives to privacy and data protection law have come under review in Chapter 5. Chapter 5's overview gives an account of possibilities that have been suggested in the literature over the past few years, and explains whether they could be of relevance in addressing big data's negative effects on individual's lives as described in this work. Due to the nature of this research, this overview gives suggestions for further research and argues for a combined approach, but it does not contain policy recommendations. When legal measures are taken to mitigate the negative effects of big data, many interests must be taken into account that have not been dealt with in this book, such as the interests of big data entities and of society in general. But the focal point throughout this work has been the protection of individuals and their individual rights and freedoms. On the basis of this analysis, no full conclusions can be drawn as to whether specific solutions should be adopted.

The alternatives discussed here, which could supplement data protection law for solving big data problems are: changing substantive data protection law, changing the scope of application of data protection law, propertisation of personal data, consumer law, competition law, non-discrimination regulation, algorithmic transparency, big data ethics, and sector-specific regulation. This overview of alternatives is derived from the legal discourse of the past few years on big data, its problems, and possible solutions. On the basis of the concise analysis in this work, consumer law, competition law, and non-discrimination regulation in the area of big data show much potential and their utility in the context of big data should be researched further. Sector-specific regulation, initiatives in the area of algorithmic transparency, and big data ethics are alternative avenues that may also be of added value. Changing the scope of application of data protection law and propertisation of personal data do not seem to lead to the desired results and have considerable drawbacks, so are therefore deemed to deserve less priority.

As argued above, big data demands a combined approach: a combination of the alternatives is the only way to deal with big data problems. There is no one-size-fits-all solution for big data, as big data's applications as well as its problems are simply too diverse. New initiatives that specifically target (parts of) the big data process, such as those concerning algorithmic transparency, can be of value as they address issues that are particular for big data, but they cannot alone mitigate all negative effects. Additionally, problems can have multiple causes, which makes a combined approach more reasonable. Often, personal data processing itself is not the problem, nor is big data analysis per se. If it is, there clearly is a role for data protection. But other problems seem to be caused primarily by information asymmetries and the weak position of the individual as a consumer vis-à-vis powerful companies. In such cases, there are clear competition and consumer protection elements, that should be addressed as such. Yet, other problems like discriminatory treatment seem to be largely the result of certain decisions, whose effects are already regulated. Such decisions should be addressed as such, through legislation designed to mitigate these issues. Likewise, some negative effects may be data-driven decisions that merit a sector-specific approach. In this respect, different sectoral laws should be allowed to evolve over time, as should data protection law in general.

It is predicted here that for the large part this approach will develop naturally, as long as it is clear that big data can affect individuals' lives in various ways, and that data protection law and authorities are not the only legitimate caretakers of individual rights and freedoms in the context of big data. Part of the negative impact of big data consists of problems that can be mitigated by other areas of law, or that trigger a response from other areas of law and supervisory authorities as soon as the negative impact becomes visible. More in general, shortly after the inception of this research the attention for solutions other than those from the privacy and data protection areas in the context of big data increased. In academic and popular science literature, particularly in the US, awareness has been raised about big data in the context of discrimination, and much has been written about algorithmic transparency and big data ethics. In Europe, consumer protection, competition law, and a more integrated approach in the context of large scale data processing are discussed. Attention for big data from various EU supervisory authorities has also increased, ranging from DPAs to authorities within the competition and consumer protection domain. It is the prediction from this research that attention for these alternatives will increase in the coming years. In time, the term 'big data' may go out of fashion, which might lead to a more technologically neutral regard for and analysis of the effects of what has been dubbed here the big data process.

Yet despite these recent positive developments, the big data discourse is at the moment still influenced by 'the law of the hammer'. For many, including many privacy scholars, everything in big data can be reduced to, or solved by, privacy and data protection (law). This perspective should be abandoned, and a more integral approach should replace it. For the protection of individuals, is requisite to see whether something is a privacy or data protection problem *pur sang*, and where it is primarily something else, such as discrimination. Personal data are a proxy for protection, but we should be honest about the scope of privacy and the limitations of data protection law. There is an important enabling effect for discrimination emanating from the rights to privacy and data protection, but this is a generally a by-effect. The rights to privacy and to data protection do not aim to achieve full individual rights protection in the context of big data, nor should this be the aim of data protection law. Doing so would lead to the erosion of the legal privacy and data protection framework. It would stretch the scope of the framework in terms of applicability and content to an extent that would make compliance impossible, would block many positive applications, and would severely aggravate existing enforcement issues. The most important point is that we should not value one solution over another, and not search for one integral solution that solves all issues. Only a combined approach, i.e., the EU privacy and data protection law framework complemented by specific solutions for the diverse array of issues, can offer individuals and individual rights and freedoms the protection that they need in the age of big data.

Bibliography

Acquisti A and Grossklags J, ‘Privacy and Rationality in Individual Decision Making’ (2005) 3 IEEE Security & Privacy 26.

Alba D, ‘50 Years On, Moore’s Law Still Pushes Tech to Double Down’ (2015) *WIRED* <http://www.wired.com/2015/04/50-years-moores-law-still-pushes-tech-double/> accessed 17 August 2016.

Amatriain X, ‘Big & Personal: Data and Models Behind Netflix Recommendations’ (2013) Proceedings of the 2nd International Workshop on Big Data, Streams and Heterogeneous Source Mining: Algorithms, Systems, Programming Models and Applications 1.

Ananny M and Crawford K, ‘Seeing Without Knowing: Limitations of the Transparency Ideal and Its Application to Algorithmic Accountability’ (2016) New Media & Society 1.

Andrejevic M, ‘The Big Data Divide’ (2014) International Journal of Communication 1673.

Angwin J and others, ‘Machine Bias: There’s Software Used Across the Country to Predict Future Criminals. And It’s Biased Against Blacks.’ *ProPublica* (23 May 2016).

Angwin J and Mattu S, ‘Amazon Says It Puts Customers First. But Its Pricing Algorithm Doesn’t’ *ProPublica* (20 September 2016)

Angwin J, Parris Jr. T and Mattu S, ‘Breaking the Black Box: What Facebook Knows About You’ *ProPublica* (28 September 2016).

Armstrong M, ‘Recent Developments in the Economics of Price Discrimination’ in Richard Blundell, Whitney Newey and Torsten Persson, *Advances in Economics and Econometrics: Theory and Applications, Ninth World Congress, Volume II* (2006).

Bibliography

Ausloos J, 'The "Right to Be Forgotten" – Worth Remembering?' (2012) 28 Computer Law & Security Review 143.

Bamberger K and Mulligan D, 'Privacy in Europe: Initial Data on Governance Choices and Corporate Practices' 81 The George Washington Law Review 1529.

Bapat A, 'The New Right to Data Portability' (2013) 13 Privacy and Data Protection 3.

Barocas S and Nissenbaum H, 'Big Data's End Run Around Anonymity and Consent' in Julia Lane and others (eds), *Privacy, Big Data, and the Public Good: Frameworks for Engagement* (1 edition, Cambridge University Press 2014).

Barocas S and Nissenbaum H, 'Big Data's End Run Around Procedural Privacy Protections: Recognizing the Inherent Limitations of Consent and Anonymity' (2014) 57 Communications of the ACM 31.

Barocas S and Selbst A, 'Big Data's Disparate Impact' (2016) 104 California Law Review 671.

Bates E, 'The Birth of the European Convention on Human Rights – and the European Court of Human Rights' in Jonas Christoffersen and Mikael Rask Madsen (eds), *The European Court of Human Rights: Between Law and Politics* (Oxford University Press 2011).

Bernal P, *Internet Privacy Rights: Rights to Protect Autonomy* (Cambridge University Press 2014).

Bernsdorff N, 'Artikel 8: Schutz Personenbezogener Daten', *Charta der Grundrechte der Europäischen Union* (Nomos Verlagsgesellschaft 2011).

Boom W van, 'Unfair Commercial Practices' in Christian Twigg-Flesner (ed), *Research Handbook on EU Consumer and Contract Law* (Edward Elgar 2016).

Bounie D and Gille L, 'International Production and Dissemination of Information: Results, Methodological Issues, and Statistical Perspectives' (2012) 6 International Journal of Communication 1001.

boyd danah, 'Untangling Research and Practice: What Facebook's "Emotional Contagion" Study Teaches Us' (2016) 12 Research Ethics 4.

boyd danah, 'Transparency ≠ Accountability' <https://points.datasociety.net/transparency-accountability-3c04e4804504> accessed 21 June 2017.

boyd danah and Crawford K, 'Critical Questions for Big Data: Provocations for a Cultural, Technological, and Scholarly Phenomenon' (2012) 15 Information, Communication & Society.

Brewster T, 'Traffic Lights, Fridges and How They've All Got It in for Us' *The Register* <https://www.theregister.co.uk/2014/06/23/hold_interthreat> accessed 13 May 2015.

Brkan M, 'In Search of the Concept of Essence of EU Fundamental Rights Through the Prism of Data Privacy' (2017) No. 2017-01 Maastricht Faculty of Law Working Paper 2.

Bublitz JC, 'Freedom of Thought in the Age of Neuroscience: A Plea and a Proposal for the Renaissance of a Forgotten Fundamental Right' (2014) 100 Archiv für Rechts-und Sozialphilosophie 1.

'Bundeskartellamt Initiates Proceeding against Facebook on Suspicion of Having Abused Its Market Power by Infringing Data Protection Rules' <http://www.bundeskartellamt.de/SharedDocs/Meldung/EN/Pressemitteilungen/2016/02_03_2016_Facebook.html> accessed 21 June 2017.

Burbergs M, 'How the Right to Respect for Private and Family Life, Home and Correspondence Became the Nursery in Which New Rights Are Born: Article 8 ECHR' in Eva Brems and Janneke Gerards (eds), *Shaping Rights in the ECHR: The Role of the European Court of Human Rights in Determining the Scope of Human Rights* (Cambridge University Press 2014).

Burrell J, 'How the Machine "Thinks": Understanding Opacity in Machine Learning Algorithms' (2016) Big Data & Society 1.

Burton C and others, 'The Final European Union General Data Protection Regulation' (2016) Bloomberg BNA Privacy and Security Law Report 1.

Busch L, 'A Dozen Ways to Get Lost in Translation: Inherent Challenges in Large-Scale Data Sets' (2014) International Journal of Communication 1727.

Butler D, 'When Google Got Flu Wrong' (2013) 494 *Nature* 155.

Bygrave L, 'Data Protection Pursuant to the Right to Privacy in Human Rights Treaties' (1998) 6 International Journal of Law and Information Technology 247.

Bygrave L, 'Minding the Machine: Article 15 of the EC Data Protection Directive and Automated Profiling' (2001) 17 Computer Law & Security Report 17.

Bygrave L, *Data Privacy Law: An International Perspective* (Oxford University Press 2014).

Bygrave L and Schartum DW, 'Consent, Proportionality and Collective Power' in Serge Gutwirth and others (eds), *Reinventing Data Protection?* (Springer 2009).

Calders T and Custers B, 'What Is Data Mining and How Does It Work?' in Bart Custers and others (eds), *Discrimination and Privacy in the Information Society: Data Mining and Profiling in Large Databases*, vol. 3 (Springer 2013).

Calders T and Žliobaitė I, 'Why Unbiased Computational Processes Can Lead to Discriminative Decision Procedures', *Discrimination and Privacy in the Information Society: Data Mining and Profiling in Large Databases*, vol. 3 (Springer 2013).

Cate FH and Mayer-Schönberger V, 'Notice and Consent in a World of Big Data' (2013) 3 International Data Privacy Law 67.

Cavoukian A, 'Privacy by Design: The Definitive Workshop' (2010) 3 Identity in Information Society 247.

Chessel M, *Ethics for Big Data and Analytics* (IBM 2014).

Chopin I and Germaine C, 'A Comparative Analysis of Non-Discrimination Law in Europe 2016' (Directorate-General for Justice and Consumers 2016) European network of legal experts in gender equality and non-discrimination.

Christian B, 'Test Everything: Notes on the A/B Revolution' (2012) WIRED.

Christman J, 'Autonomy in Moral and Political Philosophy' in Edward N. Zalta (ed), *The Stanford Encyclopedia of Philosophy* (Spring 2015, Metaphysics Research Lab, Stanford University 2015) <plato.stanford.edu/archives/spr2015/entries/autonomy-moral> accessed 8 December 2016.

Clapham A, *Human Rights in the Private Sphere* (Clarendon Press 1993).

Clifton C, 'Data Mining', *Encyclopaedia Britannica* (2014) <http://www.britannica.com/technology/data-mining> accessed 11 June 2015.

Constine J, 'How Facebook News Feed Works' <social.techcrunch.com/2016/09/06/ultimate-guide-to-the-news-feed> accessed 13 December 2016.

Craig P, 'Rights, Legality, and Legitimacy', *The Lisbon Treaty, Revised Edition: Law, Politics, and Treaty Reform* (Oxford University Press 2013).

Craig P and De Búrca G, *EU Law: Text, Cases, and Materials* (Oxford University Press 2011).

Crawford K, 'The Hidden Biases in Big Data' <https://hbr.org/2013/04/the-hidden-biases-in-big-data> accessed 14 December 2016.

Crawford K, 'Big Data: Why The Rise of Machines Isn't All It's Cracked Up To Be' (2013) *Foreign Policy*.

Crawford K, Gray ML and Miltner K, 'Critiquing Big Data: Politics, Ethics, Epistemology' (2014) 8 International Journal of Communication 10.

Crawford K and Schultz J, 'Big Data and Due Process – Toward a Framework to Redress Predictive Privacy Harms' (2014) 55 Boston College Law Review 93.

Cuijpers C and Marcelis P, 'Oprekking van het concept persoonsgegevens beperking van privacybescherming?' (2012) Computerrecht 339.

Custers B, 'Data Dilemmas in the Information Society: Introduction and Overview' in Bart Custers and others (eds), *Discrimination and Privacy in the Information Society: Data Mining and Profiling in Large Databases*, vol. 3 (Springer 2013).

Custers B, 'Click Here to Consent Forever: Expiry Dates for Informed Consent' (2016) Big Data & Society 1.

Custers B and Uršič H, 'Big Data and Data Reuse: A Taxonomy of Data Reuse for Balancing Big Data Benefits and Personal Data Protection' (2016) 6 International Data Privacy Law 4.

D'Acquisto G and others, 'Privacy by Design in Big Data – An Overview of Privacy Enhancing Technologies in the Era of Big Data Analytics' (European Union Agency For Network And Information Security (ENISA) 2015).

Dale Prince J, 'The Quantified Self: Operationalizing the Quotidien' (2014) 11 Journal of Electronic Resources in Medical Libraries 91.

Dammann U and Simitis S, *EG-Datenschutzrichtlinie: Kommentar* (Nomos Verlagsgesellschaft 1997).

Davenport TH, *Big Data at Work: Dispelling the Myths, Uncovering the Opportunities* (Harvard Business Review Press 2014).

Davis JL and Jurgenson N, 'Context Collapse: Theorizing Context Collusions and Collisions' (2014) 17 Information, Communication & Society 476.

De Hert P and Gutwirth S, 'Privacy, Data Protection and Law Enforcement. Opacity of the Individual and Transparency of Power', *Privacy and the Criminal Law* (Insertia 2006).

De Hert P and Gutwirth S, 'Data Protection in the Case Law of Strasbourg and Luxemburg: Constitutionalisation in Action', *Reinventing Data Protection?* (Springer 2009).

de Montjoye Y-A and others, 'Unique in the Crowd: The Privacy Bounds of Human Mobility' (2013) 3 Scientific Reports 1376.

Diakopoulos N, 'Algorithmic Accountability: Journalistic Investigation of Computational Power Structures' (2015) Digital Journalism 398.

Diakopoulos N and Friedler S, 'How to Hold Algorithms Accountable' (2016) MIT Technology Review.

Diggelmann O and Cleis MN, 'How the Right to Privacy Became a Human Right' (2014) 14 Human Rights Law Review 441.

Dommering E, 'Recht op persoonsgegevens als zelfbeschikkingsrecht', *16 Miljoen BN'ers? Bescherming van persoonsgegevens in het digitale tijdperk* (Stichting NJCM-Boekerij 2010).

Douglas-Scott S, 'A Tale of Two Courts: Luxembourg, Strasbourg and the Growing European Human Rights Acquis' 43 Common Market Law Review 629.

Dragland Å, 'Big Data, for Better or Worse' <http://www.sintef.no/home/corporate-news/Big-Data-for-better-or-worse, www.sciencedaily.com/releases/2013/05/130522085217.htm> accessed 7 May 2015.

Dworkin G, *The Theory and Practice of Autonomy* (Cambridge University Press 1988).

Eckes C, 'European Union Legal Methods – Moving Away From Integration' in Ulla Neergaard and Ruth Nielsen (eds), *European Legal Method – Towards a New European Legal Realism?* (Djøf Publishing 2013).

European Commission (DG Justice, Freedom and Security), 'Comparative Study on Different Approaches to New Privacy Challenges in Particular in the Light of Technological Developments' (2010) DK/100120.

European Union Agency for Fundamental Rights, 'Data Protection in the European Union: The Role of National Data Protection Authorities – Strengthening the Fundamental Rights Architecture in the EU II' (Publications Office of the European Union 2010).

European Union Agency for Fundamental Rights, *Handbook on European Non-Discrimination Law* (Publications Office of the European Union 2011).

European Union Agency for Fundamental Rights, 'Access to Data Protection Remedies in EU Member States' (2013).

European Union Agency for Fundamental Rights, *Handbook on European Data Protection Law* (Publications Office of the European Union 2013).

Fayyad U, Piatetsky-Shapiro G and Smyth P, 'From Data Mining to Knowledge Discovery in Databases' (1996) 17 AI Magazine 37.

Ferretti F, 'Data Protection and the Legitimate Interest of Data Controllers: Much Ado About Nothing or the Winter of Rights?' (2014) 51 Common Market Law Review 843.

Feuz M, Fuller M and Stalder F, 'Personal Web Searching in the Age of Semantic Capitalism: Diagnosing the Mechanisms of Personalisation' (2011) 16 First Monday.

Fontanella-Khan J and Kuchler H, 'Verizon Takeover in Doubt after Yahoo Reveals Second Cyber Hack' *Financial Times* (15 December 2016).

Forgó N, 'My Health Data – Your Research: Some Preliminary Thoughts on Different Values in the General Data Protection Regulation' (2015) 5 International Data Privacy Law 54.

Fung K, *Numbers Rule Your World: The Hidden Influence of Probability and Statistics on Everything You Do* (McGraw-Hill 2010).

Gandy O, *The Panoptic Sort: A Political Economy of Personal Information* (Westview Press 1993).

Gandy O, 'Engaging Rational Discrimination: Exploring Reasons for Placing Regulatory Constraints on Decision Support Systems' (2010) 12 Ethics and Information Technology 29.

Gatzlaff KM and McCullough KA, 'The Effect of Data Breaches on Shareholder Wealth' (2010) 13 Risk Management and Insurance Review 61.

Gavison R, 'Privacy and the Limits of the Law' in Ferdinand David Schoeman (ed) *Philosophical Dimensions of Privacy: An Anthology* (Cambridge University Press 1984).

Gellert R, 'Data Protection: A Risk Regulation? Between the Risk Management of Everything and the Precautionary Alternative' (2015) 5 International Data Privacy Law 3.

Gellert R and Gutwirth S, 'The Legal Construction of Privacy and Data Protection' (2013) 29 Computer Law & Security Review 522.

Ginsberg J and others, 'Detecting Influenza Epidemics Using Search Engine Query Data' (2009) 457 Nature 1012.

González Fuster G, *The Emergence of Personal Data Protection as a Fundamental Right of the EU* (Springer International Publishing 2014).
González Fuster G, 'Big Data and Smart Devices and Their Impact on Privacy' (European Parliament 2015) Study for the LIBE Committee PE 536.455.
González Fuster G and Gellert R, 'The Fundamental Right of Data Protection in the European Union: In Search of an Uncharted Right' (2012) 26 International Review of Law, Computers & Technology 73.
Grabenwarter C, *European Convention on Human Rights: Commentary* (CH Beck; Hart; Nomos; Helbing Lichtenhahn 2014).
Graef I, 'Market Definition and Market Power in Data: The Case of Online Platforms' (2015) 38 World Competition 473.
Graef I, Verschalken J and Valcke P, 'Putting the Right to Data Portability into a Competition Law Perspective' (2013) Law: The Journal of the Higher School of Economics 53.
Granger M-P and Irion K, 'The Court of Justice and the Data Retention Directive in Digital Rights Ireland: Telling off the EU Legislator and Teaching a Lesson in Privacy and Data Protection' (2014) European Law Review 835.
Grant H and Crowther H, 'How Effective Are Fines in Enforcing Privacy?' in David Wright and Paul de Hert (eds), *Enforcing Privacy: Regulatory, Legal and Technological Approaches* (Springer International Publishing 2016).
Groves P and others, 'The "Big Data" Revolution in Healthcare: Accelerating Value and Innovation' (McKinsey&Company 2013) McKinsey Report.
Hallinan D, 'Effects of Surveillance on Freedom of Assembly, Association and Expression' in David Wright and Reinhard Kreissl (eds), *Surveillance in Europe* (Routledge 2015).
Harris D and others, *Harris, O'Boyle & Warbrick: Law of the European Convention on Human Rights* (Oxford University Press 2014).
Harris J and others, 'Toward a Roadmap in Global Biobanking for Health' (2012) 20 European Journal of Human Genetics 1105.
Harris T, 'How Technology Hijacks People's Minds – from a Magician and Google's Design Ethicist' (2016) *Medium.*
Helberger N, 'Merely Facilitating or Actively Stimulating Diverse Media Choices? Public Service Media at the Crossroad' (2015) 9 International Journal of Communication 1324.
Helberger N, 'Profiling and Targeting Users in the Internet of Things – A New Challenge for Consumer Law' in Reiner Schulze and Dirk Staudenmayer (eds), *Digital Revolution: Challenges for Contract Law in Practice* (Nomos/Hart 2016).
Helberger N, Zuiderveen Borgesius F and Reyna A, 'The Perfect Match? A Closer Look at the Relationship Between EU Consumer Law and Data Protection Law' (2017) 54 Common Market Law Review 1427.

Helft M, 'Google Uses Searches to Track Flu's Spread' *The New York Times* (12 November 2008) <http://www.nytimes.com/2008/11/12/technology/internet/12flu.html> accessed 12 June 2015.
Hildebrandt M, 'Privacy and Identity' in Erik Claes, Anthony Duff and Serge Gutwirth (eds), *Privacy and the Criminal Law* (Insertia 2006).
Hildebrandt M, 'Profiling and the Rule of Law' (2008) 1 Identity in Information Society 55.
Hildebrandt M, 'The Dawn of a Critical Transparency Right for the Profiling Era', *Digital Enlightenment Yearbook 2012* (IOS Press 2012).
Hildebrandt M and Koops B-J, 'The Challenges of Ambient Law and Legal Protection in the Profiling Era' (2010) The Modern Law Review 428.
Hirsch D, 'That's Unfair! Or Is It? Big Data, Discrimination and the FTC's Unfairness Authority' 103 Kentucky Law Journal 345.
Hon K, Millard C and Walden I, 'The Problem of "Personal Data" in Cloud Computing: What Information Is Regulated? The Cloud of Unknowing' (2011) 1 International Data Privacy Law 211.
Hoofnagle CJ, 'How the Fair Credit Reporting Act Regulates Big Data' <papers.ssrn.com/abstract=2432955> accessed 28 May 2014.
Hoofnagle CJ, *Federal Trade Commission Privacy Law and Policy* (Cambridge University Press 2016).
Hughes K, 'The Social Value of Privacy: The Value of Privacy to Human Rights Discourse' in Beate Rössler and Dorota Mokrosinska (eds), *Social Dimensions of Privacy: Interdisciplinary Perspectives* (Cambridge University Press 2015).
Hurley M and Adebayo J, 'Credit Scoring in the Era of Big Data' (2016) 18 Yale Journal of Law and Technology 148.
Hutchinson T, 'Doctrinal Research: Researching the Jury' in Dawn Watkins and Mandy Burton (eds), *Research Methods in Law* (Routledge 2013).
Hutchinson T and Duncan N, 'Defining and Describing What We Do: Doctrinal Legal Research' (2012) 17 Deakin Law Review 83.
International Working Group on Data Protection in Telecommunications, 'Working Paper on Big Data and Privacy: Privacy Principles under Pressure in the Age of Big Data Analytics' (2014) 675.48.12.
Irion K, 'A Special Regard: The Court of Justice and the Fundamental Rights to Privacy and Data Protection' in Ulrich Faber and others (eds), *Gesellschaftliche Bewegungen – Recht unter Beobachtung und in Aktion: Festschrift für Wolfhard Kohte* (Nomos Verlagsgesellschaft, 2016).
Irion K and Luchetta G, *Online Personal Data Processing and EU Data Protection Reform* (Centre for European Policy Studies 2013).
Jacqué J-P, 'The Charter of Fundamental Rights and the Court of Justice of the European Union: A First Assessment of the Interpretation of the Charter's Horizontal Provisions' in Frederico Casolari and Lucia Serena Rossi (eds), *The EU after Lisbon* (Springer 2014).

Jefferies D, 'How the "Internet of Things" Could Radically Change Local Government' *the Guardian* (18 August 2011) <http://www.theguardian.com/local-government-network/2011/aug/18/internet-of-things-local-government> accessed 1 June 2015.

Jones A and Sufrin B, *EU Competition Law: Text, Cases, and Materials* (Oxford University Press 2016).

Kannekens E and van Eijk N, 'Oneerlijke handelspraktijken: alternatief voor privacyhandhaving' (2016) Mediaforum 102.

Klous S and Wielaard N, *Wij zijn big data* (Business Contact 2014).

Koffeman N, '(The Right to) Personal Autonomy in the Case Law of the European Court of Human Rights' (Leiden University 2010).

Kokott J and Sobotta C, 'The Distinction Between Privacy and Data Protection in the Jurisprudence of the CJEU and the ECtHR' (2013) 3 International Data Privacy Law 222.

Koops B-J, 'The Evolution of Privacy Law and Policy in the Netherlands' (2011) 13 Journal of Comparative Policy Analysis: Research and Practice.

Koops B-J, 'The Trouble with European Data Protection Law' (2014) 4 International Data Privacy Law 250.

Koops B-J and Leenes R, 'Privacy Regulation Cannot Be Hardcoded. A Critical Comment on the "Privacy by Design" Provision in Data-Protection Law' (2014) 28 International Review of Law, Computers & Technology 159.

Korff D, 'Existing Case-Law on Compliance with Data Protection Laws and Principles in the Member States of the European Union' (1998) Annex to the Annual Report 1998.

Kosinski M, Stillwell D and Graepel T, 'Private Traits and Attributes Are Predictable from Digital Records of Human Behavior' (2013) 110 Proceedings of the National Academy of Sciences 5802.

Kosta E, *Consent in European Data Protection Law* (Martinus Nijhoff Publishers 2013).

Kramer A, Guillory J and Hancock J, 'Experimental Evidence of Massive-Scale Emotional Contagion through Social Networks' (2014) 111 Proceedings of the National Academy of Sciences 8788.

Krotoszynski R, *Privacy Revisited: A Global Perspective on the Right to Be Left Alone* (Oxford University Press 2016).

Kulk S and Zuiderveen Borgesius F, 'Google Spain v. González: Did the Court Forget About Freedom of Expression?' (2014) 5 European Journal of Risk Regulation 389.

Kuner C, *European Data Privacy Law and Online Business* (Oxford University Press 2003).

Kuner C, 'An International Legal Framework for Data Protection: Issues and Prospects' (2009) 25 Computer Law & Security Review 307.

Kuner C, 'The European Commission's Proposed Data Protection Regulation: A Copernican Revolution in European Data Protection Law' (2012) Bloomberg BNA Privacy and Security Law Report 1.

Kuner C, 'The Challenge of "Big Data" for Data Protection' (2012) 2 International Data Privacy Law 47.

Lane J and others (eds), *Privacy, Big Data, and the Public Good: Frameworks for Engagement* (1 edition, Cambridge University Press 2014).

Laney D, '3D Data Management: Controlling Data Volume, Velocity, and Variety' (2001) Meta Group.

Lavrysen L, 'The Scope of Rights and the Scope of Obligations: Positive Obligations' in Eva Brems and Janneke Gerards (eds), *Shaping Rights in the ECHR: The Role of the European Court of Human Rights in Determining the Scope of Human Rights* (Cambridge University Press 2014).

Lazer D and others, 'The Parable of Google Flu: Traps in Big Data Analysis' (2014) 343 *Science* 1203.

Leisner W, *Grundrechte und Privatrecht* (Beck 1960).

Lenaerts K and Gutiérrez-Fons JA, 'The Place of the Charter in the EU Constitutional Edifice', *The EU Charter of Fundamental Rights: A Commentary* (Hart/Beck 2014).

Lerman J, 'Big Data and Its Exclusions' (2013) 66 Stanford Law Review.

Lessig L, 'Privacy as Property' (2002) Social Research 247.

Letsas G, 'The ECHR as a Living Instrument: Its Meaning and Legitimacy', *Constituting Europe: The European Court of Human Rights in a National, European and Global Context* (Cambridge University Press 2013).

Levy S, 'How Google's Algorithm Rules the Web' (2010) *WIRED.*

Linden G, Smith B and York J, 'Amazon.Com Recommendations: Item-to-Item Collaborative Filtering' (2003) 7 IEEE Internet Computing 76.

Lynskey O, 'Deconstructing Data Protection: The "Added-Value" of a Right to Data Protection in the EU Legal Order' (2014) 63.

Lynskey O, 'The Data Retention Directive Is Incompatible with the Rights to Privacy and Data Protection and Is Invalid in Its Entirety: Digital Rights Ireland' (2014) 51 Common Market Law Review 1789.

Lynskey O, *The Foundations of EU Data Protection Law* (Oxford University Press 2015).

Lyon D, 'Surveillance as Social Sorting: Computer Codes and Mobile Bodies' in David Lyon (ed), *Surveillance as Social Sorting: Privacy, Risk and Digital Discrimination* (Routledge 2003).

Krenchel M and Madsbjerg C, 'Your Big Data Is Worthless If You Don't Bring It Into the Real World' (*WIRED*, 4 November 2014) <http://www.wired.com/2014/04/your-big-data-is-worthless-if-you-dont-bring-it-into-the-real-world/> accessed 10 June 2015.

Mantelero A, 'The EU Proposal for a General Data Protection Regulation and the Roots of the "Right to Be Forgotten"' (2013) 29 Computer Law & Security Review 229.

Mantelero A, 'The Future of Consumer Data Protection in the E.U. Re-Thinking the "Notice and Consent" Paradigm in the New Era of Predictive Analytics' (2014) 30 Computer Law & Security Review 643.

Manyika J and others, 'Big Data: The Next Frontier for Innovation, Competition, and Productivity' (June 2011) McKinsey Global Institute Report.

Mascalzoni D (ed), *Ethics, Law and Governance of Biobanking National, European and International Approaches* (Springer 2015).

Mayer-Schönberger V, 'Beyond Privacy, Beyond Rights – Toward a "Systems Theory" of Information Governance' (2010) 98 California Law Review 1853.

Mayer-Schönberger V and Cukier K, *Big Data: A Revolution That Will Transform How We Live, Work, and Think* (Houghton Mifflin Hartcourt 2013).

McDonald AM and Cranor LF, 'The Cost of Reading Privacy Policies' (2008) 4 I/S: A Journal of Law and Policy for the Information Society 543.

McDonald AM and Cranor LF, 'Beliefs and Behaviors: Internet Users' Understanding of Behavioral Advertising' (2010) <https://ssrn.com/abstract=1989092> accessed 25 May 2017.

McLeod R, 'Novel But a Long Time Coming: The Bundeskartellamt Takes on Facebook' (2016) 7 Journal of European Competition Law & Practice 367.

Metcalf J and Crawford K, 'Where Are Human Subjects in Big Data Research? The Emerging Ethics Divide' (2016) Big Data & Society.

Meyer J and Bernsdorff N, *Charta der Grundrechte der Europäischen Union* (Nomos Verlagsgesellschaft 2011).

Moerel L and Prins C, 'Privacy voor de homo digitalis: proeve van een nieuw toetsingskader voor gegevensbescherming in het licht van big data en internet of things', *Homo Digitalis* (Wolters Kluwer 2016).

Monreale A and others, 'Privacy-by-Design in Big Data and Social Mining' (2014) EPJ Data Science 1.

Moore AD, *Privacy Rights: Moral and Legal Foundations* (Pennsylvania State University Press 2010).

Mowbray AR, *The Development of Positive Obligations under the European Convention on Human Rights by the European Court of Human Rights* (Hart Publishing 2004).

Mowbray AR, 'The Creativity of the European Court of Human Rights' (2005) 5 Human Rights Law Review.

Mowbray AR, *Cases, Materials, and Commentary on the European Convention on Human Rights* (Oxford University Press 2012).

Narayanan A and Shmatikov V, 'Robust De-Anonymization of Large Sparse Datasets', *IEEE Symposium on Security and Privacy, 2008. SP 2008* (2008).

Nehmelman R and Noorlander CW, *Horizontale werking van grondrechten: over een leerstuk in ontwikkeling* (Kluwer 2013).

Ó Fathaigh R, 'Article 10 and the Chilling Effect Principle' (2013) 3 European Human Rights Law Review 304.

Ohm P, 'Broken Promises of Privacy: Responding to the Surprising Failure of Anonymization' (2010) 57 UCLA Law Review 1701.

O'Neil C, *Weapons of Math Destruction: How Big Data Increases Inequality and Threatens Democracy* (Crown 2016).

Oostveen M, 'Identifiability and the Applicability of Data Protection to Big Data' (2016) International Data Privacy Law.

Oostveen M and Irion K, 'The Golden Age of Personal Data: How to Regulate an Enabling Fundamental Right?' in Mor Bakhoum and others (eds), *Personal Data in Competition, Consumer Protection and IP Law – Towards a Holistic Approach?* (Springer, forthcoming).

O'Reilly Media, *Big Data Now* (O'Reilly Media 2012).

Örücü E, 'Methodology of Comparative Law' in Jan Martien Smits (ed), *Elgar Encyclopedia of Comparative Law* (Elgar 2006).

Padova Y and Mayer-Schönberger V, 'Regime Change? Enabling Big Data Through Europe's New Data Protection Regulation' 17 The Columbia Science and Technology Review 315.

Pagallo U, 'On the Principle of Privacy by Design and Its Limits: Technology, Ethics and the Rule of Law' in Serge Gutwirth and others (eds), *European Data Protection: In Good Health?* (Springer 2012).

Pariser E, *The Filter Bubble: What the Internet Is Hiding from You* (Penguin Books 2012).

Pasquale F, *The Black Box Society: The Secret Algorithms That Control Money And Information* (Harvard University Press 2015).

Pasquale F and Keats Citron D, 'The Scored Society: Due Process for Automated Predictions' (2014) 89 Washington Law Review.

Peers S, Hervey T and Ward A, *The EU Charter of Fundamental Rights: A Commentary* (Hart/Beck 2014).

Peers S and Prechal S, 'Article 52 – Scope and Interpretation of Rights and Principles' in Steve Peers, Tamara Hervey and Angela Ward (eds), *The EU Charter of Fundamental Rights: A Commentary* (Hart/Beck 2014).

Penney JW, 'Chilling Effects: Online Surveillance and Wikipedia Use' (2016) 31 Berkeley Technology Law Journal 117.

Perrons RK and Jensen JW, 'Data as an Asset: What the Oil and Gas Sector Can Learn from Other Industries about "Big Data"' (2015) 81 Energy Policy 117.

Piatetsky-Shapiro G, 'From Data Mining to Big Data and Beyond' (*Inside Analysis*) <insideanalysis.com/2012/04/data-mining-and-beyond> accessed 23 March 2015.

Prins C, 'When Personal Data, Behavior and Virtual Identities Become a Commodity: Would a Property Rights Approach Matter?' (2006) SCRIPT-ed 270.

Prins C and Moerel L, 'On the Death of the Purpose Limitation Principle' (International Association of Privacy Professionals 2015) Working Paper.

Provost F and Fawcett T, *Data Science for Business* (O'Reilly Media 2013).

Purtova N, 'Property Rights in Personal Data: Learning from the American Discourse' (2009) Computer Law & Security Review 507.

Purtova N, *Property Rights in Personal Data: A European Perspective* (Kluwer Law International 2012).

Rainey B, Wicks E and Ovey C, *Jacobs, White and Ovey: The European Convention on Human Rights* (Oxford University Press 2014).

Reh H-J, 'Kommentar zum Bundesdatenschutzgesetz' in Spiros Simitis and others (eds), *Kommentar zum Bundesdatenschutzgesetz* (Nomos Verlagsgesellschaft 1978).

Richards N, 'Intellectual Privacy' (2008) 87 Texas Law Review 387.

Richards N, *Intellectual Privacy: Rethinking Civil Liberties in the Digital Age* (Oxford University Press 2015).

Richards N and King J, 'Three Paradoxes of Big Data' (2013) 66 Stanford Law Review Online 41.

Richards N and King J, 'Big Data Ethics' (2014) Wake Forest Law Review 393.

Rinkes JGJ, 'Europees consumentenrecht' in EH Hondius and others (eds), *Handboek consumentenrecht: een overzicht van de rechtspositie van de consument* (Uitgeverij Paris 2011).

Roberts JL, 'Protecting Privacy to Prevent Discrimination' (2015) 56 William and Mary Law Review 2097.

Robinson N and others, 'Review of the European Data Protection Directive' (RAND Corporation 2009).

Rössler B, *The Value of Privacy* (Polity Press 2005).

Rouvroy A, 'Of Data and Men: Fundamental Rights and Freedoms in a World of Big Data' (Bureau of the Consultative Committee of the Convention for the Protection of Individuals with Regard to Automatic Processing of Personal Data [ETS 108] 2016) T-PD-BUR(2015)09REV.

Rouvroy A and Poullet Y, 'The Right to Individual Self-Determination and the Value of Self-Development: Reassessing the Importance of Privacy for Democracy' in Serge Gutwirth and others (eds), *Reinventing Data Protection?* (Springer 2009).

Rubens P, 'Can Big Data Crunching Help Feed the World?' (*BBC News*) <http://www.bbc.com/news/business-26424338> accessed 24 April 2015.

Rubinstein I, 'Big Data: The End of Privacy or a New Beginning?' (2013) 3 International Data Privacy Law 74.

Samuelson P, 'Privacy as Intellectual Property' (2000) Stanford Law Review 1125.

Sartor G, 'The Right to Be Forgotten in the Draft Data Protection Regulation' (2015) 5 International Data Privacy Law 64.

Sartor G, 'The Right to Be Forgotten: Balancing Interests in the Flux of Time' (2016) 24 International Journal of Law and Information Technology 72.

Schauer F, 'Fear, Risk and the First Amendment: Unraveling the "Chilling Effect"' (1978) 58 Boston University Law Review 685.

Schermer B, 'The Limits of Privacy in Automated Profiling and Data Mining' (2011) 27 Computer Law & Security Review 45.

Schermer B, Custers B and van der Hof S, 'The Crisis of Consent: How Stronger Legal Protection May Lead to Weaker Consent in Data Protection' (2014) 16 Ethics and Information Technology 171.

Schoeman FD (ed), *Philosophical Dimensions of Privacy: An Anthology* (Cambridge University Press 1984).

Schreurs W and others, 'Cogitas, Ergo Sum. The Role of Data Protection Law and Non-Discrimination Law in Group Profiling in the Private Sector' in Mireille Hildebrandt and Serge Gutwirth (eds), *Profiling the European Citizen: Cross-Disciplinary Perspectives* (Springer 2008).

Schwartz P, 'Property, Privacy, and Personal Data' (2004) Harvard Law Review 2056.

Schwartz RL, 'Internal and External Method in the Study of Law' (1992) 11 Law and Philosophy 179.

Science Europe, 'How to Transform Big Data into Better Health: Envisioning a Health Big Data Ecosystem for Advancing Biomedical Research and Improving Health Outcomes in Europe' (2014) Workshop Report.

Seife C, '23andMe Is Terrifying, but Not for the Reasons the FDA Thinks' (2013) *Scientific American* <www.scientificamerican.com/article/23andme-is-terrifying-but-not-for-reasons-fda> accessed 8 June 2015.

Siegel E, *Predictive Analytics: The Power to Predict Who Will Click, Buy, Lie, or Die* (Wiley 2013).

Siemen B, *Datenschutz als Europäisches Grundrecht* (Duncker & Humblot 2006).

Singh RI, Sumeeth M and Miller J, 'A User-Centric Evaluation of the Readability of Privacy Policies in Popular Web Sites' (2011) 13 Information Systems Frontiers 501.

Solove D, 'Privacy Self-Management and the Consent Dilemma' (2013) 126 Harvard Law Review 1180.

Solove DJ, 'A Taxonomy of Privacy' (2006) 154 University of Pennsylvania Law Review 447.

Solove DJ, *Understanding Privacy* (Harvard University Press 2008).

Solove DJ, *Nothing to Hide: The False Tradeoff between Privacy and Security* (Yale University Press 2011).

Sorel J-M and Boré Eveno V, 'Article 31', *The Vienna Conventions on the Law of Treaties: A Commentary* (Oxford University Press 2011).

Spiekermann S and others, 'The Challenges of Personal Data Markets and Privacy' (2015) 25 Electronic Markets 161.

Spiekermann S and Cranor LF, 'Engineering Privacy' (2009) 35 IEEE Transactions on Software Engineering 67.

Spiekermann S, Korunovska J and Bauer C, 'Psychology of Ownership and Asset Defence: Why People Value Their Personal Information beyond Privacy', *Proceedings of the International Conference on Information Systems* (AIS Association for Information Systems 2012).

Stucke M and Grunes A, *Big Data and Competition Policy* (Oxford University Press 2016).

Sunstein CR, *Infotopia* (Oxford University Press 2006).

Sunstein CR, *Republic 2.0* (Princeton University Press 2007).

Swan M, 'Sensor Mania! The Internet of Things, Wearable Computing, Objective Metrics, and the Quantified Self 2.0' (2012) 1 Journal of Sensor and Actuator Networks 217.

Swire P and Logos Y, 'Why the Right to Data Portability Likely Reduces Consumer Welfare: Antitrust and Privacy Critique' (2013) 72 Maryland Law Review 335.

Taleb N, 'Beware the Big Errors of "Big Data"' [2013] *WIRED* <http://www.wired.com/2013/02/big-data-means-big-errors-people> accessed 12 June 2015.

Tene O and Polonetsky J, 'Big Data for All: Privacy and User Control in the Age of Analytics' (2013) 11 Northwestern Journal of Technology and Intellectual Property 239.

Tene O and Polonetsky J, 'Judged by the Tin Man: Individual Rights in the Age of Big Data' (2013) 11 Journal of Telecommunications and High Technology Law 351.

Tene O and Polonetsky J, 'Beyond IRBs: Ethical Guidelines for Data Research', *Future of Privacy Forum – Big Data Ethics* (2015).

'The Zettabyte Era: Trends and Analysis' (Cisco 2014) White Paper <http://www.cisco.com/c/en/us/solutions/collateral/service-provider/visual-networking-index-vni/VNI_Hyperconnectivity_WP.pdf> accessed 6 May 2016.

Thielman S, 'Yahoo Hack: 1bn Accounts Compromised by Biggest Data Breach in History' *The Guardian* (15 December 2016).

Tjong Tjin Tai E, 'Aansprakelijkheid bij datalekken' (2016) 150 WPNR: Weekblad voor Privaatrecht, Notariaat en Registratie 459.

Topol E, *The Creative Destruction of Medicine: How the Digital Revolution Will Create Better Healthcare* (Basic Books 2012).

Turner V and others, 'The Digital Universe of Opportunities: Rich Data and the Increasing Value of the Internet of Things' (International Data Corporation 2014) White Paper <idcdocserv.com/1678> accessed 6 May 2016.

Turow J, *Niche Envy: Marketing Discrimination in the Digital Age* (MIT Press 2008).

Tyrrell JS and others, 'Parental Diabetes and Birthweight in 236 030 Individuals in the UK Biobank Study' (2013) 42 International Journal of Epidemiology 1714.

Tzanou M, 'Data Protection as a Fundamental Right Next to Privacy? "Reconstructing" a Not so New Right' (2013) International Data Privacy Law 88.

UK Biobank, 'Dad's Influence on Birth Weight Linked to Diabetes Genes' <http://www.ukbiobank.ac.uk/2013/12/dads-influence-on-birth-weight-linked-to-diabetes-genes/> accessed 10 June 2015.

UK Biobank, 'Keeping Active in Middle Age May Help Cut Breast Cancer Risk, Study Shows' <http://www.ukbiobank.ac.uk/2014/11/keeping-active-in-middle-age-may-help-cut-breast-cancer-risk-study-shows/> accessed 10 June 2015.

UK Biobank, 'Research Gives New Insights into Ménière's Disease' <http://www.ukbiobank.ac.uk/2014/04/research-gives-new-insights-into-menieres-disease> accessed 10 June 2015.

van der Sloot B, 'Do Data Protection Rules Protect the Individual and Should They?' (2014) 4 International Data Privacy Law 307.

van der Sloot B, *Privacy as Virtue: Moving Beyond the Individual in the Age of Big Data* (Dissertation University of Amsterdam 2017) 189–193.

van Hoecke M, 'Legal Doctrine: Which Method(s) for What Kind of Discipline?' in Mark van Hoecke (ed), *Methodologies of Legal Research – Which Kind of Method for What Kind of Discipline?* (Hart Publishing 2011).

van Hoecke M, *Methodologies of Legal Research – Which Kind of Method for What Kind of Discipline?* (Mark van Hoecke ed, Hart Publishing 2011).

Vayena E and others, 'Elements of a New Ethical Framework for Big Data Research' (2016) Washington and Lee Law Review.

Vested-Hansen J, 'Article 7 (Private Life, Home, and Communications)', *The EU Charter of Fundamental Rights: A Commentary* (Hart/Beck 2014).

Wade W, 'Horizons of Horizontality' (2000) Law Quarterly Review 217.

Wagner B, 'Draft Report on the Human Rights Dimensions of Algorithms' (Council of Europe 2016) MSI-NET(2016)06.

Walkila S, *Horizontal Effect of Fundamental Rights in EU Law* (Europa Law Publishing 2016).

Waterman K and Bruening P, 'Big Data Analytics: Risks and Responsibilities' (2014) 4 International Data Privacy Law 89.

Weigel E, 'A/B Testing – Concept!= Execution' <https://blog.booking.com/concept-dne-execution.html> accessed 18 May 2017.

Wheatley M, 'Big Data Goes Green: How Data Analytics Is Saving the World's Forests' <siliconangle.com/blog/2013/07/02/big-data-goes-green-how-data-analytics-is-saving-the-worlds-forests> accessed 6 May 2015.

Whitman J, 'The Two Western Cultures of Privacy: Dignity versus Liberty' (2004) 113 Yale Law Journal 1151.

Wohlsen M, 'Tech's Hot New Market: The Poor' (2013) WIRED.

Xenos D, *The Positive Obligations of the State under the European Convention of Human Rights* (Routledge 2012).

Yeung K, '"Hypernudge": Big Data as a Mode of Regulation by Design' (2016) 1 Information, Communication & Society.

Zanfir G, 'The Right to Data Portability in the Context of the EU Data Protection Reform' (2012) 2 International Data Privacy Law 149.

Zarsky T, '"Mine Your Own Business!": Making the Case for the Implications of the Data Mining of Personal Information in the Forum of Public Opinion' (2003) 5 Yale Journal of Law and Technology.

Zarsky T, 'Understanding Discrimination in the Scored Society' (2014) 89 Washington Law Review 1375.

Zuboff S, 'The Secrets of Surveillance Capitalism' (2016) *Frankfurter Allgemeine Zeitung*.

Zuiderveen Borgesius F, 'Behavioural Targeting', *Improving Privacy Protection in the Area of Behavioural Targeting* (Kluwer Law International 2015).

Zuiderveen Borgesius F, *Improving Privacy Protection in the Area of Behavioural Targeting* (Kluwer Law International 2015).

Zuiderveen Borgesius F, 'Online Price Discrimination and Data Protection Law' (2015) Amsterdam Law School Research Paper No. 2015-32 1.

Zuiderveen Borgesius F, 'Singling out People without Knowing Their Names – Behavioral Targeting, Pseudonymous Data, and the New Data Protection Regulation' (2016) Computer Law & Security Review.

Zuiderveen Borgesius F, 'Should We Worry about Filter Bubbles?' (2016) 5 Internet Policy Review.

Zuiderveen Borgesius F, van Eechoud M and Gray J, 'Open Data, Privacy, and Fair Information Principles: Towards a Balancing Framework' (2015) 30 Berkely Technology Law Journal 2074.

Zweigert K and Kötz H, *Introduction to Comparative Law* (Tony Weir tr, Clarendon Press 1998).

Zwenne G J, 'De verwaterde privacywet' (inaugural lecture, Leiden, the Netherlands, 12 April 2013).

Websites and Others

<http://www.23andme.com> accessed 10 June 2015.

'2016: The Year of the Zettabyte' *Daily Infographic* (23 March 2013) <http://www.dailyinfographic.com/2016-the-year-of-the-zettabyte-infographic> accessed 6 May 2016.

A/B Testing: Test Your Own Hypotheses & Prepare to Be Wrong – Stuart Frisby (Booking.Com) (2015) <https://www.youtube.com/watch?time_continue=3&v=_sx5LV23hIE> accessed 18 May 2017.

<http://www.acxiom.com> accessed 26 May 2016.

'A Very Short History Of Big Data' (*Forbes*) <http://www.forbes.com/sites/gilpress/2013/05/09/a-very-short-history-of-big-data> accessed 22 April 2015.

<http://www.bigdatascoring.com> accessed 12 December 2016.

<http://www.biobankdenmark.dk> accessed 7 May 2016.

<https://www.coe.int/en/web/conventions/full-list/-/conventions/treaty/005/signatures> accessed 26 May 2017.

<http://en.parelsnoer.org> accessed 7 May 2016.

<http://www.fitbit.com/uk/about> accessed 10 June 2015.

<http://www.generationscotland.org> accessed 7 May 2016.

<http://www.globalforestwatch.org> accessed 6 May 2016.

<http://www.intelliq.co.uk/solutions.htm> accessed 6 May 2016.

<http://jawbone.com> accessed 10 June 2015.

<http://www.kreditech.com> accessed 12 December 2016.

<http://quantifiedself.com> accessed 12 May 2016.

<http://www.tylervigen.com/spurious-correlations> accessed 13 May 2016.

<http://www.ukbiobank.ac.uk> accessed 7 May 2016.

<http://www.zestfinance.com> accessed 12 December 2016.

'ZestFinance Introduces Big Data Model For Collections Scoring: New Industry-Specific Models Can Increase Collections by 30%' <https://www.zestfinance.com/pdf/ZestFinance_Collections_Model.pdf> accessed 6 May 2016.

Table of Cases

Table of Legislation

Opinions, Reports, and Communications

Article 29 Working Party, 'Opinion 4/2007 on the Concept of Personal Data' (2007) WP 136, 116, 117, 124

Article 29 Working Party, 'Opinion 2/2010 on Online Behavioural Advertising' (2010) WP 171, 123

Article 29 Working Party, 'Opinion 15/2011 on the Definition of Consent' (2011) WP 187, 138, 141

Article 29 Working Party, 'Opinion 03/2013 on Purpose Limitation' (2013) WP 203, 34, 49, 57, 132, 142, 157

Article 29 Working Party, 'Advice Paper on Essential Elements of a Definition and a Provision on Profiling within the EU General Data Protection Regulation' (2013), 133, 148

Article 29 Working Party, 'Opinion 6/2014 on the Notion of Legitimate Interests of the Data Controller under Article 7 of Directive 95/46/EC' (2014) WP 217, 139

Article 29 Working Party, 'Opinion 5/2014 on Anonymisation Techniques' (2014) WP 261, 119, 121

Article 29 Working Party, 'Statement of the WP29 on the Impact of the Development of Big Data on the Protection of Individuals with regard to the Processing of Their Personal Data in the EU' (2014) WP 221, 110

Autorité de la concurrence and Bundeskartellamt, 'Report "Competition Law and Data"' (2016), 180, 189

Council of Economic Advisers, 'Big Data and Differential Pricing' (2015) White House Report, 30

European Commission, 'Commission Staff Working Document – Guidance on the Implementation/Application of Directive 2005/29/EC on Unfair Commercial Practices' (2016) SWD(2016) 163 final, 187

European Commission, 'Mergers: Commission Fines Facebook €110 Million for Providing Misleading Information about WhatsApp Takeover' (2017) Press Release, 189

European Data Protection Supervisor, 'Privacy and Competitiveness in the Age of Big Data: The Interplay between Data Protection, Competition Law and Consumer Protection in the Digital Economy' (2014) Preliminary Opinion, 30, 180, 186

European Data Protection Supervisor, 'Meeting the Challenges of Big Data: A Call for Transparency, User Control, Data Protection by Design and Accountability' (2015) 7/2015, 34, 49, 134, 135

European Data Protection Supervisor, 'Opinion 4/2017 on the Proposal for a Directive on Certain Aspects Concerning Contracts for the Supply of Digital Content' (2017) 4/2017, 183

Holdren JP and Lander ES, 'Big Data and Privacy: A Technological Perspective' (2014) White House Report, 30

'KPN En XS4ALL – Onderzoek Naar de Verwerking van Persoonsgegevens via Interactieve Televisie van XS4ALL' (Autoriteit Persoonsgegevens (Dutch DPA) 2016), 121

'Onderzoek CBP Naar de Verwerking van Persoonsgegevens Door Snappet – Bijlage 1: Zienswijze Snappet, Met de Reactie Daarop van Het CBP' (College Bescherming Persoonsgegevens (Dutch DPA) 2014), 121

'Onderzoek CBP Naar de Verwerking van Persoonsgegevens Met Cookies Door de Publieke Omroep (NPO)' (College Bescherming Persoonsgegevens (Dutch DPA) 2014), 121

Podesta J and others, 'Big Data: Seizing Opportunities, Preserving Values' (2014) White House Report, 30

'Rapport de La Commission Informatique et Libertés I (Le Rapport Tricot)' (1975), 113

'The Commercial Use of Consumer Data – Report on the CMA's Call for Information' (Competition and Markets Authority (UK) 2015), 189

'Towards a Thriving Data-Driven Economy' (2014) Communication from the Commission to the European Parliament, the Council, the Economic and Social Committee and the Committee of the Regions COM(2014) 442 final, 157

INFORMATION LAW SERIES

1. Egbert J. Dommering & P. Bernt Hugenholtz, *Protecting Works of Fact: Copyright, Freedom of Expression and Information Law,* 1991 (ISBN 90-654-4567-6).
2. Willem F. Korthals Altes, Egbert J. Dommering, P. Bernt Hugenholtz & Jan J.C. Kabel, *Information Law Towards the 21st Century,* 1992 (ISBN 90-654-4627-3).
3. Jacqueline M.B. Seignette, *Challenges to the Creator Doctrine: Authorship, Copyright Ownership and the Exploitation of Creative Works in the Netherlands, Germany and The United States,* 1994 (ISBN 90-654-4876-4).
4. P. Bernt Hugenholtz, *The Future of Copyright in a Digital Environment, Proceedings of the Royal Academy Colloquium,* 1996 (ISBN 90-411-0267-1).
5. Julius C.S. Pinckaers, *From Privacy Toward a New Intellectual Property Right in Persona,* 1996 (ISBN 90-411-0355-4).
6. Jan J.C. Kabel & Gerard J.H.M. Mom, *Intellectual Property and Information Law: Essays in Honour of Herman Cohen Jehoram,* 1998 (ISBN 90-411-9702-8).
7. Ysolde Gendreau, Axel Nordemann & Rainer Oesch, *Copyright and Photographs: An International Survey,* 1999 (ISBN 90-411-9722-2).
8. P. Bernt Hugenholtz, *Copyright and Electronic Commerce: Legal Aspects of Electronic Copyright Management,* 2000 (ISBN 90-411-9785-0).
9. Lucie M.C.R. Guibault, *Copyright Limitations and Contracts: An Analysis of the Contractual Overridability of Limitations on Copyright,* 2002 (ISBN 90-411-9867-9).
10. Lee A. Bygrave, *Data Protection Law: Approaching its Rationale, Logic and Limits,* 2002 (ISBN 90-411-9870-9).
11. Niva Elkin-Koren & Neil Weinstock Netanel, *The Commodification of Information,* 2002 (ISBN 90-411-9876-8).
12. Mireille M.M. van Eechoud, *Choice of Law in Copyright and Related Rights: Alternatives to the Lex Protectionis,* 2003 (ISBN 90-411-2071-8).
13. Martin Senftleben, *Copyright, Limitations and the Three-Step Test: An Analysis of the Three-Step Test in International and EC Copyright Law,* 2004 (ISBN 90-411-2267-2).
14. Paul L.C. Torremans, *Copyright and Human Rights: Freedom of Expression – Intellectual Property – Privacy,* 2004 (ISBN 90-411-2278-8).
15. Natali Helberger, *Controlling Access to Content: Regulating Conditional Access in Digital Broadcasting,* 2005 (ISBN 90-411-2345-8).
16. Lucie M.C.R. Guibault & P. Bernt Hugenholtz, *The Future of the Public Domain: Identifying the Commons in Information Law,* 2006 (ISBN 978-90-411-2435-7).

17. Irini Katsirea, *Public Broadcasting and European Law: A Comparative Examination of Public Service Obligations in Six Member States,* 2008 (ISBN 978-90-411-2500-2).
18. Paul L.C. Torremans, *Intellectual Property and Human Rights: Enhanced Edition of Copyright and Human Rights,* 2008 (ISBN 978-90-411-2653-5).
19. Mireille van Eechoud, P. Bernt Hugenholtz, Stef van Gompel, Lucie Guibault & Natali Helberger, *Harmonizing European Copyright Law: The Challenges of Better Lawmaking,* 2009 (ISBN 978-90-411-3130-0).
20. Ashwin van Rooijen, *The Software Interface between Copyright and Competition Law: A Legal Analysis of Interoperability in Computer Programs,* 2010 (ISBN 978-90-411-3193-5).
21. Irini A. Stamatoudi, *Copyright Enforcement and the Internet,* 2010 (ISBN 978-90-411-3346-5).
22. Wolfgang Sakulin, *Trademark Protection and Freedom of Expression: An Inquiry into the Conflict between Trademark Rights and Freedom of Expression under European Law,* 2011 (ISBN 978-90-411-3415-8).
23. Stef van Gompel, *Formalities in Copyright Law: An Analysis of their History, Rationales and Possible Future,* 2011 (ISBN 978-90-411-3418-9).
24. Nadezhda Purtova, *Property Rights in Personal Data: A European Perspective,* 2012 (ISBN 978-90-411-3802-6).
25. Brad Sherman & Leanne Wiseman, *Copyright and the Challenge of the New,* 2012 (ISBN 978-90-411-3669-5).
26. Ewa Komorek, *Media Pluralism and European Law*, 2012 (ISBN 978-90-411-3894-1).
27. Joris van Hoboken, *Search Engine Freedom: On the Implications of the Right to Freedom of Expression for the Legal Governance of Web Search Engines,* 2012 (ISBN 978-90-411-4128-6).
28. Natali Helberger, Lucie Guibault, Marco Loos, Chantal Mak, Lodewijk Pessers & Bart van der Sloot, *Digital Consumers and the Law: Towards a Cohesive European Framework*, 2012 (ISBN 978-90-411-4049-4).
29. Tatiana-Eleni Synodinou, *Codification of European Copyright Law: Challenges and Perspectives,* 2012 (ISBN 978-90-411-4145-3).
30. Heather Ann Forrest, *Protection of Geographic Names in International Law and Domain Name System Policy*, Second Edition, 2017 (ISBN 978-90-411-8839-7).
31. Sari Depreeuw, *The Variable Scope of the Exclusive Economic Rights in Copyright*, 2014 (ISBN 978-90-411-4915-2).
32. Vikrant Narayan Vasudeva, *Open Source Software and Intellectual Property Rights*, 2014 (ISBN 978-90-411-5228-2).
33. Frederik J. Zuiderveen Borgesius, *Improving Privacy Protection in the Area of Behavioural Targeting*, 2015 (ISBN 978-90-411-5990-8).
34. Paul L.C. Torremans, *Intellectual Property Law and Human Rights*, Third Edition, 2015 (ISBN 978-90-411-5836-9).

35. Irini A. Stamatoudi, *New Developments in EU and International Copyright Law*, 2016 (ISBN 978-90-411-5991-5).
36. Lodewijk W.P. Pessers, *The Inventiveness Requirement in Patent Law: An Exploration of Its Foundations and Functioning*, 2016 (ISBN 978-90-411-6731-6).
37. Susy Frankel & Daniel Gervais, *The Internet and the Emerging Importance of New Forms of Intellectual Property*, 2016 (ISBN 978-90-411-6789-7).
38. Axel M. Arnbak, *Securing Private Communications: Protecting Private Communications Security in EU Law – Fundamental Rights, Functional Value Chains, and Market Incentives*, 2016 (ISBN 978-90-411-6737-8).
39. Christina Angelopoulos, *European Intermediary Liability in Copyright: A Tort-Based Analysis*, 2017 (ISBN 978-90-411-6835-1).
40. João Pedro Quintais, *Copyright in the Age of Online Access: Alternative Compensation Systems in EU Law*, 2017 (ISBN 978-90-411-8667-6).
41. P. Bernt Hugenholtz, *Copyright Reconstructed: Rethinking Copyright's Economic Rights in a Time of Highly Dynamic Technological and Economic Change,* 2018 (ISBN 978-90-411-9103-8).
42. Manon Oostveen, *Protecting Individuals Against the Negative Impact of Big Data: Potential and Limitations of the Privacy and Data Protection Law Approach*, 2018 (ISBN 978-94-035-0131-4).